KU-722-506

Structure in Thought and Feeling

SUSAN AYLWIN

Structure in Thought and Feeling

METHUEN · London & New York

First published in 1985 by
Methuen & Co. Ltd
11 New Fetter Lane
London EC4P 4EE

Published in the USA by
Methuen & Co.
in association with Methuen, Inc.
733 Third Avenue, New York, NY 10017

© 1985 Susan Aylwin

Typeset by Nene Phototypesetters Ltd
Printed in Great Britain at the
University Press, Cambridge

All rights reserved. No part of this
book may be reprinted or reproduced
or utilized in any form or by any
electronic, mechanical or other means,
now known or hereafter invented,
including photocopying and recording,
or in any information storage or
retrieval system, without permission
in writing from the publishers.

British Library Cataloguing in
Publication Data

Aylwin, Susan
Structure in thought and feeling.
1. Consciousness
I. Title
153   BF311

ISBN 0–416–35990–6

Library of Congress Cataloging in
Publication Data

Aylwin, Susan.
Structure in thought and feeling.
Bibliography: p.
Includes index.
1. Emotions.   2. Thought and thinking.
I. Title.
BF531.A96   1985   152.4   84–20758

ISBN 0–416–35990–6

To Robert Schneider;
and to the memory of Karl Britton.

Contents

List of figures

List of tables

Acknowledgements

Many people have helped in the making of this book. My foremost debt is to all the people who willingly filled in questionnaires, talked into tape recorders, or kept diaries. Without their help there would have been no book.

I am grateful to a number of people who have acted as second judges in coding the qualitative data: Brenda Shrensky, Chris Simms, Sean Hammond, Richard Bird, Bob Michell, Gay Ó Crualaoich, Seamus Feehan and Elizabeth Dunne. I am grateful also to George Delafield, Des MacHale, Grace Neville and Tony O'Mahoney, who all helped in various ways with the MOTQ standardization work.

Elizabeth Dunne and Sean Hammond are included among the second judges, but my debt to them extends well beyond this: they were my co-workers on some of the studies of chapters 5 and 6, and I have often had reason to be thankful for their advice, expertise and general civilizedness. The National Board for Science and Technology financed this part of the work.

Some of the writing was done while on sabbatical in Australia. Alan Richardson, at the University of Western Australia, was especially generous with his time and thoughts, and I have profited greatly from discussions with him. Both he and Robin Winkler made useful suggestions on some draft chapters. I would also like to thank Peter Sheehan for arranging my sojourn in Brisbane.

At a later stage David Salter and John Antrobus read the entire manuscript for Methuen, and made a number of sensible and sensitive suggestions for improvement.

The writing has only been the final stage of a longer journey. On that journey many people have provided the right kind of academic stimulation, or support of more general kinds: I am grateful in various ways to Roy Davis, John Brown, Peter Dempsey, Richard Donovan, Michael Howley, David Routh, Rom Harré, Judy Kravis, Theo Dorgan, the Hardy family, my own family and to my colleagues and students at Newcastle and Cork.

Susan Aylwin
Réidhleán
April 1984

Part 1

The three forms of representation

1

Introduction

This book is about the relationship between thought and feeling; which is not a simple matter.

At their closest, thought and feeling are inextricably linked. Many cultures account for the beginning of all things by saying that first there was chaos, and then the chaos was partitioned into two: an upper part called sky or heaven, and a lower part called earth. At a single stroke the universe acquired both structure and value. The imposition of a cognitive opposition had direct affective complements: there was then a spatially higher part, which was also the spiritually better part, with human beings, for complicated reasons, being confined to the spatially and morally lower part. In such mythological accounts the same structure, opposition, has both cognitive and affective aspects.

An equally close relationship between thought and feeling is found in the experience of insight. Here the excitement accompanying the cognitive content is what tells the thinker the idea is a good one. At the moment of insight, truth is as much a matter of feeling as it is of thought. Polanyi (1958) assigns these 'intellectual passions' a vital role in science because they indicate what is scientifically important. Unguided by them, he says, research would spread out into a desert of trivialities.

The relationship is not always so close. Often thought and feeling come far enough apart for one to be seen as the cause of the other. Some people tell themselves how awful they are, and how hopeless their life is, and manage to think themselves into depression (Beck, 1963). The relationship may work both ways here, and people can sometimes be helped to think their way out of depression again, using one of the techniques of cognitive behaviour therapy.

The thoughts cannot always be assumed to lead the feelings however. Wolpe (1978a and b) describes how some patients remain phobic even though they know, rationally, that the object of their terror will not harm them. Here feeling is immune to cognitive interference, either because the feelings come first, or because thought and feeling are simply separate. Zajonc (1980) has recently suggested that in many situations affective processing has primacy over cognitive processing, and that in some situations the two may be virtually independent of each other.

Sometimes thought and feeling are the two inseparable facets of a single process; sometimes one causes the other; sometimes they are separate. When a number of accounts can be given of the relationship between two things, it is safest to assume that the relationship is complex. There are many ways of thinking and many ways of feeling, and there may be many kinds of relationship between them.

An anchoring of terms

Ryle (1949), in discussing the word *emotion*, lets the term range freely over a number of common-sense equivalents. In the present work the meaning of the term *feeling* is allowed to range freely in a similar way and over much of the same territory. *Feeling* may thus refer to evaluations, motives, personality traits, emotions; and generally to any of the loose aggregate of phenomena which psychologists normally class as 'affective'.

In everyday speech the term *thinking* has almost as many uses as does *feeling*. However, with the meaning of one term left open it is as well to have some stringency in the definition of the other. The empirical work that follows looks at thinking in terms of the different kinds of representation that may be used in the thought process. This has the effect of anchoring the cognitive end of the relationship between thought and feeling in a substantial body of research on the topic of representations.

The developmental evidence suggests that there are three main forms of representation: enactive, visual and verbal, each originating in a different period of childhood.

> At first the child's world is known to him principally by the habitual actions he uses for coping with it. In time there is added a technique of representation through imagery that is relatively free of action. Gradually there is added a new and powerful method of translating action and image into language, providing still a third system of representation. (Bruner, 1966, p. 1)

The three systems of representation begin as ways of interacting with the real world, and gradually become internalized, so that as adults we have three different though interconnected forms of representation available to us: *inner speech*, or verbal representation; *visual imagery* or 'pictures in the mind's eye'; and *enactive imagery*, a kind of imagined action or role play.[1]

All three are available for a wide variety of tasks. When reading a novel some people will mutter the words to themselves under their breath and rely mainly on inner speech; some will follow the plot through pictures in their mind's eye; and some will identify with the hero or heroine and follow the plot through imagined action. Most people can switch their strategy depending on what they are reading: verbal representation for abstract and technical matters; visual and enactive representations for good escapist fiction.

One of the advantages of elaborating thinking in terms of different forms of representation is that much of recent cognitive psychology has also been concerned with the topic of representation. This cognitive work has focused on the topic at two different levels: an abstract level, concerned with the representation of meaning in semantic memory; and a phenomenal or holistic level, concerned with the surface properties of the different forms of representation. Both these approaches will turn out to be useful in exploring the relationships between thought and feeling.

The research on representations at both levels has been in a primarily cognitive tradition, with relatively little reference to affective phenomena.[2] Some additional idea is therefore needed as an intellectual springboard to project an initial tentative link between thought and feeling. The notion of cognitive style is useful here.

Cognitive style

The idea of cognitive style is rooted in the psychoanalytic tradition, from which it arose as a way of explaining how the impulsive and passionate id could be controlled by the more intellectual and reality-orientated ego. Klein (1958) describes cognitive styles as involving particular patterns of cognitive structures, with the structures being responsible both for making sense of reality and for channelling instinctual energy into it. *Cognitive styles thus involve the idea of structural relationships between thought and feeling.*

Within cognitive style research itself, the structural component remained rudimentary, and was never articulated further than Rapaport's reference to 'information; habits; concepts; anticipatory, grammatical, syntactic, and other logical patterns, etc.' (1959, p. 126). Many changes have taken place in psychological theory since he was writing, and it may now be possible to interpret the structures underlying cognitive styles in a new way, in terms of the structures used to describe the organization of semantic memory. This provides the following interrelated set of ideas which serve as the starting-point for the empirical work.

Firstly: verbal, visual and enactive modes of thought may utilize different kinds of cognitive structures.

Secondly: if these structures do have the dual cognitive and affective role assigned to them in the cognitive style tradition, then the different cognitive structures should have particular kinds of affects and feelings associated with them. More generally this means that there should be systematic and structural relationships between thought and feeling in the three forms of representation.

Thirdly: there may be 'representational styles' just as there are cognitive styles of other kinds, with people showing biases in the use they make of the three forms of thought.

Fourthly: these representational biases should be associated with particular styles in personality. Verbalizers, visualizers and enactive imagers should be different kinds of people, with distinct personality characteristics.

The empirical exploration of these interconnected ideas has required the detailed qualitative examination of both cognitive representations and affective experiences, using relatively simple observational and descriptive techniques. It has seemed important to observe what there is first, and to quantify it afterwards; and much of the work that follows therefore uses initial qualitative analyses, followed by quantification.[3]

Plan of the book

The book is divided into three parts. Part one is mainly concerned with comparisons between verbal, visual and enactive representations: chapter 2 provides background sketches of some of the things already known about each mode of thought; and chapter 3 elucidates the characteristic cognitive structures of each form of representation, using a modified free-association technique. It also examines the problematic notion of structure, and suggests that structures be seen as describing patterns of temporal organization. Chapter 4 sketches the affective concomitants of these cognitive structures by looking at day-dreams which occur in verbal, visual and enactive modes. As a more formal approach to the same general topic, chapter 5 describes some work with the Modes of Thought Questionnaire, which assesses representational biases on the basis of cognitive structures; and chapter 6 uses this questionnaire to relate the structures to personality.

Part two takes up affective issues specific to particular modes of thought. Chapter 7 looks at evaluative aspects of the hierarchical organization of inner speech; chapter 8 explores the affective consequences of an important visual structure – the relationship between object and environment; and chapter 9 examines the strong emotions important in enactive imagery.

Part three returns to general issues and attempts to integrate the findings. It consists of two chapters. Chapter 10 reviews what has been discovered of the relationships between thought and feeling in the three forms of representation, and makes some suggestions about how they can be accommodated within a unified theory. The final chapter considers the three forms of representation as integrated aspects of a single cognitive system. It looks at the accounts of reality given by the three modes of thought, and at how science equilibrates them against each other.

2

Preliminary sketches of the three modes of thought

Speech, vision and action are the three main ways human beings have of interacting with, making sense of, and contributing to their world. Verbal, visual and enactive modes of thought are their internalized versions.

All three forms of representation have been proposed, at one time or another, as the main bearer of meaning, though it is only for language that there exists any detailed account of semantic structure. Within visual imagery there are heated debates about structure; and for enactive imagery there is no coherent body of work at all. It may be that action, as the foundation of all later cognitive development, is buried deepest and is the most difficult to articulate.

This chapter reviews some of the general characteristics of the three forms of representation, focusing where possible on two kinds of properties: the affective aspects of the representations, which usually emerge in the context of psychotherapeutic work; and the structural features, which will be important later in elaborating the notion of cognitive style. Though some work has been done on comparing the three forms of thought, it is convenient at this stage to consider each mode of representation separately.

Inner speech

Intuition suggests that inner speech is quieter and often less polite than outer speech, but is fundamentally the same sort of thing. Internalized verbal representation is derived from external language, and thus shares many of the same properties. For example, inner speech, like the external form, can be seen as having a linear and sequential organization, which makes it useful for coding information organized in the same way (Paivio and Csapo, 1969). It is also seen as being conceptual and abstract in nature: internal words, like external ones, refer to general *classes* of objects and events, and can be useful for remembering abstract information (Paivio and Foth, 1970).

The internalization of speech occurs at about school age. A transitional stage is egocentric speech, where children talk out loud, but to themselves rather than to anyone else (Piaget, 1959). It is a short step from talking to oneself outside the head to talking to oneself inside it.

Inner speech has an important self-directive function (Luria, 1961), in that people use it to tell themselves what they ought to do. Children also do this out loud. Adults only do it out loud if there is no one else listening, or if they are thinking about something very difficult.

Adults may also talk to themselves in negative and non-coping ways. Hollon and Kendall's work (1980) indicates that many depressed people tell themselves such things as, 'I feel like I'm up against the world', 'I'm no good', 'I've let people down', 'I don't think I can go on', and 'It's just not worth it'.

On the positive side, modifying what people say to themselves can be therapeutically helpful. The classic treatment is Coué's 'Every day, in every way, I am becoming better and better.' Formal training in self-instruction (Meichenbaum, 1976; Meichenbaum and Cameron, 1974) is also useful in supplementing verbal controls over behaviour. It may be especially useful for people liable to outbursts of anger, who can thus learn to talk themselves into self-restraint (Camp, 1977; Novaco, 1979).

Structure in language

Vygotsky (1962) claims that there are structural differences between inner speech and speech destined for others. The most noticeable of these differences is that inner speech characteristically consists of predicates without subjects; a commentary on topics which themselves are linguistically unspecified. Inner speech may also occur in a highly contracted form, as Sokolov (1972) has confirmed. Only when thinking encounters problems does the telegraphese need expanding into a semblance of external grammar.

Lacking a detailed grammar for inner speech itself, we must assume, provisionally, that its structures are those of language, though perhaps it includes only some of them, or in simplified form.

Although Chomsky first introduced cognitive psychology to linguistic structures, the syntactic emphasis of his work makes it less relevant here than systems whose concern extends to semantics. One of the key figures here is Charles Fillmore (1968, 1971), who sees some important linguistic structures as being both syntactic and semantic. His ideas have clear psychological relevance and have been incorporated into several models of semantic memory (e.g.: Kintsch, 1972; Rumelhart, Lindsay and Norman, 1972). They have also been widely used in developmental psycholinguistics (e.g.: Braine and Wells, 1978; Braine and Hardy, 1982; Gleitman and Wanner, 1982).

For Fillmore, in order to make sense of the world we need to be able to make a small number of key judgments about it. If something happens, we need to know who did it, where, what with, why, who to, and with what result. These judgments are reflected in language in particular *cases*.[1]

If the answer to *Who did it?* is *Daniel did it*, then *Daniel*, as the agent of the action, takes agentive case; and he takes it in both *Daniel planted the cabbages* and *The cabbages were planted by Daniel*. Agency is thus a semantic relationship independent of the particular syntactic form of the sentence.

The cases that seem to be required are given in the following list, taken from Fillmore (1971), with some modifications from Chafe (1970), and Braine and Hardy (1982).

Agent – the animate being who instigates the action.

Instrument – the thing causally involved in the action.

Locative – where the action occurs, or more generally, where something is.

Resultant – the result of the action.

Experiencer – the animate being who feels or experiences something.

Subject of attribution – that to which qualities, locations and intransitive actions are attributed.

Objective – the case used for anything else, including things acted upon or experienced.

Some examples:

Sean (agent) unlocked the car (objective) in the garage (locative) with a key (instrument).

Jane (experiencer) was happy. She (agent) had just carved a wooden bowl (resultant).

The pigeon (subject of attribution) was sitting on the roof (locative).

Are linguistic structures only linguistic?

One of the questions that needs to be raised about case grammar is the extent to which the structures it describes are specifically linguistic. Fillmore sees case structures as having both syntactic and semantic properties, and as representing kinds of judgments people make about the world and events in it. Some developmental psycholinguists go further, and claim that the structures seen in language are largely derivative, originating in the structures of perception or action (see Gleitman and Wanner, 1982, for a recent review).

As long ago as 1971, Osgood pointed out that the subject–verb–object structure of language has the same form, and may be derived from, the actor–action–object form of real actions. He maintains that the non-linguistic cognitive system is 'where sentences come from' in sentence creating by speakers, and where sentences 'go to' in being understood by listeners. In similar vein, Bever (1970) provides a long list of features of linguistic processing which appear to be taken over from perception.[2] On case categories specifically, Bruner (1975) suggests that these originate in interactive relationships between mother and child. Language structure would thus have a social origin, at least in part.

Though the dependence of language on non-linguistic functioning is most visible in early childhood, it can also be spotted in adults. Occasionally people use language 'magically' (Werner and Kaplan, 1963), confusing symbol and referent, and attributing the properties of the object to the word. Swear words most clearly retain this potency, and the words themselves become taboo along with whatever unmentionable it is that they refer to. Werner and Kaplan discuss spells, general invective and love talk in this context. They point out that ostensibly neutral words are also contaminated by their referents. The word *lowering*, for example, tends to be apprehended as lower in the visual field than does the word *raising*.

The dependence of language, even for its structure, on other modes of cognition, means that we cannot be sure whether the structures described for language are its own, or borrowed. The medium (noise, words) is its own, but the structures may not be.

I take the unravelling of which form of representation is responsible for which type of structure to be an empirical matter.

Pending the evidence, I shall use *verbal representation* or *inner speech* to refer to what is peculiarly linguistic, to what words can do without the support of other forms of representation; and *language* or *linguistic* to refer to the full range of effects of which words are capable, including those cases where the effects are dependent on the presence of some non-verbal representation.

Visual imagery

To explain to a non-psychologist that 'visual imagery' refers to 'pictures in the mind's eye' is enlightening. To explain the same thing to psychologists is contentious. The difficulty is that, as with all metaphors, the idea of mental pictures has a good deal of aptness, but it also has limits, noticed only when one has passed beyond them and is well into nonsense. Nonsense in this case would include the idea that there is a place called 'mind' which has things called 'images' in it.

Ryle (1949) suggests that images do not involve the real seeing of ephemeral 'pictures', but the as-if 'seeing' of real ones. For him the difference between image and reality is not in the ontological status of the thing (or 'thing') perceived, but in the act of perceiving (or 'perceiving') itself. Sarbin (1972) takes this further in describing imagining as 'hypothetical instantiation', or *as-if* behaviour. Neisser's (1976, 1978) analysis of imagery as the *anticipation* of perceiving a state of affairs though without that state of affairs actually arriving to be perceived, attempts to tackle the same problem.

These are important analyses, but it still remains true that 'pictures in the mind's eye' provides a useful metaphor for those wishing to communicate with ordinary mortals, and perhaps to enlist their aid as subjects in imagery experiments.

The metaphor is useful too in pointing up parallels between the processing of real pictures and the processing of imaginary ones. That the two use the same processing system is shown by the fact that images and pictures may sometimes be mistaken for one another (Perky, 1910; Segal, 1971), and may sometimes interfere with one another (Brooks, 1968; Atwood, 1971).

One of the most important properties of this shared system is its spatial-parallel organization. This allows a number of items to be depicted simultaneously in space, and has powerful effects on learning (Paivio, 1971). The general effect has been known since the time of the poet Simonides of Ceos, who, in about 500 BC, was fortunate enough to be called away from a banquet just before the roof collapsed. According to Frances Yates's account, he managed to identify the victims, although they were crushed beyond recognition, by remembering where they had been sitting. Thus was born the 'Method of Loci', whereby items to be remembered are imagined as arranged in the mnemonic niches of some well-known place.

That imagery is a spatial medium is supported by Kosslyn's work (1973), which shows the resemblance between scanning the 'space' of mental pictures and scanning actual pictures. The greater the distance between the two parts of the 'picture', the longer it takes to scan between them.

The spatial capacity of visual imagery is such that up to twenty items may all be imaged together in one composite imaginal scene without interfering with one another (Bower, 1972). Not surprisingly, when a mere two items have to be integrated together, as in paired-associate learning, visual imagery has an equivalently powerful effect.

Imagery in psychotherapy

The similarity between imaginary 'seeing' and real seeing allows images to be used as substitutes for the real thing. This is important in psychotherapy (Singer, 1974; Tower and Singer, 1981; Strosahl and Ascough, 1981). If people show similar emotional responses to images as to real equivalents, then treatment may proceed using convenient mental representation rather than inconvenient and unwieldy reality. Thus in Wolpe's (1958) systematic desensitization of phobias, the spider phobic imagines a sequence of scenarios which are increasingly related to spiders, and eventually imagines spiders themselves. In Cautela's (1970) covert conditioning, positive reinforcements for imagined healthy conduct consist of imagined rewards (chosen from Cautela and Kastenbaum's reinforcement survey schedule (1967)); and imagined undesirable behaviour is covertly punished with images of nauseating occurrences (Cautela and Wisocki, 1971).

Where comparisons have been made, images are not quite as good as the real thing (see Bandura, 1977; Dyckman and Cowan, 1978), but then real things are expensive, and may be difficult for even therapists to manipulate (real snakes, real spiders, real nauseating occurrences).

Imagery does not only function in psychotherapy as a substitute for reality. It is also used as a vehicle of communication between unconscious and conscious parts of the mind. Visual images may reveal important information in much the same way as dreams. Kanzer (1958) reports that in classical psychoanalysis, images cropping up during the free-association process were considered as 'secret islands of repression'. This is partly because the free-associative process was supposed to be a matter of bringing things into words. When people are encouraged to make use of such images they often reveal material less easily accessible to language (Reyher, 1963; Reyher and Smeltzer, 1968).

A number of techniques, including Leuner's (1977, 1978) guided affective imagery, systematically exploit the close relation between images and the unconscious for diagnostic and therapeutic purposes. It is assumed that if a person's unconscious processes can be tapped, they are the best source of information about what is wrong, and about what may heal it. Jaffe and Bresler (1980) refer to the 'Inner Advisor' as a personification of this source of intuitive inner guidance, and Emmons's (1980) 'Inner Source' serves similar functions.[3]

Role of vividness

One of the more researched characteristics of visual imagery is its vividness. Vividness is often interpreted, if tacitly, as a measure of the extent to which the image approaches reality. The most frequently used instrument for assessing vividness, Sheehan's (1967) version of the Betts's (1909) Questionnaire upon Mental Imagery, asks people to rate the vividness of their images in comparison with actual sensory experiences.

If vividness assesses how close an image approaches a 'percept', then it stands to reason that a vivid image is a first-class honours sort of image, and a faint image is a mere lower second. Whatever can be done with images ought to be done better with a vivid one.

This assumption has been proved true in one area. In incidental learning, people with more vivid images are able to remember more. This is true particularly of pictorial material (Sheehan and Neisser, 1969) but is also found with words (Morris and Gale, 1974).

As soon as we start looking at intentional learning the matter becomes confused, with occasional positive relationships, but with the majority of studies showing that vividness does not have any significant effect (Morelli and Lang, 1971; Rehm, 1973; Calvano, 1974). Imagery does promote learning, as many studies using imagery instructions show, but it does not seem to matter how vivid the images are. Bartlett (1921) suggested that vivid imagery may in fact increase a person's confidence in their recall far more than it increases their accuracy.

One source of the confusion may be that people who are capable of vivid imagery are not necessarily using it in the learning situation examined. This analysis is supported by the fact that there is a relationship between vividness and intentional learning when they are assessed on the same task (Danaher and Thoresen, 1972; Marks, 1973b).

The confusions over the role of vividness in learning also arise in its role in psychotherapy. Vividness does not seem to relate to the emotional intensity of imagery in phobics (Weerts and Lang, 1978; Lang, Melamed and Hart, 1970), nor does it predict the outcome of systematic desensitization (McLemore, 1972).

One of the problems may be that here, as in learning, people who are capable of vivid imagery may not be using it in the therapy situation. If they do use it then the relationship between vividness and therapeutic improvement becomes stronger. Wisocki (1973) found that covert reinforcement was more effective in changing anxiety level, the more vivid the reinforcing image. Similarly Dyckman and Cowan (1978) found that the vividness of the imagery actually used in therapy was a better predictor of the outcome than pretherapy vividness ratings. Phillips (1971) has tried training people in the use of imagery, with preliminary but hopeful results.

A further problem here is that the emotions being treated are not unitary phenomena, and imagery might be impinging only on one aspect of them. Lang (1968) suggests that fear is represented in three systems: the verbal (cognitive), the overt motor, and the somatic. Odom, Nelson and Wein (1978) found that different therapies had different effects on these three systems (though imagery based systematic desensitization was relatively ineffective in all three).

Structures in visual imagery

Whether or not visual imagery has a structure, equivalent to the syntactic-semantic structure of language, has been a topic of considerable debate.

The general argument can be polarized around two positions. One is represented by Paivio's (1971, 1976) dual-coding hypothesis. This supposes that the meaning of a concrete word is the image it refers to. The images derive originally from perception and are stored in one half of long-term memory. The other half of the dual-coding hypothesis is that the meaning of abstract words is represented in verbal form and stored as such in the verbal half of long-term memory.

Paivio's account is related to a long philosophical tradition of seeing meaning as 'thing' rather than as relationship. Within such a general view, structure is relatively unimportant and Paivio only talks about 'associations' of rather general kinds (e.g. between words or between words and images).

The other pole of the argument is represented by Pylyshyn (1973, 1979), who maintains that images are not stored in long-term memory, being themselves only epiphenomena. The real phenomena consist of abstract and a-modal propositional structures which underlie images, and to which we have no conscious access. In other words, there *are* structures related to imagery, but they are in abstract rather than imagistic form. They are behind or beneath imagery, rather than in it.

We either have no structure to speak of, only mental 'things' (images, pictures), or a structure independent of imagery. An important intermediate position is put by Kosslyn (1973, 1978; Kosslyn and Pomerantz, 1977; Kosslyn, Pinker, Smith and Schwartz, 1979) for whom imagery does have a structure, which may be represented in analogue (i.e. imagistic) form.

The general tendency now is towards compromise positions of one kind or another (e.g.: Marschark and Paivio, 1977; Kieras, 1978; Anderson, 1978; Palmer, 1978), with people tending to assume that it may be expedient to include both imagistic and propositional representations. Even when they both code the same state of affairs one form may have processing advantages. For example, the image rotation data of Shepard and his colleagues (Shepard and Metzler, 1971; Cooper and Shepard, 1973) are more easily accounted for by analogue representations.

The question of why it has been a matter of so much contention that imagery may have a structure, and particularly a structure of its own, is an interesting one in its own right. The problem originates in the fact that the effectiveness of imagery as a mnemonic occluded for a long time the possibility of any other role being envisaged for it. This contrasts with work in linguistics, which has emphasized linguistic creativity as providing vital insight into linguistic structure.

Chomsky (1959) emphasized that we can all use language creatively, and, at least in principle, produce sentences hitherto unheard in the universe. This is because any sentence framework can be used to generate an enormous number of different sentences. It is the exercise of this creativity that reveals structure, because it allows us to see that the syntactic skeleton may remain the same, while the contents, the particular words, may vary. The constraints on what may be changed while we still get sense reveal the structures governing the sense.

In classical memory studies it is accuracy rather than creativity that is important. Indeed creativity would be seen as responsible only for errors. If we focus on the information that remains unchanged between going into and coming out of memory, then nothing, not even language, would be seen as having any structure. A sentence unchanged between input and output would be functioning as a structureless unit, and not as language as we know it. Not surprisingly, the image that passes unchanged through memory does not show any structure either. The memory task is simply not one conducive to the exhibition of structure.

In other words, we lack a grammar of the image because the tasks used in much imagery research have not been such as to reveal one. Linguists have notoriously stretched linguistic creativity to its limits in order to unravel its structure. Psychologists working with imagery have been distinctly less imaginative.

That images do have a structure is indicated by the fact that there are certain things we can do, and others we cannot, even in imagination. We can, for example, change the colour of an imagined swan to black, or green, or pink, leaving the rest of the image untouched. We can probably take the legs off and put wheels on (at least after some experience of cartoon films). We have to replace the legs with something of a broadly similar sort, something that will count as part-of-an-object, or as a means-of-locomotion. We cannot replace the legs with the pink, for legs are parts and pink is an attribute, and with different ontological statuses these cannot replace one another and yield visual sense.

Further and more formal evidence that it should be possible to formulate a grammar of the image comes from two directions: from artificial intelligence work on scene recognition (see D. J. McArthur, 1982); and from the elegant neurophysiological work of Hubel and Wiesel (1979). Whether the specifics of work in these areas can be transferred to a distinctly psychological account of imaging remains a moot point.

Enactive imagery

The study of enactive representation is not a well-defined area, and the following sketch draws on a range of sources which use a variety of terminologies. At this stage asserting that the variety may be comprehended under a single heading is a matter of intuitive judgment.

A foundation for all knowledge

In developmental psychology enactive representations are taken to be the foundation of all subsequent intelligence, and the means whereby the most basic aspects of reality are constructed (Piaget, 1954; Bruner, 1966). Space, time, the idea of an object, and the concept of causality, all begin here; and here adult thought remains rooted.

Action has also been seen as basic by some sociologists. The 'general theory of action' of Parsons and Shils (1951) sees action as the foundation of the personalities of the actors; and of the social system; and of the wider cultural system. Following on from this notion there has been a good deal of work on *social* action (e.g.: Brenner, 1980; von Cranach, Kalbermatten, Indermühle and Gugler, 1982).

The relative neglect of action in current cognitive psychology contrasts rather strongly with this developmental and social emphasis. In the past, however, action has been seen as epistemologically important for adults and individuals, and there are some signs that it is beginning to be so again.

On the historical side there have been a number of motor theories of thought and consciousness. Washburn (1916) assumed that all consciousness depended upon 'tentative movements' which were reduced and inhibited versions of real actions. Similarly, Titchener (1909), saw action and bodily attitude as being at the origin of meaning, with the sensations deriving from how one physically confronts a particular situation being what gives that situation meaning. He did, however, criticize motor theories in general for their lop-sidedness, and for disregarding the fact that we had developed modes of thought apart from the motor.

One of the problems with motor theories has been the precise contribution of the bodily component, and whether this is centrally or peripherally represented. Assuming particular kinaesthetic sensations to represent the meaning of particular actions is problematic in so far as for many actions (assassinating the president; going to the library) no specific muscular contribution is necessarily implicated. It should be noted that not all motor theories are entirely naïve on this point. Despite the crude neurophysiology of the times, Washburn speculated that the cortex, not the muscles, was the organ of the tentative movements responsible for consciousness.

Weimer (1974, 1977) has recently argued that motor theories of the mind may be more appropriate to cognitive phenomena than some of our currrent 'sensory' conceptions. A motor theory would hold that we represent knowledge of objects in terms of the actions we use in interacting with them. A sensory theory sees knowledge as thing rather than process. Weimer's conception of a motor theory is elaborated in terms of both neurophysiology and information processing. His stress on representing knowledge in terms of the procedures used to acquire it is similar to the recent interest in 'procedural semantics' (e.g.: Winograd, 1972, 1975; Miller and Johnson-Laird, 1976). Norman (1973) also holds that we represent knowledge in terms of 'plans', and suggests that some of these are in sensori-motor form. Thus *walking* would be represented in terms of the sensorimotor routine used for performing it (and not in terms of an abstract semantic description).

All these recent trends do not together amount to a new motor theory, but they do suggest a renewed awareness of the epistemological importance of action and of the internal or central representation of action.

Action, agency and the first person

The relative neglect of action is grounded historically in the behaviourists' demotion of action to objectively observable and meaningless muscle twitches. It is grounded more recently in the dominance of the computer as the epistemological standard to which human activity must be compared, and which has been the unwitting host of a new objectivism.

The crucial feature of action is that, in the end, it is what each individual must do for him or herself. It involves a first-person-singular agent, who cannot be replaced by the second-person observer, or the third-person reporter. Watching someone else doing the action is not the same as doing it; and hearing about it afterwards is even further removed. But according to the impersonal logic of the computer, these are not significant differences.

For artificial intelligence, the proposition *A does X* remains true regardless of whether I, my sibling, or the man on the Clapham omnibus happens to be *A*, and to do X. Organic life, for better or worse, does not offer this serene impartiality. Most of us must recall as children being the resentful B when it was A who was getting to ride the pony or shoot the airgun. To individual human beings it can be a matter of enormous significance who is involved in the action, who is watching, and who is only told about it. It matters also in law.

There are some signs, within cognitive psychology, of an awareness that the first-person singular has a unique epistemological position. Pichert and Anderson (1977) and Anderson and Pichert (1978) report work which shows the importance of taking a particular individual's viewpoint for remembering details of a story only accessible from that viewpoint. Bower (1978) extends this to memory for moods and feelings: to remember how a character was feeling it is helpful to have identified with that character during learning.

Agency is, however, more than a viewpoint, and though the notion of agency may be philosophically problematic, there can be no doubt of its psychological importance. Human beings denied agency and the freedom of action that supports it, lapse into helplessness, self-deprecation and other signs of depression, and even death (Seligman, 1975; Maier and Seligman, 1976; Bandura, 1977, 1980). Conversely, people who feel they have some choice in what they do, express greater satisfaction with their lot, whether this be the lot of a university student (Liem, 1975) or that of an old person in an institution (Schulz, 1976).

A number of terms have been used to describe what people are exercising when acting as agents. White (1959) calls it *competence*; de Charms (1968) calls it *personal causation*; Bandura (1977) calls it *self-efficacy*. Agency, under whatever heading, is complex. It includes an assumption of motivation; that there are reasons (including emotional ones) for making one decision rather than another, or for wanting to exercise one's competence in a particular way. Agency also involves the notion of purpose and intention, and envisages a future in which it will be better if we do X than if we fail to do X or if we do Y. Agency, motive, purpose and the future are interrelated concepts here.

Kinaesthesis in psychotherapy

Overt action and covert enactive imagery must have a central representation, but they are also *embodied*. Action which is blocked can lead to the chronic muscular tension which is a feature of many forms of emotional maladjustment (Plutchik, 1954). It is sometimes therapeutically effective to work directly on these tensions.

Jacobson (1938) found that attention, thought and emotion all diminish with progressive relaxation; and because of this, relaxation training is often used as a prelude to or in combination with other forms of therapy. Work by Wolpin and Kirsch (1974), examining the effects of relaxation and tension in systematic desensitization, showed that general muscular tension significantly increases the emotionality of images, without having any effect on their vividness.

A similar divorce between vividness on the one hand, and emotion and bodily involvement on the other, is found in Lang's work (1979a and b). He distinguishes between images which represent 'stimulus propositions' and those which represent 'response propositions'. The difference is between the representation of an event, such as being trapped in an overheated sauna, through its objective properties (stimulus propositions: 'Thick clouds of white mist swirl round you. . . . The large wooden door is tightly closed.'), and its representation through the effect on oneself as the person involved (response propositions: 'You sweat great buckets of perspiration. . . . You pull with all your strength on the door.'). His distinction between stimulus propositions and response propositions parallels the distinction between visual and enactive imagery. Enactive representation is emotional representation, and is conceptually distinct from visual imagery which contributes vividness.

Other bodily oriented techniques used in psychotherapy have received less formal testing and are difficult to assess. Some therapists (e.g.: Reich, 1968; Rolf, 1977) maintain that physical work on particular muscle groups and their skeletal attachments may be helpful. Others emphasize the importance of bodily expression in a variety of dance and movement therapies (e.g.: Danehy, 1980; Dendinger, 1980; Dosamantes-Alperson, 1980). Imagined role play has also been used as a way of exploring the factual and the emotional possibilities of the future. In their counselling for decision making, Janis and Mann (1977) ask clients to imagine that they have already decided on first one and then another of their possible courses of action, and to explore the consequences. They are then in a better position to take the real decision.

Mental practice and other functions

It is widely assumed that internal enactive representations share some characteristics with the real actions whose covert versions they are. This interrelation gains support from the fact that mental practice can lead to improvement of physical skills. If one lacks a private gymnasium or swimming pool, mental practice can be used as a convenient alternative. The technique has been used with considerable effect in the coaching of a number of sports (Vandell, Davis and Clugston, 1943; Start, 1960; Jones, 1965; Richardson, 1967a and b). Start and Richardson (1964) found no relationship between the efficacy of mental practice and the vividness of the imagery used, and Mahoney (1979), commenting on his interviews with Olympic gymnasts, suggests that what is important here is a proprioceptive sense of actually doing the action rather than any visual component.

Two important functions have been discussed in the context of both visual and enactive representations. One is spatial flexibility. This has commonly been assumed to be a visual ability, despite repeated failures to show any relationship between it and imagery vividness (Ernest, 1977; Richardson, 1977b; DiVesta, Ingersoll and Sunshine, 1971; Forisha, 1975; Neisser, 1970). Piaget and Inhelder's

(1971) developmental work on spatial flexibility shows that while there is a visual component, this alone is not sufficient, and the active principle derives from internalized action. Yuille and Catchpole (1977) use a Piagetian framework to separate these two components into the *figurative* (the visual image) and the *operative* (operations carried out on the image). McGee (1979) suggests a similar distinction between an orientation/location component, and a transformational one. Failures to show empirical relations between spatial flexibility and purely visual imagery may be because the task in fact requires an enactive component to transform what is otherwise only a static image.

Creativity has also been discussed in the context of both forms of representation. Visual imagery is mentioned by McKellar (1957), Tauber and Green (1959), Forisha (1978), and Shepard (1978); and enactive representations are also included by Walkup (1965), and Harrington (1980).

The evidence here is largely anecdotal. Einstein (1954) wrote that his thinking tended to consist of visual and muscular elements, and the theory of relativity originated in his imagining what it would be like to travel at the speed of light alongside a lightwave. S. T. Coleridge (quoted in Gerard, 1954) claimed that he would imagine himself identified with anything that especially took his interest. Gordon (1961) follows up such anecdotes in his brainstorming groups, and encourages people to use what he calls 'personal analogy' in thinking through problems. This consists of getting people to imagine that they are physically identified with the problem they are trying to solve.

Summary

The three modes of thought have unique sets of properties. Verbal representation is linear and sequential, adapted to dealing with abstract and sequential information, and useful in a variety of self-instructional ways. Visual imagery is spatially organized, making it a very effective mnemonic tool. It is also useful in psychotherapy for both diagnosis and treatment, and sometimes serves as a therapeutically adequate substitute for either pleasant or unpleasant realities. Vividness is an important attribute of visual imagery, and one to which a good deal of research has been devoted, though its importance remains unclear. Enactive imagery is studied under a number of different headings. It involves covert action, a first-person-singular perspective, an agent and muscular tension. It appears to be the most emotional of the three forms of representation.

Semantic structure has only been fully articulated for language, but it is evident that some of its structures may have originated in non-linguistic representations. Fillmore uses the idea of *cases* which have general psychological significance, and his case grammar is a useful general starting-point for describing representational structures.

3

Free associative structures

Of all the techniques used in psychology, free association is one of the most venerable. It has been widely used by clinicians as a diagnostic tool (e.g.: Jung, 1918; Rapaport, Gill and Schafer, 1968); and it has also been employed by cognitive psychologists as a way of elucidating associative and semantic relationships in memory (e.g.: Deese, 1965; Cramer, 1968). Galton (1907) used free association to investigate his own thought processes and even divided his associations into three representational types; verbal, visual, and what he called 'histrionic'.

This chapter looks at how free association can be used to elucidate the cognitive structures of verbal, visual and enactive representations. The discussion is based on the results of three studies; two of these have been published elsewhere (Aylwin, 1977 and 1981), and the technical details of the third can be found in appendix A.

In all three studies the free association technique was used in a modified form. People were given a stimulus item, asked to represent it in a particular way – by saying it to themselves, seeing a picture of it in their mind's eye, or imagining they *were* it – and then required to free associate to their representation. By looking at how the response relates to the stimulus item it is possible to discern the kind of cognitive structure characterizing the association.

The need to use stimuli that could be represented in all three ways posed something of a problem. Any word at all can be said; most, and especially the concrete ones, can be visualized; but only the ones referring to animate beings can easily be identified with. Of the two available kinds of animate being, humans and animals, animals are the more interesting (as associative stimuli), and dominated the stimulus materials. The different kinds of animals have a range of visual appearances and a range of behaviours far in excess of that permitted to the different kinds of human being.

The first study (Aylwin, 1977) in fact used only animal stimuli: people were presented with individual animal names, were asked to represent the stimulus in a particular way, and then to give a single word response. Here for example the stimulus *parrot* might evoke the association *bird* (in which case the association process exemplifies an object–superordinate structure), or the stimulus *reindeer* might evoke the response *grey* (exemplifying an object–attribute structure).

The restriction to individual stimulus and response words is limiting, and the second study (Aylwin, 1981) used sentences as stimuli and allowed free-flowing speech as response. The sentence stimuli were again about animals, for example, *parrot is in the same forest as gorilla*, or *crocodile snaps at flamingo*. Here people were asked to represent each sentence by either saying it to themselves (inner speech); or getting a picture in their mind's eye of the state of affairs described by the sentence (visual imagery); or by imagining they *were* the first animal in the sentence and that whatever the sentence said about that creature applied to them (enactive imagery). The responses to this were complex, and allowed a correspondingly complex characterization of structural features.

The third study (appendix A) reverted to single word stimuli, but included words from the human realm, particularly kinship roles (e.g. *uncle*) and job roles (e.g. *mechanic* and *doctor*), as well as a variety of abstract words.

As a general summary, the results of these studies indicate that the same stimulus represented in different ways can have quite different meanings. In other words, verbal, visual and enactive forms of representation each lead thought along particular cognitive pathways and into different semantic domains; with the result that people may make sense of the same thing in rather different ways.

In brief, inner speech or verbal representation is concerned with a relatively abstract domain, in which objects are categorized or pigeon-holed into a hierarchical classification system: *tigers are a kind of cat, cats are a kind of animal*. It is also concerned with the acoustic properties of words, and thus results in rhyming associations (*tiger → geiger*) and phrase completions (*tiger → by the tail*).

Visual imagery is concerned with where things are (their environment), and with how things look (their parts and attributes): *the tiger is in the forest, it is yellow with black stripes and long white whiskers*.

Enactive imagery, imagining being the tiger, leads to an awareness of action and affect. Interactions are very important, both actual and potential, and there is an awareness of the motives which prompt action and the consequences which follow: *tiger is hungry and he goes and stalks a deer in the hope of getting himself a meal*.

The same starting-point, *tiger*, can thus lead to quite different associative patterns, depending on how it is represented. Table 3.1 summarizes in a more formal way the characteristic cognitive structures used by the three forms of representation. There are problems with interpreting the precise nature of the cognitive structures reached through the free association technique, but because it is easier to discuss concrete findings than abstract principles, a consideration of these difficulties is deferred until the end of the chapter ('Some thoughts on "structure" ').

The following sections discuss the associative characteristics in detail for each of the three forms of representation in turn.

Structures in inner speech

The instruction to represent the stimuli verbally resulted in a set of associations which indicate that inner speech has three important general properties. These are its propensity for hierarchical or taxonomic order; its focus on typical instances; and its dereferentialization (its tendency to become detached from what it refers to).

Taxonomic organization

Hierarchical classification presupposes two operations: the division of things into superordinate categories (which Rosch, 1978, calls the vertical dimension of categorizing), and differentiation between classes of objects (which she calls the horizontal dimension). Inner speech involves both these types of operation.

The vertical dimension of classifying is seen in superordinate associations such as *lobster* → *crustacean*, and *peacock* → *bird*. The horizontal dimension is seen in polar oppositions (study 3) and differences (study 2), which in many cases seem to be abstract and concrete versions of the same kind of operation. Abstract words encourage polar opposites of a dichotomous sort (as in *fast* → *slow*). When dealing with concrete creatures the polarities are less stark and people use the dimension between the poles to make comparisons (*Antelope is a deer, like gazelle* → *but slower*).

Polar opposites have received a good deal of discussion in the clinical literature. They require little mental effort, and become more frequent under time pressure (Siipola, Walker and Kolb, 1955) or conditions of distraction (Jung, 1918). On the one hand these contrast responses indicate ability to think with a certain degree of abstractness, and they may thus be a predictor of 'normality' (Tendler, 1945) or even of educational level (Jung 1918). On the other hand they are what Rapaport, Gill and Schafer (1968) call 'stimulus-bound'. They are relatively superficial, and in staying close to the stimulus word may be used as a defence against plumbing, or indeed against drowning in, the psychic depths.

Focus on the typical

Consider the following:

Table 3.1 Free associative characteristics of verbal, visual and enactive representations

Study	Characteristics*	Examples	General description
	Verbal		
1,3	superordinate	lobster → crustacean	
3	opposite	fast → slow	taxonomic ordering based on prototypes
2	difference	→ live in different places	
1,3	rhyme	parrot → carrot	
1,3	phrase completion	April → showers	dereferentialized language
2	assertion of falsity/meaningless	→ is not true	
	Visual		
2,3	environment	reindeer → in the forest	
1	part	reindeer → antlers	
3	attribute	peacock → colourful	
3	instantiation (of abstract word)	thought → philosopher	vivid, picture-like qualities; absolute spatiality
2	nominalization	kangaroo → is a jumper	
2	metaphor	lobster → like a man in armour	
2	spatial relation	→ behind the rock	
2	intransitive action	→ walking	
2	– present-continuous tense	→ is walking	static without direct interaction or temporal flow
2	– locative adjunct	→ walking in the forest	

Table 3.1 Free associative characteristics of verbal, visual and enactive representations (continued)

Study	Characteristics*	Examples	General description
	Enactive		
1,2	transitive action	→ A bites B	direct interaction
2	– instrumental use of body part	→ sinks his teeth into	defining relative
2	– passive	→ is bitten by	spatiality
2	– ordinary present tense	→ bites	
2	– future and conditional modes	→ could, can, will bite	
2	– negative	→ could bite but doesn't	awareness of
2	– infinitives	→ wants to bite	possible futures and
2	reason for action	→ because he doesn't like it	of moral choice
2,3	physical consequence of action	→ and it makes him fall over	
2,3	emotional consequence of action	→ which makes him feel sad	
2	mental awareness	→ watching	affectivity
2,3	personality traits and emotions	→ proud, angry	

* Significantly different (p < .05, two-tailed) from one, or more usually both, the other two modes of thought in one or more of the three studies.

Camel could spit at kangaroo → Again that's highly improbable, er, they live in different areas.

Wallaby feels inferior to bison → This seems grossly unlikely as wallabies come from Australia and bison come from America.

Fair enough. In fact these judgments about the truth of the stimulus sentences represent a degree of reality testing far superior to anything found in either visual or enactive imagery. Freud (1911) distinguished between two principles of mental functioning: there is language, operating according to the reality principle in the functioning of the ego; and there are non-verbal representations, operating according to the pleasure principle in the functioning of the more fantastical id. The factual reference frame of inner speech sees in fantasy only falsehood. It cannot countenance what might implausibly be the case, but only what typically is the case.

Verbal representation focuses on the typical because its taxonomic categories are conceptually represented in terms of their prototypes. Rosch and her colleagues (Rosch, 1975a and b, 1978; Rosch and Mervis, 1975; Rosch, Mervis, Gray, Johnson and Boyes-Braem, 1976) have shown that categories have an internal structure and are organized with respect to the prototype at the centre. The prototype sums up both what the members of the category have in common (their 'family resemblances'), and how they differ from members of other categories. Thus for Rosch herself an alsatian is a prototypical dog, being both the most doggy sort of dog and the most different from members of such contrast categories as cats. The focus on typical cases in verbal representation is a natural adjunct to the conceptual order exhibited in the superordinates and differences.

Detachment from referents

The distance of verbal representation from particular objects and events starts with its conceptual nature and its concern with the typical rather than with the individual. There are two further stages in this dereferentialization. The first is the production of phrase completions, as in freedom → of speech and zebra → crossing. These, like contrast responses, are stimulus-bound associations, based this time on well-known phrases and sayings, which once triggered roll glibly off the tongue.

The extreme of dereferentialization is seen in rhyming associations, such as weasel → easel, and parrot → carrot. Here words are no longer referring symbols at all, but are taken as entities in their own right, their associations based on acoustic rather than semantic properties. Jung (1918) thought such responses to be highly defensive, judging by their unusually long associative reaction times. The remarks made by some of the participants in the studies suggest that rhymes are more available as responses if the stimulus word is repeated sub-vocally more than once, and that such repetition may be a deliberate strategy to exclude images which otherwise naturally flood in, in association to concrete words.

The dereferentialization of language is not something that most people worry about, or even have a name for. Those who do worry about it tend to be either poets or French intellectuals rather than psychologists). Barthes (1972) and Lefebvre (1971) have both discussed the ideological consequences of dereferentialization, and describe how a language which loses contact with its referents is vulnerable to use for propaganda purposes. The power of this language is seen in the fact that we can be seduced by patter like 'the sunshine breakfast' even while eating our bowl of soggy cereal on the ninth day of unremitting drizzle.

The general properties of verbal representation are shown in figure 3.1, which may be read as a map of the associative transitions that inner speech affords.

Structures in visual imagery

Many of the characteristic association types in visual imagery achieve their linguistic realization through some form of the verbs *to be* and *to have*. The reindeer *has* antlers, (which *have* a metaphorical likeness to certain Cladonia lichens), the reindeer *is* brown, it *is* in the forest and in the favourite present continuous verb tense it *is* walking. Being and Having are sometimes seen as the great poles of Human Existence, alternative ways of standing breast to breast with the Universe. Linguistically they have no such grandiose status. Indeed Lyons (1968) refers to them as mere 'dummy verbs' with no reality at a deep-structure level, and necessary only to carry information about number, person and tense. Lyons was writing when deep structures were supposed to be linguistic. Within the subsequent cognitive interpretation it is possible to speculate that relations of *being* and *having* are not primarily linguistic at all, but visual in origin. The mapping from the visual representation into language here is fixed only within very loose limits. A dog *has* four feet, but also *is* four-footed. It is brown, but might, if one wished to be pedantic about it, be said to possess the quality of brownness. Or one can simply conjoin the words and talk about brown dogs.

In terms of case grammar there is a remarkable uniformity in the case structures of all the visual association types. In the version of case grammar used by Braine (Braine and Wells, 1978; Braine and Hardy, 1982), the animal to which parts, attributes, locations and intransitive actions are attributed would be the *subject of attribution*.

The semantic nature of this subject and what is attributed to it can be discussed under three interrelated headings: the static spatiality of the visual image; its ontological depth; and its propensity for metaphor.

Static spatiality

One of the first things a typical visualizer does with a stimulus sentence about two

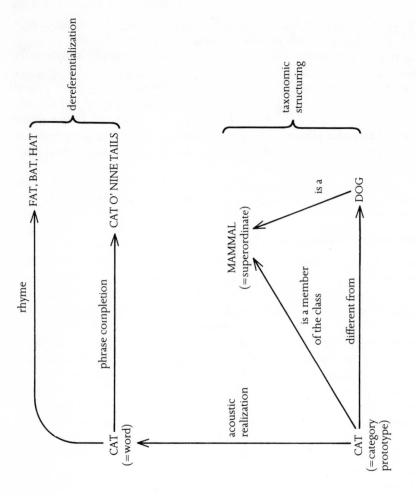

Figure 3.1   Map of semantic territory for verbal representation

animals is to find an environment that will accommodate both. This is what counts as making sense of the sentence. Once found, the environment becomes the reference frame to which all else is related. Animals are in it, their actions are in it, on it, through it, etc., and relationships between the two animals are mediated through their common relation to it:

Jellyfish could sting goat → On a raft, the goat going across a raft on the river and jellyfish is up through the logs.

Stallion is by the side of leopard → Paradise. . . I just suddenly saw a stallion and a leopard drinking from the water, rather the way you see in the pictures, paradise mixture, you know, sun and dappled pool.

These environments are often detailed and presumably take up considerable processing capacity, but they form in consciousness without apparent mental effort. Mandler, Seegmiller and Day (1977) suggest that the processing of locative information is automatic, unlike the processing of information about the internal constitution of objects. It may be that the object–locative relationship is a version of the primitive figure–ground relationship. That this operates 'automatically' is shown in von Senden's (1960) work with congenitally blind people who first gain their sight in adult life. They can at first make little sense of their new visual world beyond an awareness of colour, and an awareness that there are some things, figures, that stand out from the rest, the ground.

In the free association studies, animals relate to their environments through spatial relations, which may be elaborated in terms of intransitive actions. These are actions like running or sitting which do not 'carry over' to a direct object (in contrast to transitive actions like chasing or eating something which do take a direct object).[1] A beaver might be in the river, or, a little more elaborately, swimming in the river. Even when the environment is not mentioned, the frequent use of spatial prepositions indicates the continuing presence of a spatial framework in which up, down, to the left of, and so on, continue to have meaning. One gets the impression of a stage set, proscenium arch and all:

Zebra has a round belly, like rhino → They are on the same plain . . . somewhere . . . it's sort of my notion of Africa with flat trees on that, and zebra is on the left of the picture, looking left, and the rhino is sort of standing looking vaguely towards the front.

There are indications that even when the intransitive verbs denote energetic happenings, the image itself fails to depict this, and consists only of snapshots which have caught the action in mid-air.

Piaget and Inhelder (1971) maintain that purely visual imagery (as in children under 7) is itself static. It may represent movement, just as comic strips do, by using stance and location as movement cues. The Mighty Thor, spreadeagled between buildings, is seen as leaping between them, not as nailed uncomfortably to the sky. Visual images operate similarly. To say that something is flying is to say that it is apprehended with wings outspread, located against a background of sky. The characteristic verb tense here, the present continuous, is what one would expect in a description of arrested movement.

The presence of a detailed environment in visual imagery can cause problems in trying to get animals to interact:

> Donkey is kicking crocodile→I can't, I can't see, I can't imagine a donkey kicking a crocodile. I can see a sort of cross section of sky and grass and a river bank; so blue sky, green grass and a brown river bank, and sort of greeny-brown water. The donkey is in fact on the river bank and it's kicking, it's got one of its hind legs up in kicking position, and the crocodile is just sort of submarining along the surface of the water but certainly the donkey isn't kicking the crocodile.

Ontological depth

One of the striking features about visual imagery is that it involves a number of relationships between entities of different ontological types: object and environment, whole and part, object and attribute. The last two are especially important in the constitution of an individual object because they ensure that properties are united in something and are not just concatenated. The alternative to a world of Being and Having is a world of And. It would perhaps contain the following associative scenario: 'Legs & ears & black & white & tail & hooves'. The world of Being and Having provides a more hospitable arrangement, and also contains the cows which manage to hold all these properties together.

The object–attribute relationship appears to operate symmetrically. Objects may be analysed in terms of their attributes, as in peacock→colourful, and niece→little: and conversely, attributes may be instantiated in objects, as in wide→river, and yellow→daffodils.

The other important constitutive relationship, whole–part, plays a number of roles in the semantic structure of the image. Palmer (1977) suggests that it may serve as a backbone in the hierarchical organization of perception. It can do this because whole and part are defined relative to each other, so that parts may be wholes relative to other and smaller parts. A fish is whole in relation to its skin, which is a whole in relation to its scales, each of which is a whole with regard to the cells which make it up, and so on. If the relationship between two things is that of whole to part, then they count as being at different levels of discourse. Confusing them leads to category mistakes (Ryle, 1949), such as assuming that the fish's skin is hungry or its scales are swimming to the Sargasso sea. The whole–part relationship, as the Gestalt psychologists realized, is a brace against reductionism, not an invitation to it.

As well as constituting the ontological backbone along which levels of description are arranged, the whole–part relationship has another vital function: that of defining what kinds of physical action are possible. Anything at all may move, but only a thing with legs can walk or run; and only a thing with wings can fly. Body parts are the tacit instruments of the actions carried out by the whole. When albatrosses fly and swoop, they do so with wings. The wings are not explicitly mentioned as instruments in visual imagery, perhaps because flying is 'marked' for wingedness, and needs no explicit statement. Perhaps too, it would increase the complexity of the image unduly to include whole and part simultaneously. There is evidence from developmental studies that this is a sophisticated accomplishment, achieved only during the period of concrete operations (Elkind, Koegler and Go, 1964). Before this, children are aware of either whole or part, but not of both.

Metaphor

I use the term 'metaphor' to cover a variety of associations, including cases of visual metamorphosis, where one thing actually changes into another (as a badger into a zebra, or a camel into a toy camel on wheels); also substitutions, where something is represented by something else without any actual metamorphosis being involved (a kangaroo represented by a cartoon kangaroo); and similes, where a likeness between two things is acknowledged explicitly (hedgehog's spikes are like zoo bars). Relations of isomorphy are always involved:

> Stallion is by the side of leopard → Stallion is by the side of leopard . . . Stubbs . . . yes, yes, Stubbs picture isn't it of a lion or is it horses as well? Yes, that's what, a picture, I've a painting in mind.

> Camel could spit at kangaroo → Well the first image I suppose is of a camel being in a . . . standing with a frown on its face (laugh) being of the . . . no, I can't express it . . . feeling so angry that he's capable of spitting and there's a subs . . . and the next image came immediately of a kind of bullet-shaped piece of spit about a yard out of the camel's mouth, flying like a kind of rocket across the horizon (laugh).

> Scorpion is segmented like lobster → Oh, a scorpion and a lobster and an an idea of a man . . . in . . . a nice shiny red suit of armour.

There has been a recent upsurge of interest in metaphor (see e.g. Ortony, 1979), which allows us to say that while such concrete isomorphisms are only one kind of metaphor, many of the processes involved may hold true for the whole class. Lakoff and Johnson (1980) show that metaphor is an all-pervasive cognitive phenomenon, but the idea that at least some metaphors have a visual origin is supported by Paivio (1979) and Miller (1979).

The importance of similarities in metaphor has been recognized since Aristotle wrote about the topic. The similarities involved in the metaphors of visual imagery are usually of parts, attributes, or spatial relationships. A possible mechanism here is that in the transition from object to attribute, the whole becomes indistinct, and the attribute is then reinstantiated in something different. The *shiny red suit of armour* case takes off from a lobster (boiled). The reference to *segmented* leads to a focus on just the hard and jointed exoskeleton. This image fragment is then instantiated in a *nice shiny red suit of armour*, which is just as accommodating to it as was *lobster*. Indeed, at the time, more accommodating: images may have a refractory period, and thought is more likely to go on than to go back. You cannot, to misquote Heraclitus, look into the same image twice. Not only because it is flowing but because it is changed by the looking.

The general properties of visual imagery are summarized in figure 3.2.

Structures in enactive imagery

Enactive imagery relates animals together through the transitive interactions possible between them, and the motives that legitimate these actions. The important cases are: *agentive*, for the instigators of the actions; *instrumental*, for the body parts used in them; *experiencer*, for the subject of the feelings; and *objective*, for what is acted on (in fact, in many cases, *patient*, or even *victim*, would be more appropriate terms).

The following discussion separates what are *in vivo* four interrelated features of enactive imagery: the agency involved in transitive action; the relative spatiality determined by transitive action; the subjectivity which informs action in a number of ways; and the future towards which much action is oriented.

Agency in transitive action

In linguistics the distinction between transitive and intransitive verbs is as much one of usage as of type. Some verbs can be used in both forms. *Moved* is transitive in *somebody moved the stone*, but intransitive in *the stone moved*.

In cases where verbs have a preferred form, transitive and intransitive verbs may belong to the same verb family, and differ from one another in systematic ways.[2] In the large class of movement verbs, *move* is the nuclear form (Dixon's, 1971, term), being a basic kind of action which may be done by virtually anything. Non-nuclear verbs, which describe more specific kinds of moving, are derived from *move* by additional specifications: thus *walking* is *moving with legs*, *running* is *moving fast with legs*, and so on. An important kind of additional specification is with regard to intent, and Miller and Johnson-Laird (1976) suggest that this is what makes the difference between an intransitive action and a transitive one. It is the difference between *tiger is running after hyena*, and *tiger is chasing hyena*. The intransitive *running after* could be just happening to be running in the same direction, but slower, or later; or it could be running with malice aforethought.

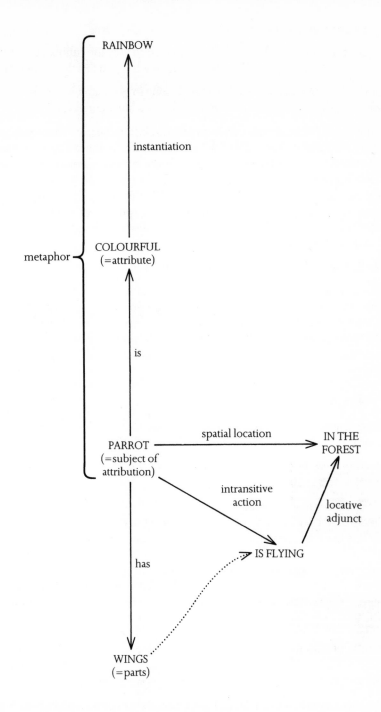

Figure 3.2 Map of semantic territory for visual imagery

The transitive verb is not so neutral with regard to why the running is occurring. Transitive verbs have eaten of the tree of knowledge, and lost their innocence:

Donkey is kicking crocodile → And he's going to get quite a lot of money when he manages to kill him and sell the skin to the white hunter.

Only those without innocence need develop a morality; and in enactive imagery, to balance the potential for violent action there are a number of mechanisms for controlling it. These include the fact that action does not happen without some loosely legitimating motivation. As a moral stance this is low grade, but it is a start. A little more sophisticated is the ability to envisage possible consequences, admittedly usually from the perspective of harm to self. One further control derives from the morally more advanced ability to empathize with the victims of one's acts:

Hedgehog sniffs at walrus → Walrus'll get pricked by the spikes.

This indicates an intersubjective perspective in so far as there is identification both with the actor, at least according to the enactive encoding instructions, and with the victim of that actor's action, expressed in the passive voice. This intersubjective perspective is an important social prerequisite for the emergence of moral agency, as distinct from the more impulsive kind.

Relative spatiality

Most transitive verbs include a surprising amount of information about the kind of spatial relationship involved in them. Consider nibbling:

Bulldog is in the same field as stallion → AND is about to aggressively nibble the stallion's ankles.

Nibble tells us that it is being done with teeth; that it involves several little bites rather than one big one; and that contact is necessary to do it. About to nibble tells us therefore that it is the toothed end of bulldog that is critically approaching stallion. The spatial relation is further clarified by reference to the stallion's ankles as the portion most threatened. Motivating these spatial arrangements is the aggressive intent of the bulldog. Enactive space is thus relative in the sense that bulldog and stallion are here considered wholly in relation to one another, and without regard to the field mentioned in the stimulus sentence; but it is also affective, structured by intent.

In some cases the instrument involved in the action is made explicit, even though it is not semantically necessary to do so. Everyone knows that pecking is done with beaks, but it may still make sense to spell it out:

Peacock despises jellyfish → And gives it a couple of pecks with its beak to make sure the jellyfish knows that it's despised.

It is evident that visual and enactive representations operate with different versions of spatiality. In visual imagery, space is absolute, organized with reference to an environmental framework; in enactive imagery it is relative, mediated through transitive actions and their complements.

Subjectivity

Enactive imagery is thoroughly permeated with subjective awareness. This shows up in the intentfulness of the transitive verbs (*running after* can be perceived from outside, but it takes inside information to realize that it is really *chasing*); it is revealed in desires, such as *wanting to bite*; it shows up in references to sensory and intellectual processes such as *watching* and *thinking about*; and at its most strongly affective it emerges in personality dispositions like *kindliness*, and in emotions like *being scared of* or *adoring*.

These subjective occurrences are usually embedded in the general context of action, either actual or potential. Some actions are the fulfilment of affective intentions:

Parrot is in the same forest as gorilla→(laugh) And it . . . it's humiliating the gorilla by perching upon its head.

Some potential actions lack motivational justification and never achieve actuality. This causes most of the negations produced in enactive imagery:

Badger could bite wallaby→But he's too fat and lazy to be bothered to.

In fact it is often when action is *not* happening that subjectivity is most evident. This is what Freud would have predicted. For him the inhibition of impulsive action was the foundation of all later intellectual development. Compare:

Crocodile snaps at flamingo→And breaks it in two

where the action proceeds with a minimum of subjective fuss, with the following, where at first the action is conditionally suspended pending the exploration of its possible legitimations:

Elephant is fond of badger→Yes and he could in foot, fact, put his foot on badger and break badger's back if it was necessary, or if it, or if he was feeling that way inclined . . . there wouldn't have to be a real reason 'cause he's very very big, and has got a very wide foot, with tremendous power for crushing badgers' backs.

Desire is also tied up with action that is as yet only potential. One cannot want what one already has, and conversely, one may be busy with wanting to act only because not busy acting:

Jackal could attack peacock→Has a rabid desire to do so, all those poncey feathers make him sick.

Sometimes action is not mentioned at all and the relation between the animals is affective. However the feelings only seem justified by reference to a prescience which foresees probable future interactions:

Parrot is in the same forest as gorilla → It'd be frightened.

The parrot's paranoia here may be a consequence of the fact that those who are not exercising their own agency are liable to become the victim of someone else's.

The future

Enactive imagery has a temporal organization, with actions having beginnings (reasons), dynamic middles (present tense) and ends (consequences). As well as the simple present, distinctive verb tenses include a variety of modal auxiliaries, indicating potential action which for some reason or another hasn't actually happened yet. The present tense has two uses. The most frequent is episodic, indicating dynamic action: tiger chases the hyena describes movement, not a snapshot of movement. The other use is dispositional: tigers chase their prey as a matter of general tiger-nature. Here chase is similar to can chase.

The future orientation of enactive imagery is revealed minimally in the marking of transitive verbs for intent. Even the current chases is oriented toward the future, in being directed towards some goal: elevenses, or tea. It is given more explicit linguistic realization in a variety of ways. These include the use of could, can and will as auxiliaries; in the use of forms of the verb to go, as in he's going to do something dreadful; and in the use of concatenative constructions like hoping to, wanting to and trying to:

Porcupine is bristling at albatross → Wants to get the albatross, wants to fix it on the ends of its spines.

Looking towards the future extends beyond the particular action itself, to its possible consequences. This provides the kind of moral foresight discussed earlier, which may be important in inhibiting foolish actions:

Reindeer charges at porcupine → But realizing that he's got sharp quills all over his body, slithers to a halt in the snow and walks away again.

In human beings too, a sense of future is considered desirable. Delinquents have a rather poor future-time sense (Siegman, 1961); and temporal disturbances are involved in many emotional disorders (Minkowski, 1958; Ellenberger, 1958; Wallace and Rabin, 1960).

Fillmore treats the future as external to case frameworks themselves. This makes the future a kind of present that hasn't happened yet, which is clearly an inadequate account. The difficulty lies in formulating anything better.[3]

The general properties of enactive representation are summarized in figure 3.3.

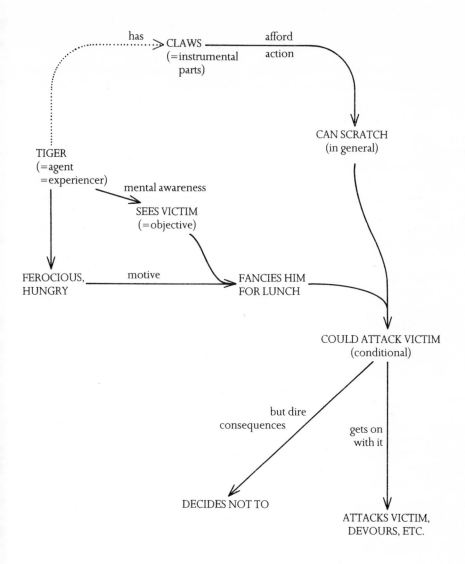

Figure 3.3 Map of semantic territory for enactive imagery

Some of the pathways here are more tentative than those for verbal or visual representations.

Making up the mind: a triptych of meanings

Each mode of thought operates over a distinct semantic territory, and gives its own account of reality. In inner speech there are words and concepts; in visual imagery there are environments and subjects of attribution with properties; and in enactive imagery there are agents, actions and experiencers.

Each mode of thought has an internal equilibrium, balancing a way of taking things apart with a way of holding them together. In inner speech the fission of opposites and differentiations is balanced by fusion in superordinate classes. In visual imagery parts and attributes are only analysed in the context of their co-ordination in the whole. In enactive imagery the separate individuals of agent and patient are brought together through action and feeling.

A possible interpretation of the differences between the three modes of thought would be that they involve primarily differences of complexity, reflecting the fact that there are different numbers of coding systems involved. The argument would be that the original stimuli in the free-association studies are words, to which a visualizer adds images, and to which someone using enactive imagery adds also internalized action. There are reasons for claiming that this is not true in a simple sense, though it may be partially true in a complex one.

The composition of inner speech is not like that of visual imagery minus the characteristically visual bits. It is different. Enactive imagery is not just visual imagery plus internalized action. At the very least the addition of the action liberates images of objects from their environment and converts them to agents or patients. Piaget and Inhelder's work (1971) shows, however, that there are developmental grounds for suggesting that enactive imagery does develop out of visual imagery and to that extent is an addition to it. A case grammatical interpretation of this developmental sequence is that visual imagery involves a basic two-case system (with subject of attribution and either locative or objective, but not both at once), and that adding internal action converts this to a three-case system (agent plus instrument plus either objective or experiencer).[4]

The following features of the data from the second study can be accounted for on the assumption that while enactive imagery may depict three-termed (three-case) relationships, visual imagery may only depict two-termed ones.

1   Parts and environments, though both characteristically visual, rarely co-occur.
2   A detailed environment is inimical to the representation of transitive action.
3   The instrumental use of body parts is not mentioned in visual imagery, though the parts themselves are. In enactive imagery parts occur as instrumental to transitive actions, but not otherwise.

Other kinds of structural continuity are also evident, and it is generally the case that while verbal, visual and enactive representations have sufficient distinctiveness to justify their treatment as separate systems, there are strong and important semantic connections between them. These ensure that we have one mind, not three of it. There are connections in two general regions: between verbal and visual domains, and between visual and enactive.

Relations between verbal and visual representations have to do with the criteria by which concrete objects are assigned to abstract superordinate categories, and the categories differentiated from one another. Rosch, Mervis, Gray, Johnson and Boyes-Braem (1976) talk about the world and objects in it exhibiting correlational structure: beings with feathers usually also have wings. It is this correlational structure that is encapsulated in the abstract prototype defining the superordinate category. The abstract conception of *bird* is erected upon the concrete foundation of such visual properties as *wings* and *feathers*. The situation is complicated by the fact that for low levels of abstraction (*bird* or *dog*) we can use a generic image as an alternative to an abstract representation; and at higher levels of abstraction (like *mammal*) we can represent the generic by a concrete exemplar. The fact that verbal superordinates are generated from visual properties results in the relatively poor differentiation between verbal and visual representations seen in the data here.

Attributes also play a role in verbal structures, particularly in differentiating classes of objects from one another. The attributes of the visual domain are matter for comparison and polar opposition in the verbal.

The contact between visual and enactive modes is through parts and action. The whole–part relationship is characteristically visual, and tacitly determines the repertoire of possible actions. These same parts are the explicit instruments of enactive transitive actions. Furthermore these transitive actions frequently belong to the same family of actions as the visual intransitive ones, differing in the additional specification of intent.

What these cross-connections amount to is that the semantic territory covered by the free-association studies is best described as a triptych, in which visual structures form the central panel, with verbal and enactive ones hinged on either side. A sample of this arrangement is given in figure 3.4.

Some thoughts on 'structure'

Though the details may vary, most of the kinds of structures shown in the figure are familiar from a number of memory models. What is different is that figure 3.4 is divided into three semantic domains, corresponding to verbal, visual and enactive representations. Each domain depicts the cognitive structures characteristic of the relevant form of representation.

In the light of the empirical findings which have been discussed, it may not appear contentious to say that particular cognitive structures are characteristic of particular forms of representation. In fact there is a considerable tangle of conceptual problems lurking in this statement, which need to be pulled out and

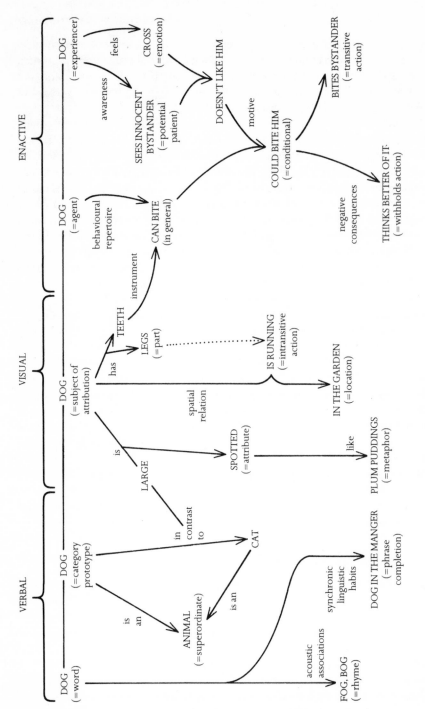

Figure 3.4 A semantic triptych: the free-associative lives of dogs

unravelled. These problems include how the structures are accessed; the nature of the relationship between the structures and the surface representations; and at bedrock, the very nature of the structures themselves.

The only safe ground here is given by the bare findings of the free-association studies. These can be summarized thus: the same stimulus, used with a different representational instruction, leads to structurally different associations. For example: *parrot* represented in inner speech might evoke the superordinate *bird*; represented in visual imagery it might evoke the attribute *green*; represented in enactive imagery it might evoke the transitive action *cracking nuts*.

A possible interpretation of these findings is to say that these are just three different language samples, which should be treated as such, without reference to internal happenings of any sort. The difficulty with this interpretation is in the question why the language samples should be different; and indeed there seems to be no parsimonious way of explaining this.

The alternative is to assume that the external language refers to internal representations which themselves may or may not be linguistic in form. This raises the question of the reliability of verbal reports on mental processes. Nisbett and Wilson (1977) have indicated that under some circumstances verbal reports may be highly inaccurate, especially when people are asked about the *causes* of their behaviour. Fortunately it seems unlikely that the same degree of scepticism is warranted by other, simpler kinds of report. For example the use of the 'verbal report' of the items remembered in a memory task may be liable to some suspicion, but total scepticism would amount to sawing off the methodological branch that much of psychology is still sitting on. The possibility of inaccuracies in verbal reports, whether of real-world events or of internal ones, is probably reduced by asking people for simple expressive or descriptive information rather than for complex interpretations. For simple reports it is difficult to see why *I have an image of a reindeer* or *I feel hungry* should be treated with much greater scepticism than *I went to the theatre last night* or *I see a guillemot*. People may sometimes lie or make mistakes, but they cannot be assumed to do so *all* the time.

If language can be used to access other and internal forms of representation, there then arises the problem of the extent to which the properties of these forms of representation have been distorted because they have been filtered through the language used to express them.

In some ways this is not a peculiarly psychological problem, but one shared by all sciences which have to access their phenomena indirectly, through instruments. All instruments 'distort' what they access. The gas chromatograph breaks biological molecules into fragments under high temperature, but still remains a valuable instrument of biochemical analysis. Techniques in atomic physics similarly 'distort' the nature of the particles examined in order to explore that nature. In the case of accessing internal representations, to worry about how 'the phenomena accessed' are distorted by 'the means of access' implies that under normal circumstances mental phenomena happen without ever being accessed.

This is not the case. People often express a good deal of what they are thinking, so that asking them to do this in psychological studies is only tapping a natural process; it is not introducing a highly artefactual procedure liable to twist thought out of any semblance to its normal form.

The content of thought, verbal and non–verbal, may be expressed through language, just as the properties of biological molecules may be 'expressed' in the recordings which form the output of gas chromatography, or the properties of subatomic particles may be 'expressed' in their tracks in bubble chambers. Language is a viable, if not a wholly transparent, means of access to mental representations. Thus if a person visualizing a *parrot* produces the associate *green*, whereas a person verbalizing *parrot* never produces the associate *green*, it makes sense to say that the object–attribute structure involved here derives from the visual image. It may be expressed through language but it did not originate there.

Interpreting the structures as originating from the various forms of internal representation raises a further problem: the problem of the precise relationship of the cognitive structure, in this case the object–attribute structure, and the surface representation, the visual image.

The discussion in chapter 2 mentioned a number of interpretations of the relationship between structural and phenomenal levels, ranging from accounts which focus exclusively on one level (as Paivio, 1971, does on the phenomenal, or Pylyshyn, 1973, on the structural), to accounts which accommodate representations at both levels (e.g.: Kosslyn *et al.*, 1979; Anderson, 1978, 1983; Rosenberg and Simon, 1977). Glucksberg (1984) suggests that there is an emerging consensus of some kind, evident in a general agreement that the question of whether there are only modality specific stores or whether there is in addition a common underlying propositional store, is not an issue to be decided by empirical evidence. Most investigators find it useful to include both kinds of store. This has led to structural and surface representations being included indifferently; either in the sense of there being a network in which the elements may be indifferently visual, verbal or propositional (as in Anderson, 1983), or in the sense of underlying propositions being indifferently instantiated in any of a number of surface representations (as in Rosenberg and Simon, 1977). The free-association data indicate a less arbitrary relationship, and show that particular surface representations have specialized and characteristic structural properties; or conversely, that particular structures cannot equally well be instantiated in different surface representations.

One of the points that can be drawn from this structural division of labour between the three forms of representation is that abstract structure and surface content cannot be wholly separated. There is a non-arbitrary relationship between them, and it is therefore not sufficient to see the structures as entities separate from the surface representations, lying either beneath or alongside these other representations.

The key problem here is that traditionally the structures have been seen as distinct from modality specific or surface representations. Most theorists preserve the distinction itself, though they define it in different ways.

Pylyshyn's (1973, 1979) work provides a very clear version of this 'autonomous structures' viewpoint. For him the structures are abstract a-modal propositions, inaccessible to consciousness. It is these abstract structures that form the functional elements in cognition, and not the surface conscious representations of which they are essentially descriptions. One of the criteria Pylyshyn uses for distinguishing structures and surface representations is that the structures are inaccessible to consciousness, while the surface representations are accessible to it.

This inaccessibility claim for structures is an interesting one, given the source from which much of the original information about structures is derived. The notion of structure in cognitive psychology derives largely from discussions in linguistics about syntactic and semantic structures. In fact these structures are not at all inaccessible to consciousness, being originally discovered by people using only their linguistic intuition. Intuition revealed the structures just sitting there in the language, apparent to anyone who cared to look. The distinction between structural and phenomenal therefore cannot be preserved by an appeal to the inaccessibility of the one as opposed to the accessibility of the other.

There is, however, another important way of drawing the distinction. Kosslyn et al. (1979) and Snodgrass (1984) use the initially appealing idea that the abstract structures lie behind the surface ones, and are distinguished by virtue of being their causes. Structures are generative; and surface representations are generated from them.

To see why this account cannot work, and to see the kind of ontological sleight of hand it involves, requires another appeal to psycholinguistic history. Noam Chomsky, the linguist who brought the notion of structures into prominence, carefully stated that he was interested in a competence model of language rather than a performance one; and outlined a theory of transformational generative grammar in which surface structures were 'generated' from more abstract deep structures. The choice of words was perhaps unfortunate. In a competence model the fact that the symbol S (for sentence) can be rewritten as NP + VP (noun phrase + verb phrase) means that what is S at the most general level of description may legitimately be analysed into a noun phrase and a verb phrase at a more specific level. This is *logical* generativeness. It does not mean that when we speak we *actually* generate sentences in the same way, by starting with deep and abstract form and working up to concrete and surface content. The distinction between deep and surface structures has gradually been eroded in linguistics (see e.g. Lakoff, 1971), though it lingers in other areas, including cognitive psychology. The free-association data suggest that to talk about structure is to say that there is a pattern in phenomena; it is not to say there is a pattern *and* phenomena, with the pattern lying behind. Linguistic structures are conceptual patterns discernible in language; they do not lie behind and cause the language. Cognitive structures are the conceptual patterns discernible in thinking; they do not lie behind and cause the thinking. *Structures are patterns evident in phenomena, not the causes of these patterns. Structures are in phenomena, not lurking behind them.*

To see precisely how they are in phenomena it is necessary only to go back to the data. If a person free-associates *feathers* to their visual image of a *parrot*, it is going beyond the evidence to say that they are using a whole–part structure to form their association. What the bare evidence shows is that when people focus on their visual image of a parrot, the next thing that comes into their focus of attention is the feathers. Attention shifts from the image of the parrot to the image of the feathers. Indeed, typically the mental representation of the parrot apparently evolves into the more close-up image of just the feathers. There is no mental entity called a cognitive structure evident here, but only a transition from one thought to the next. The whole–part structure is not an entity either 'behind' or 'in' the image, it is a temporal patterning, a transition of attention between one image and its successor.

All the cognitive structures evident in the free-association data are in fact essentially temporal. There is no direct evidence for structures as independently existing entities, as quasi-things occupying the mind. There is only direct evidence for temporal structuring. In free-associating, people are making transitions, for example from whole to part, or from object to superordinate, and the structures are the pathways or transitions that thought may take from one idea to the next in the associative process. The structures which can be picked out in the free associative data are thus indicative of the pathways thought may take. Different forms of representation *afford* different pathways (to borrow a term from Gibson, 1977). In the process of making sense of a stimulus, people therefore move their attention around it in particular ways, and this leads to the different constructions of meaning seen in the three forms of representation.

This view attributes to cognitive structures a status similar to that of biochemical equations. The structure *whole → part* describes a metamorphosis of one mental representation into another, just as the biochemical equations in a metabolic pathway describe how one biologically important molecule is metabolized into another. *Structures are descriptions of processes, they are not entities participating in those processes.*

One last problem remains. This is the type–token problem, which is a traditional philosophical minefield. The type–token problem is essentially the problem of the relationship between universal and particular. In cognitive psychology it takes the form of the problem of the relationship between the generic representations of semantic memory (types), and their particular instances in episodic consciousness (tokens).

It is useful here to compare the metabolic account with some recent 'spreading activation' models of memory (e.g.: Bower, 1981; Anderson, 1983), because the comparison makes it clear that the two views cope with the type–token problem in rather different ways.

According to the spreading activation view, memory is represented in terms of a propositionally structured network, with associative linkages between the nodes (the concepts or types) in the network providing the route along which activation spreads to particular nodes when they are in use. The types (general concepts) are represented as nodes in the network, and tokens (particular events) are represented by the spreading activation which links and activates the set of concepts involved in the event. For Bower the particular token *Mary kissed me* is represented by the activation of the generic types (the nodes), for *Mary*, *kiss*, and *myself*, by the passage of activation spreading between them. Roughly speaking, the types are mental entities (nodes or concepts), and tokens rely on the structures between them (these are the associative linkages along which activation spreads; they are based on particular experiences and give rise to particular representations when activated).

In the metabolic account the arrangement is different: roughly, the mental entities (the representations in consciousness, e.g. images) are particular tokens, and the structures between them are types (i.e. generic kinds of transitions). Here the particular representations in consciousness do not arise by the activation of any underlying generic representation, rather they arise from the preceding particular representation in consciousness (this is not to preclude neural processing, which is presumably where they 'arise from' in another sense). Particular representations arise from their predecessors not (or at least not solely) on the basis of particular experience with the transition which is being used, but because of generic kinds of transitions, the cognitive structures, which mental processing relies on. Experience undoubtedly is important in determining the transitions, but generic types of change may override particular experiences of change. This is seen with especial force in the case of the 'metaphorical' transitions of visual imagery. No one has ever actually seen a lobster turning into a man in a shiny red suit of armour, so there is no direct experience to support or encourage so bizarre an occurrence, yet in terms of mental events it is a simple and compelling kind of shift.

The metabolic account, with its interpretation of cognitive structures as descriptive of generic kinds of transformation that may occur between particular mental representations, is in some ways not greatly different from other models in cognitive psychology. But the small differences have large implications. Where there are differences they may stem mainly from the reliance of the metabolic account solely on observations of human thought processes, in contrast to many information processing models which have a considerable investment both in memory and in computer modelling.

The shift from a metaphorically spatialized notion of structures (as particularizing links between generic concepts), to a temporal notion of structures (as generic transformations that may occur between particular representations) has some important implications. The metabolic account will allow a dynamic and attentional interpretation of the personality correlates of cognitive styles in chapter 6, and will allow a dynamic and temporal interpretation of the relationship between thought and feeling in chapter 10.

Summary

This chapter has been concerned with the structural properties of the three modes of thought. It uses free association on the practical side and case grammar on the theoretical side, to articulate the different ways of making sense of the world that are afforded by verbal, visual and enactive representations. Inner speech is abstract and concerned with words and hierarchically organized concepts. Visual imagery focuses on the parts and attributes, the environment and intransitive actions of its subject of attribution. Enactive imagery is organized affectively and with a future time perspective, and involves experiencers of feelings and agents who act transitively and with goals in mind. Figure 3.4 summarizes the findings. This threefold distinction is not new. One of the *Upanishads* puts the same matter more tersely: *this universe is a trinity and this is made of name, form and action.*

Each mode of thought may be said to involve different kinds of cognitive structures, provided that these structures are interpreted as descriptive of the patterns of transformation that occur between one thought and the next in the stream of consciousness.

4

Day-dreams, fantasies and other idle thoughts

The free association studies were concerned primarily with the cognitive features of verbal, visual and enactive representations. This chapter involves a preliminary and in vivo exploration of the affective aspects. It looks at day-dreams, fantasies and other idle thoughts, and at how thought and feeling are interrelated in them. Day-dreams and kindred phenomena are here used more as a method through which the relationships between thought and feeling can be explored than as the focus of study in their own right.

Cognition and affect in day-dreaming

If dreams are the royal road to the unconscious, day-dreams are surely one of the busier by-roads. They are less dramatic and more plebeian, but appear to involve the same fundamental processes (Freud, 1900, 1908b; Starker, 1974; Cartwright and Munroe, 1968). Night-dreams often have a symbolic grandeur which disguises their latent content and allows people to recount them over the breakfast table without feeling unduly exposed. Day-dreams come into consciousness wearing flimsier symbolic cladding and sometimes reveal our needs and feelings with what Singer (1966) refers to as an embarrassing propensity for soap-opera and cliché.

Freud (1908b) saw all day-dreams, like all night-dreams, as being attempts to gratify in fantasy wishes unmet by reality. Recent writers have tended to emphasize that day-dreaming may also have cognitive functions.

Singer and Antrobus (1967) show that at the very least day-dreaming may keep people awake when doing some task that is otherwise so boring that they might drop off to sleep over it. Rather more productively, Klinger (1971) suggests that day-dreaming may be a way of mulling over some of our 'current concerns'; and Varendonck (1921) describes some of his day-dream sequences as being in a question and answer format, as if at each stage the day-dream were trying out possible solutions to problems. Occasionally our wool-gathering may be of a high order, and Freud (1908a) and Singer (1966) both speculate that many works of literature are but reworked day-dreams.

In all these instances a motivational component is intimately intertwined with the cognitive. Fantasy-based therapies, such as Leuner's (1977, 1978) Guided Affective Imagery, assume that the cognitive and affective aspects are related sufficiently strongly at this level for the feelings to be modified through the thoughts, and projective tests such as the Rorschach and the Thematic Appreception Test also tap this level.

There is evidence that day-dreaming is not a homogeneous phenomenon, and that there exist a number of different day-dreaming 'styles'. The most important work here is that of Jerome Singer and his colleagues (Singer and McCraven, 1961; Singer and Antrobus, 1963, 1972). Their factor analytic work with the Imaginal Processes Inventory suggests the existence of three, or possibly four, main patterns of day-dreaming: 1) anxious distractible day-dreaming; 2) obsessional emotional day-dreaming; 3) positive, vivid day-dreaming; and the final factor, which sometimes merges with the third, 4) controlled thoughtfulness. The last two patterns are typical of what Singer (1976) calls 'the happy day-dreamer', the person who enjoys day-dreaming and who can put it to positive use. The first two day-dreaming styles involve a greater preponderance of negative emotions. In a recent reanalysis of a large amount of data collected on the Imaginal Processes Inventory, Giambra (1980) found thirty three factors. This greatly adds to the complexity of the original picture while furthering the general notion that there are different kinds of day-dream with different affective atmospheres. Unfortunately this work does not give much guidance on whether particular affective tones are associated with day-dreams in particular representational forms, as the Inventory concentrates, though not exclusively, on visual day-dreams.

The following study used 'idle thoughts' as a general term, rather than 'day-dreams', in order to pre-empt any assumption that the only phenomena of interest are visual fantasies with reasonably elaborate plots. Preliminary work showed that many purely verbal idle thoughts consist of brief phrases or sentences, which are too short to have anything like a plot, or even much temporal extension. Some purely enactive idle thoughts were of equivalent brevity, and it was often only when these forms of representation appeared in conjunction with visual imagery that the idle thought approached the level of complexity that most people associate with a proper day-dream.

The study of idle thoughts

The idle thoughts study involved people keeping a 'Journal of Idle Thoughts' over a period of ten days. The introductory pages of the Journal indicated the general focus of the study as being on different forms of idle thought – verbal, visual and enactive – and the kinds of feelings and emotions that accompany the different types. The notion of 'idle thoughts' was elaborated as follows:

> Probably all of us spend at least part of our time engaged in 'idle thought' – when the stream of consciousness is not focused on any particular task. Sometimes these idle thoughts may interrupt our directed thought processes; sometimes they are interpolated very rapidly between one focused thought and the next; sometimes we discover a fantasy stream that has been going on in a subterranean way beneath the more conscious processes.
>
> Idle thoughts generally are a kind of thinking that 'happens in me' rather than thinking that 'I do'.

Table 4.1   Summary of themes of idle thoughts

Verbal
1   Critical or belittling, especially of taxonomic misfits.
2   Evoke a sense of alienation, as if someone else were speaking them.
3   May compensate for unpleasant episodes in real life.

Visual
1   Sometimes sparked off by memories.
2   Involve groups or crowds of people.
3   Concern with sex and romance.
4   Preoccupation with how others view the self.

Enactive
1   Usually sparked off by present experience.
2   Involve identifying with people or objects.
3   Preponderance of morbid themes.
4   Strong emotions, both positive and negative.
5   Various mythological and supernatural themes.

Verbal-visual composites
1   Arise in compensation for unsatisfactory past experience.
2   Themes of power and pride.
3   Involve negative feelings toward others.

Visual-enactive composites
1   Predominance of sexual and romantic themes.
2   Generally positive affective tone.

The analysis of the idle thoughts collected by this procedure showed that distinctive affective themes were indeed associated with different forms of representation. Characteristic features are shown in table 4.1, and fuller technical data on the procedure and results are given in appendix B.

There are some features which appear to be characteristic of idle thoughts generally, regardless of form of representation, and which presumably distinguish them from more directed thought processes. For example, the results show broad agreement with Singer's (1966) finding that day-dreaming most often occurs in drowsy or undemanding situations. This interpretation of the current results requires the (reasonable) assumption that studying sometimes counts as a drowsy or undemanding situation. Interestingly, visual-enactive day-dreams, which tend to be both elaborate and positively toned, were most frequent in the pre-sleep context particularly picked out by Singer. Pure enactive idle thoughts never occurred in this kind of situation, perhaps because a pre-sleep muscular relaxation precludes the kinaesthetic component of enactive imagery.

Singer found that many day-dreams were orientated towards the future, a result which is not paralleled in the present study. The discrepancy appears to have arisen for two reasons. One is that in so far as future-oriented thinking involves planning, it would not count as idle, and would thus not be recorded. The other has to do with how one interprets the idea of the future; from beforehand, or with the benefit of hindsight. If someone sees a stranger on a train and wonders what it would be like to make love to him or her, this seems more like doing something in fantasy now than working towards doing something in reality later. Day-dreaming may incidentally serve as practice of social and indeed of sexual skills which will be useful in the future, but this is not (at least phenomenologically) why it is done. Day-dreaming resembles children's play here. Both are effortless fun at the time, but turn out to be useful learning with the benefit of hindsight.

The following sections discuss the particular affective properties of the different representational forms of idle thought, including some of the more important composite forms.

Verbal idle thoughts: taxonomy and castigation

The idle thoughts which occur in purely verbal form are typically brief and isolated comments rather than elaborate narratives. Their most striking feature is that they are highly critical. A significant number of these criticisms are directed towards innocent strangers who have done nothing at all to justify castigation, but who are unfortunate enough to be noticeably odd:

It is dark, I am walking across campus. Approaching the arch someone comes up fast from behind, and precedes me through the arch. I notice a certain silhouette and then: 'He's a darkie', the words spoken in an 'appropriate' tone of voice.

I think the immediate feeling was an appropriate feeling – simply of prejudice! So it was very quickly repressed and replaced by horror.

Somewhere behind was my father speaking.

Sometimes the criticism is expressed in humorous terms:

> This afternoon while walking down a main street in a city centre area I saw a man and a woman walking in front of me with hands joined. Suddenly I heard a voice from within saying,
>
> 'If she was only two feet smaller, and he was about four stone lighter, there may be some hope.'!!!!
>
> *Type* verbal
>
> N.B. The emotion here was one of extreme joviality.

To be oversized for one's sex, or overweight, or black in a white community, is to be peculiar, and, as if that were not enough to cope with, it is evidently also to be the butt of rude remarks inside the heads of local strangers.

In the free-association studies, inner speech emerged as characteristically conceptual in nature, exhibiting a hierarchical organization based on typical instances of categories. The focus of criticism in these verbal thoughts appears to be precisely those entities which do not fit within this conventional order, and which therefore constitute a threat to it. Criticism is a way of coping with those objects that would unwittingly subvert the foundations of the semantic edifice.

An awareness of the impersonal basis of these criticisms and of their manifold injustice, may underlie the sense of alienation people frequently felt. The voices which spoke these idle thoughts were often experienced as 'not me', as if emanating from someone else. This may be partially a defence against taking responsibility for the prejudices they express. The following occurred during a visit to a unit for handicapped children. Some of the preamble, and some interpretations are omitted:

> The first group we visited were the severely handicapped. The minute I entered the door to their room I felt a stranger and uncomfortable. The children gathered around us, stared at us, pulled at us, touched us and spoke incoherently to us. I felt very uncomfortable, afraid and somehow sad. The room where they were staying was big, with a high ceiling, wooden seats – empty. The atmosphere was cold and strange. But the children get to me. They didn't seem to like people and I was really afraid of them and wanted to get out. Then this thing started going through my head – 'Hitler was right!' And I felt confused. 'Hitler was right!' And I repeated it (or IT was repeated) again and again. (The experience was definitely VERBAL.) But the thing that got to me was that this was NOT ME. 'I' thought I could never say anything like that. That Hitler was right to kill all the handicapped and maimed children and adults in Germany – something I have often condemned and abused. But here I was in an unsure

situation and all my high ideals and philosophy momentarily were thrown out
of the window when in my head I was repeating 'Hitler was right!'

Much of the trauma of keeping the journal of idle thoughts derived from
experiences of this type, the *Angst* of which is very apparent here. One person
commented on confrontations with the *Shadow* (in Jung's sense), as if there is a
distinctly nasty part of ourselves that we can ignore until such times as we
innocently agree to record our idle thoughts for research purposes.[1]

To mitigate the nastiness it should be said that there may be some validity
beyond that of simple defensiveness in the claim that these criticisms are alien and
that one is therefore not personally responsible for them. It could be argued that
in order to make sense of the world at all we must draw conceptual lines across it,
yet because of the nature of that world there will always be some entities that are
marginal with regard to the lines we have drawn. Criticism is one strategy for
coping with these marginal cases.

That we do have difficulties in coping with ambiguous stimuli has long been
known. Bruner and Postman (1949) show that perception becomes extremely
difficult, and may break down altogether, when people are tachistoscopically
faced with such unexpected things as playing cards showing red spades or black
hearts. Pavlov's (1927) work on experimental neurosis in dogs goes further, in
showing how under some circumstances behaviour may also disintegrate. The
generative semanticists (Korzybski, 1933; Hayakawa, 1965) maintain that both
neurosis and authoritarianism can be construed as unfortunate consequences
of efforts to preserve a rigid conceptual system against the perceived threat of
entities that fail to fit it.

In anthropology also there is evidence that anomalous objects get special
treatment. Edmund Leach (1964, 1969) claims that objects which are marginal
with respect to major category boundaries tend to become taboo. Blood, urine,
faeces, spittle and nail and hair clippings, all start out as *me* but end up as *not me*,
and are thus ambiguous with respect to the major category boundary between self
and world. Tabooed objects often evoke both dread and respect, and are seen as
imbued, where culturally appropriate, with a magical potency. The special status
of such ambiguous objects is also indicated by the use of the language referring
to them as a form of invective. One way of being rude consists of shifting one's
rather ordinary enemies to marginal territory and proceeding to insult them
thereon:

> When listening to a close relation speaking I have adopted the habit of drifting
> in thoughts so as not to hear what I do not need to hear. Today, however, whilst
> listening to her prattle, without realizing it, I went to reply but what I mumbled
> was in fact 'Kinky bitch'. This is completely uncharacteristic of me and certainly
> had nothing to do with the conversation. Try as I might I simple could not
> remember anything of what I was thinking to result in such words 'Kinky bitch'.

The general background of cultural and individual problems in dealing with anomalous objects provides a context within which the critical idle thoughts can be understood. Criticism acknowledges the threat posed by the unusual to the conceptual order, and attempts to defuse it. Criticism phrased in humorous terms (as in 'If she were only two feet smaller') may be particularly effective here, in belittling its object without resorting to obvious insult.[2]

Misfits are not the only focus for criticism. Another favourite butt is the self. Sometimes the idle thought is in the voice of exasperatingly sweet reason, debunking overambitious plans:

> The thought was verbal.
>
> I was on the point of sleep and was planning some work I had to do. I was worried about not having finished the work and was trying to calm myself by saying that I would do it the next night before I washed my hair. Suddenly a voice which I knew not to be mine said 'You'd be surprised' just after I said 'I'd get it done in an hour'. I wouldn't get it done in an hour but I was trying to relieve the anxiety which the voice succeeded in turning back on me again.
>
> The emotion was anxiety intrinsic in the situation but only re-evoked by the voice.

Quite often these self-criticisms crop up in day-dreams which are attempts to compensate for unsatisfactory social encounters:

> When Chris was here I found myself having lots of conversations in my head but with no visual or really enactive images. I used what I was saying to myself in fact about 60 per cent of the time. The conversations were often of the simultaneous talking type – going on in my head while I was saying something else. Content-wise they were phrasings of what I wanted/should say & there was a fair amount of stuff like 'You fool, you should have said. . . . '

Criticisms of the misfits appear to be on the basis of their divergence from the prototypical; criticisms of the self appear to be on the basis of divergence from the ideal. In these cases the hortatory inner voices sound remarkably like a super-ego trying to call its person to order:

> I had a funny kind of thought today.
>
> I play rugby in College. And my attitude towards it isn't very serious, unlike most of my team-mates. Many get very worked up about it before games and during training – but I don't. It isn't an attitude I express very much during team situations but I keep it to myself.
>
> I was talking to a friend of mine, who takes his game very seriously, about this last night. Today, while I was reading a book, I lost concentration and my mind began drifting. I cannot remember the trend or course of my mind but the final result was that I said to myself 'I must take my rugby more seriously' . . . I did feel a little puzzled at the time at the way the idea appeared.

Its implications for me personally were more serious I think ... I have a
difficulty in applying myself to something, especially in the face of adversity.

This parallel between the voice of the verbal idle thoughts and the voice of the
super-ego is worth exploring further: the super-ego develops at about the same
time as inner speech becomes possible through the internalization of language;
the super-ego is derived not from what parents do but from what they *say*. The
super-ego is the cultural representative in the personality, and how better could
the conventions of a culture infiltrate a psyche than in the form of language, itself
an essentially cultural product. In fact Freud himself remarked upon the
dependence of the super-ego on 'word-presentations (concepts, abstractions)'
(1923, p. 52). This idea of a verbal-auditory super-ego was elaborated further by
Isakower (1939), and accords with what most parents tell their children about the
conscience (which is part of the super-ego) being a little voice inside the head
which is critical of bad behaviour.

It may therefore be that some aspects of super-ego functioning are manifestations of the conventional conceptual structures embodied in internalized language. It would then make sense that the voices expressing the criticisms in verbal
idle thoughts are less a matter of a personal voice directed against a personal
enemy, than a public voice, a voice which is 'not mine', directed against an enemy
which is also 'not mine', but which represents a threat to the cultural conventions
found in the culture as a whole and in the language which codes them.[3]

*

To summarize the properties of verbal idle thoughts it can be said that they
operate with a conception of how things should be, and criticize deviations from
this standard. In dealing with objects and people apart from the self, the standard
is set by the norm of how things as a matter of fact are. Here it is the
unconventional, the taxonomic misfit, that comes in for castigation. In dealing
with the self the standard appears to be a version of the 'ideal self', and criticism
is meted out for shortfalls. The frequently alien properties of both the taxonomic-
ally critical and the self-critical voices, along with their other characteristics,
suggest some similarities with the super-ego.

Visual idle thoughts: social space and the importance of being seen

Of the three pure forms, visual idle thoughts are closest to our normal conception
of what a day-dream should be. They often involve the larger than life-size self and
the predilection for a world seen through rose-tinted spectacles that are conventionally associated with day-dreaming. One aspect of the generally romantic
constellation of visual day-dreams is their tendency towards nostalgia. The
following example occurred at a concert, and is almost pure memory:

Pleasure at the fact a girl sitting by me was wearing a familiar-looking check shirt (viyella or something), then realized that it reminded me of a similar, but differently coloured shirt worn – and not worn – by Elizabeth during several delightful days before Christmas.

Visually evoked. Emotions – I suspect none intrinsic, but evoked an obvious delight at nice memories and also a pleasant surprise at such clear response to a small visual detail (the person wearing the shirt bore not the slightest resemblance to Elizabeth).

An important feature of most visual day-dreams, as of this one, is their social orientation. This has a number of manifestations, the most diffuse being the fact that these day-dreams frequently refer to social environments which constrain and support particular social behaviours. 'The Honan' in the following example is the College Chapel:

In the home of married friends, they being out. I imagine myself marrying in the Honan, a feast of music and friends. I am particularly pleased with my cream linen suit. Now my rule begins and will be wise and carefree. Comment. Help!

That references to environments should be included in visual day-dreams is not surprising. What is noteworthy is the social character of these environments. Physical space is almost entirely subordinated to the people contained within it, who provide an audience before whom one appears:

I have been thinking of doing the H. Dip. once (if) I get my BA. I went recently to get my dip hours [the teaching hours of a student teacher]. Having asked for them and being told I would more than likely get them I began on my way home to imagine myself teaching in the school. I could see the difficulties I would have and as the day-dream continued I could feel the tension and nervousness beforehand and the embarrassment at certain things that could go wrong in the class. I could experience the relief at being regarded as a teacher and the fun it would be to have someone I knew in the class (the latter being quite possible).

I think it is a way of preparing myself for the things that may happen. I know things don't always go the way you may want them to. Things go wrong and I must prepare for situations I will have to put up with.

'The class' here is as much audience as place, and this social–spatial fusion is typical of visual day-dreams. The idea that space may have social connotations is familiar from work on metaphor (e.g.: Asch, 1958; Lakoff and Johnson, 1980; De Soto, London and Handel, 1965). Lee (1981) uses the example of a traditional courtroom to illustrate how spatial organization can be used to encode precisely the social roles and relationships involved in the legal drama. Within the visual day-dreams also, location may be an important cue to social role: the one in the aisle is the bridegroom; the one at the front of the classroom is the teacher.

Within social space most of the realities are socially constructed (Berger and Luckman, 1966). Of particular importance is the construction of one's own social persona, which is manifest as an appearance in the eyes of others. Groups of people are important in ratifying these personae, particularly if newly acquired through status passage. The proper social constitution of bridegroomliness requires a congregation of well-wishers, and the social constitution of teacherliness requires schoolchildlike behaviour and attitudes to authority.

One of the problems with socially constituted statuses is that one cannot manipulate them directly. 'Social space' is as intransitive as the visual space of the free-association studies. People cannot interact directly with Society-in-general to induce its good opinion; they must instead mould their own appearance or performance along socially approved lines and hope that the spectators will have the decency to notice or, even better, to applaud, or best of all, to fall desperately in love. The following must be a classic:

The thought was visual.

I was simply listening to some songs by Olivia Newton-John and I began to imagine myself singing those songs dressed in a pure white dress and to a huge audience (as well as being televised). I was very well received and afterwards the agents were fighting to sign me but I already had an agent who was also madly in love with me. The whole episode was like the things you would read about in a newspaper about a star marrying her manager. These kind of day-dreams, which I may have fairly often, are often fragmented and broken in that I seem to add new things as I go along. (Like I start singing to an audience then add the TV and then the adoring managers. . . .) The dramatic points are very exaggerated in these types of day-dreams.

The feelings are naturally pleasurable and make me feel comfortable. It is probably my way of coping with the less romantic and successful life I lead.

It is tempting to talk about 'social desirability' here. While undoubtedly appropriate, such comfortable jargon should not dispose us to think that something has been explained when it has scarcely been pointed at. The language of existentialist philosophy catches some of the complexity involved in trying to be socially desirable. Sartre (1957) distinguishes betweeen Being-for-itself and Being-for-others, and sees a fundamental human dilemma arising from the split between them. Part of the human condition is to be torn between how we feel ourselves to be and how we think others view us, which is a schism that manages to cause agonies for many during adolescence. There is a temptation to collude with the views of the other in order to be liked; and this is what is happening in many of the visual day-dreams. Sartre saw this as 'bad faith', a moral defect to which humanity is irretrievably prone. But if we shift the discussion from the austere climate of existentialism it can be seen as having some positive value: existentialists' bad faith is a lot of other people's social sensitivity. And once we are accustomed to the idea of having two selves, a private I and a socially constituted me, their relationship can afford considerable pleasure. Here is a civilized encounter between the two:

> That 'I' am the person who lives in this room, who has collected all these books and can be seen next to them.
>
> 'Simply' a phenomenon of jotted noticing? reasserting the familiar by introducing a stranger who is actually – I realize after the briefest moment of doubt – me. Emotion – immense surprise, as if someone had come into the room. Then still more surprise when I realize that no one has. (This is recurrent, I like it. It's as if it releases me from some penance inside my own head. It usually happens when I'm sitting still in the room, pausing between doing things. Histrionic self-identification – making another self come in and point to the original, now momentarily displaced self – is curiously cheering. It gives you a certain freedom, but not so much as to cause terror. Self hasn't vanished; it's merely playing games.)

The French psychoanalyst Lacan (1977) traces the origin of the I–me split to a period he terms the 'mirror stage', occurring between the ages of 6 months and 18 months. In this period the child first learns to recognize the image seen in the mirror as his or her own. The self in the mirror, the me, always remains somewhat alienated from the I, since the me is on a par with the selves of others who are also present to us primarily as visual appearances. However, it is only this equivalence of visible selves that allows us to empathize with others, since the appropriative act linking the I to the me can be extended also to the perceived selves of others.

Mead (1934) also saw our capacity for social empathy as related to the I–me split. For him however the relationship is the other way round, with social empathy coming first, and the I–me distinction, along with the kind of consciousness it allows, being consequences.

While the speculations of Lacan and Mead are difficult to test directly, there is some experimental evidence which supports their common contention that the I–me distinction is socially important. This is work on *objective self-awareness*, and was initiated by Duval and Wicklund (1972) as an attempt to test some of Mead's ideas. People can be precipitated into a state of objective self-awareness in a number of ways: for example, by seating them in front of a mirror, or by having them perform in front of an audience. Once aware of themselves from the outside, people become acutely conscious of social evaluations, and tend to modify their behaviour in socially desirable directions. Visual day-dreams function in a similar manner, also endowing people with an objective self-awareness in which social desirability is important.

*

In summary, visual day-dreams are predominantly social in tone. They depict social environments which are peopled with groups of spectators before whom the day-dreamer appears. There is a concern with the good opinion of others, and people may trim their social personae to encourage it. This collusion takes on romantic overtones when the audience is of one.

Enactive idle thoughts: metamorphoses of being and feeling

Enactive idle thoughts are often fairly brief. They are usually triggered by noticing a person who then becomes the focus of identification; or noticing an object which then becomes the target of imagined action. There is often an intimate mix of fantasy and reality, with the imagined elements being projected on to a real world. Enactive idle thoughts are similar in this regard to verbal ones, and both differ from the visual, which are more self-containedly inside the head.

The cases involving imagined action are usually very simple, consisting of a brief impulse to act, for no apparent reason, which the person does not as a matter of fact carry out:

> Last night when I was watching TV I suddenly got this feeling I was going to grab the chair I was sitting on and throw it through the TV. A split second thought. For a brief second I felt like doing it. It was enactive but certainly non-emotional. A funny kind of thing.
> (I just got this idea that the difference between the 'mad' and the 'normal' is that the normal can smother the unsuitable thoughts.)

This comment on the difference between the 'mad' and the 'normal' is in line with much psychological work from Freud onwards which holds that the ability to restrain impulse is a sign of psychological health. Psychologists apart, many parents must have tried to teach their offspring the social art of counting to ten before acting.

Simple impulses to act, perhaps because so brief, are a less frequently recorded enactive theme than the slightly more elaborated fantasies in which people identify with some person or object.

Identifications with other people show a marked bias in that these people are rarely the figures of power or status whom one might reasonably wish to emulate, but tend to be more properly figures of compassion; for example, a character in a film who is being driven mad, a woman mentioned in a newspaper who is dying of cancer, or a destitute figure seen on a night street. In imagination people identify with these unfortunates and experience what their lives must be like:

> Blindness. We have a lecturer in the French department who is going – has nearly gone – blind. I frequently see him (I don't really know him) at lunch time. I also have sometimes to counter students' criticisms of his teaching – he doggedly struggles on at his lecturing, but is so blind that he sometimes writes two sets of notes over the top of one another on the blackboard – the students naturally feel that they are not getting adequate teaching, but the situation inhibits them from any other than muted and apologetic criticism.

One day I was at lunch when he walked into the corner of a table and nearly dropped his tray – suddenly I found myself in the position of a blind man.
Obviously enactive.
Emotions – intrinsic – fear, I think, and helplessness. Evoked – envy of the sighted, anger, sadness at memories of past times of sightedness.

Verbal and enactive thoughts evidently cope with misfits in very different ways: the handicapped person who is the target of criticism in verbal idle thoughts may be the subject of empathy in enactive ones.

These compassionate projections are not confined to the human world. The following is an example from a zoologist, showing equivalent empathy for a unicellular organism:

Death of a *Paramecium*. Cells die if they get too much calcium inside them. I have done experiments in which I have let too much calcium in *Paramecium*, a ciliated protozoan, and I have watched their death-throes under the microscope. Suddenly I found myself in their position, feeling 'discomfort' and 'anguish' of a condemned paramecium moving in an uncontrolled way around the bottom of a petri dish.
Enactive, the main evoked emotions a helplessness, and compassion, together with a feeling of guilt for inflicting this 'suffering'.

The general emotivity of enactive fantasies is underscored by their concern with various morbid themes – disease, death, handicap, physical or emotional injury – and it may be that the relative rarity of enactive fantasies is partly because not everyone is interested in subjecting themselves to the anguish consequent upon such morbid identifications. Beyond the anguish, however, there appears to be a brighter prospect, as if exploring the possibility of death or illness can also be cathartic, leading to a sense of acceptance and a genuine cherishing of the existence which, in fantasy at least, is under threat:

Feeling very fed up. Sitting in my room knowing I have 1000 things I ought to attend to. Thoughts revolve around all sorts of morbid ideas. Not so much connected to death as to physical harm and violence. Try to imagine how women feel when they are being battered by their husbands, and kids too – these ideas probably have to do with an item I heard on the news today talking about domestic brutality. Thinking perhaps is a way of relieving tension or something – having thought all that out makes me feel better (be thankful for small mercies).

There is more, however, to these enactive identifications than compassionate-ness and catharsis, since the sympathetic and human were only one end of a wide spectrum. In enactive fantasies people also imagined identifying with a milk bottle, a bottle of Southern Comfort and a fish. While human identifications can be construed as a laudable empathy, some of these non-human ones cannot; and they often have a bizarre flavour when what is countenanced in fantasy is not in any way possible to human beings in actuality:

> I remember one day (few weeks ago) sitting at the breakfast table and, while looking at it, I tried to imagine what it is like to be a milk bottle. I really tried to imagine it. And would you believe it I did. For a few seconds I knew what it was like to be a milk bottle. ENACTIVE. No emotional content (milk bottles don't have emotions).

Such fantasies involve what is a traditional mythological theme, that of the shape changer, the person capable of metamorphosing his or her physical form at will, and often capable of supernatural powers in the changed identity. The supernatural element sometimes occurs without explicit translocations of identity:

> The white kitten vomits. In the vomit is a round worm, thin but about 4 inches long. I put it in the shit box with a cloth. Later have a histrionic fantasy of what it would be like to eat this worm – thing from inside another to living inside me. Immediate associations to this one are worm as phallus, as pregnancy, life within, the conception of heroes (by mouth, not sure whether or no by worm).
> Had had tea with Mary and the babies. (At the time no feelings of disgust, though aware this would be normal, but a kind of wrapt wonder – at the thing, and the feeling of living thing within. Enactive.)

If visual fantasies manipulate appearances in order to attract social esteem, enactive ones seem to manipulate physical being in order to express actions and, especially, feelings. As far as enactive fantasies are concerned, the nature of one's physical self strongly determines what one does and feels with it. Thus the emotional form of a milk bottle is unconducive to emotional reactions ('milk bottles don't have emotions'). In other enactive day-dreams the physical form of the bottle of Southern Comfort was conducive to, or possibly symbolic of, drunkenness; and the physical form of the fish added to the enjoyment of swimming. Within the human domain one person found that imagining being mad was productive of a kind of serenity, and several confronted feelings of sadness in identifying with someone with severe physical illness. Being and feeling, which were closely related in the free-association studies, maintain this link in enactive fantasy.

It is unclear whether the primary motivation involved in the enactive idle thoughts is compassion, emotional self-indulgence, or sheer if sometimes sombre playfulness. Whatever the case may be, enactive day-dreams show the full emotional range from despair to delight, with feelings being directed towards others in addition to (though slightly less often than) just being felt. An odd kind of decency operates in the fact that other people are more often the recipient of positive emotions than of negative ones. People feel affectionate towards others but keep their blues to themselves.

Feelings include a tacit evaluative dimension, and involve what Arnold (1960) called an 'appraisal' of their object. In enactive fantasy the feeling is dominant and the appraisal or value judgment tacit. I *feel depressed* presupposes I *don't think much of myself at the moment*; and I *am ecstatic about X* involves at least X *is rather good*. In verbal and visual idle thoughts the balance between value judgment and feeling tends to be the other way up, with judgment dominant and feeling subdued. It is difficult to envisage what very palpable pleasure might accompany the visual value judgment of 'being famous', for example; and the verbal criticisms often just get on with the criticizing without bothering to dwell on the hostility that might be assumed to motivate it.

A comparison of the emotive aspect of the enactive fantasies with the more muted affects of the visual ones suggests that emotions may be highly asymmetric relationships. In enactive day-dreams people are concerned with loving and caring, in visual ones they are concerned with being loved and being cared about. What is logically reversible (A loves B: B is loved by A) is not psychologically so, for the needs satisfied by being the active lover or carer are very different from those satisfied by being the passive beloved.

Enactive idle thoughts may be part of a process of emotional digestion which people use to cope with some of the harsher aspects of reality, and which involves a rather literal assimilation of emotional trauma to the self. This emotional digestion appears to be a form of low-level catharsis that can take on other motivational guises, such as the self-indulgent and the pitying. Catharsis here is not restricted to painful occurrences, though these predominate; positive events may also need to be worked over before they can be assimilated.

The cathartic potential of enactive representations is exploited in a number of therapeutic techniques. Gendlin's (1980) 'focusing' emphasizes the importance of getting into bodily touch with one's thoughts, and many therapists use role play, sometimes combined with overt action, to enable clients to work through feelings in a manner not possible if more cerebral techniques are used.

In summary, enactive fantasies involve imagined action, and imagined changes of physical identity, with concomitant emotional changes. Some of the non-human identifications have a bizarre and supernatural quality, and the human ones tend to focus on emotionally traumatic experiences. The wide range of emotions expressed suggests the cathartic potential of enactive representations.

Composite forms: revenge, heroic lovers and missing links

The properties of the idle thoughts including more than one form of representation can in general be accurately predicted from a knowledge of their constituents. Some interesting features do, however, emerge from the conjunctions.

Day-dreams which contain both verbal and visual elements retain the criticism theme of the pure verbal forms and the audience theme of visual ones. When the two are put together we get a way of thinking that has a peculiar potency for revenge – which is typically a matter of publicly humiliating one's victim. Some personal or social power is necessary to conduct the humiliation with panache, and an audience is desirable to ratify the humiliation and watch the victim grovel. An upsurge of personal pride is an understandable consequence. Sometimes simply being successful (and being seen to be so) is sufficient to cause a due contrition in those who have evidently failed to show respect for the day-dreamer in real life. Negative feelings directed towards others are particularly associated with this form of day-dream.

It is as if revenge were a board game, with the board itself, the evaluative social environment, being visual; and the moves, the changes of relative status wrought by the humiliation, being verbal.

> Today I had a most enjoyable wallow in my traditional death-list fantasy. The holy orders were very much in evidence and Bishop **** (of whom I know nothing except the name and some gossipy fragments) was sentenced to parade round the city in his ecclesiastical underclothes until he died from exposure.
>
> The fantasy mixes verbal and visual modes: the verbal element accounts for the court hearing in which I eloquently refute his faith and bigotry and in which he refuses ardently to accept that his credibility has been so thoroughly compromised.
>
> Others to feel the vengeance of the revolutionary committee were **** (an old favourite), the Pope, Khomeni, **** and **** (other favourites).
>
> The fantasy is a well-used one and sometimes seems to be ritualistic – occurring after a frustrating event. I can't remember what brought it on but judging by the anti-church element it was some moral dilemma. The emotions evoked are satisfaction and an intrinsic emotion, sometimes evoked as well, is quite often pity. This was present in today's example.

Day-dreams which have both visual and enactive elements have a generally rosy affective tone, with feelings like happiness and pleasure predominating. They combine the larger than life-size version of the self characteristic of pure visual fantasies with the propensity for transitive action seen in some of the enactive ones. There is only one kind of transitive action that is worthy of this sort of day-dreaming treatment: making love. To romantic fluff (visual) is added sexual action (enactive). Not surprisingly, these fantasies tend to occur in bed, before one falls asleep. The following luscious example is an exception in that it occurred while hitch-hiking:

> Hitching from Dublin.
>
> I imagine entering a room at a party, drink in hand. Few people in the dark room, music, mellow. In the corner, in an armchair, a young woman in a black dress; grey, sea-grey eyes, long blond hair. A great stillness in her, the stillness of contained purpose. She rises, crosses the room, takes my drink, then me by

the hand, leads me to a wide, carpeted staircase. No words. Great ease. In a red-panelled room, at twilight we make love on a green bed, soundlessly, with perfect understanding. It is like being in and under the sea. After, we look and travel forever back and forth through each other's eyes. My eyes are grey now and through them she sees sky, clouds, infinite space blocked in by reassurance.

No issue, no outcome, a forever.

Day-dreams combining verbal and enactive elements, or containing all three forms of representation, occurred too infrequently for adequate analysis.

There were only two verbal-enactive examples in the entire corpus, as if these forms of representation normally only come together through the mediation of visual imagery. This interpretation is coherent with the semantic triptych elaborated in chapter 3 where there was little contact between verbal and enactive structures. It is also coherent with the common-sense assumption that feelings can be remarkably difficult to verbalize, certainly relative to perceptions. This difficulty reflects the problems of acquiring an emotional vocabulary when the referents have to be interpreted from the more obvious signs of facial, bodily, or behavioural expression (Skinner, 1957). Some people never learn to label their feelings and somatize them as psychosomatic ailments, a syndrome known as 'alexithymia' (Sifneos, 1975). Even normal people can manage to not attach words to feelings as a defence. Bucci (1982) shows that being able to verbalize painful affect is the beginning of positive adaptation in depression, and the beginning of asserting self-control after stressful life events. She talks of a 'need to name' feelings as an adaptive urge we can maladaptively inhibit.

Day-dreams containing all three forms of representation were a little more common, but the majority came from a small number of people, so that it is difficult to know to what extent the themes are biased by individual characteristics. For what it is worth, a remarkable 90 per cent of these day-dreams involved power themes of some kind, and over 50 per cent showed evidence of physical violence, which was a power theme rather rare elsewhere. These day-dreams appear to combine the revenge motif of verbal-visual composites and add an enactive component in the form of physical aggression to supplement verbal criticism.

Concluding remarks

The idle-thoughts study was undertaken as an enquiry into the affective and evaluative complements of the three modes of thought. As a result of it the hope expressed in chapter 1, that there would be structural relationships between thought and feeling, can be preliminarily unpacked into what is already a quite complex picture.

The relationship between semantic organization and value judgments is simplest in inner speech. The taxonomic organization that was an important way of making cognitive sense of things in the free association studies turns out also to be an important way of making evaluative sense of them. The norm, that which fits neatly into the conventional order, is good (tacitly). The odd, the misfit which cannot be easily categorized, threatens the conventional order and is therefore bad. It is punished by insult and prejudice.

In visual day-dreams, matters are more complex. While the emphasis on the environment, on intransitive relations to it, and on appearances, all show some continuity with the free-association studies, new features have entered. Of major importance is that space is now imbued with social meaning and social value. Within the social space people constitute and evaluate their social personae by reference to how they appear in the eyes of others: to be beautiful is good, to be famous is good, to be beloved is good; and generally to be approved by the social environment is good. To be repudiated, or ostracized is bad.

Enactive idle thoughts are most difficult to interpret. As in the free-association studies, action and most of the stronger emotions are concentrated in this mode, and are intimately related to the imagined vicissitudes of Being. In enactive fantasies, however, doing and feeling tend to be divorced from each other, so that emotions rarely have the motivational quality of the free-association studies. Some of the transformations of being that occur in enactive fantasies seem to be ways of evoking or releasing feelings. This may be part of an emotional digestion process, involving a natural form of catharsis, through which people cope with emotionally important experiences. While it is evident that value judgments are implicit in the emotional tone of the enactive day-dreams, it is not clear what principles underlie these value judgments.

5

A cognitive interlude: individual differences in modes of thought

Although adults evidently *can* use all three ways of thinking, it seems likely that when left to their own devices they will use whatever best balances task demands with personal preference. The idea that people show some systematic biases in their use of different forms of representation is about as old as the idea that people use forms of representation at all.

Galton (1880), having examined his own imagery, sent out a 'Breakfast Table Questionnaire' to his acquaintances; the responses indicated that some could visualize their morning breakfast table with extraordinary vividness and clarity, while others only 'knew' that marmalade was on it because marmalade was always on it. By the turn of the century interest in imagery differences was running high, but the matter had become so confused that, according to Horowitz (1978), the American Psychological Association called in James Angell to chair a committee to clarify the chaos. Angell's paper (1910) is still a useful compendium both of various imagery assessment techniques and of the problems attendant upon their use. Despite confusions about how to measure representational biases, and despite the behaviourism which did little to encourage the study of internal events, the interest in representational biases continued intermittently and soared in the 1970s, stimulated by the publication of Sheehan's (1967) revision of the Betts (1909) Questionnaire upon Mental Imagery. In consequence of this long history, there are numerous options now available for assessing individual differences.

There are tests which look at one mode of representation (Marks, 1973a), at two (Paivio, 1971; Richardson, 1977a; Riding and Calvey, 1981), at three (Spindler, 1907; Diehl and England, 1958), at six (Reing, 1978), or at seven (Betts, 1909; Sheehan, 1967).

There are tests of imagery control (Gordon, 1949); of image elaboration (Slee, 1980); of vividness (Marks, 1973a; Sheehan, 1967); and of dominance (Griffitts, 1925, 1927; Diehl and England, 1958; Leibovitz, London, Cooper and Hart, 1972; Reing 1978).

Most of these tests rely on subjective ratings or reports. It is also possible to use objective measures, such as tests of spatial ability (Ernest and Paivio, 1971), or measures of improvement in paired-associate learning after imagery instructions (Hiscock and Cohen, 1973).

To judge by the amount of experimental energy devoted to test development and test use, the idea of individual differences in cognitive biases has long been an attractive one. The results of this work have, however, sometimes been rather disappointing, particularly if imagery vividness is the focal variable (see reviews in White, Sheehan and Ashton, 1977; Ernest, 1977). Tests involving vividness usually correlate with one another, but do not reliably relate to measures of spatial ability, to learning (unless incidental), or to therapeutic improvement in clinical situations using imagery techniques. Furthermore, ratings of vividness tend not to differentiate between different forms of representation, as Betts (1909) was the first to note.

This chapter looks at an alternative way of assessing representational biases, through their characteristic cognitive structures. It then examines how this structural approach to individual differences relates to some of the other approaches that have been used to explore representational biases.

The Modes of Thought Questionnaire

The Modes of Thought Questionnaire (MOTQ for short) was developed with Sean Hammond and Elizabeth Dunne as part of a project on cognitive style. It is based on the free-association work of chapter 3, but involves a radical modification of format. Instead of giving people stimulus words and asking them to produce associative responses, it gives people items consisting of stimulus–response pairs, and asks them to rate how good the association is. For example, the item:

say   FAST $-----$ slow . . .   (   )

requires that the person *says* the word *fast* to him or herself, and then rates, on a five-point scale, whether *slow* is an immediate or a distant associate to it. Items are chosen to exemplify particular cognitive structures, which in turn are characteristic of particular modes of thought. There are in all thirteen structural subscales, for which example items are as follows:

Verbal subscales

say	WIDE – – – – – narrow	(opposite)
say	SCARLET – – – – – fever	(phrase completion)
say	REGAL – – – – – legal	(rhyme)
say	ALUMINIUM – – – – – metal	(superordinate)

Visual subscales

see	BOAT – – – – – harbour	(environment)
see	HANDKERCHIEF – – – – – square	(attribute)
see	PENSIONER – – – – – strolling	(intransitive action)
see	KETTLE – – – – – spout	(part)

Enactive subscales

be	OBLITERATING – – – – – gone	(consequence)
be	GREEDY – – – – – tummy ache	(affective consequence)
be	TELEPHONIST – – – – – curious	(affective)
be	LEOPARD – – – – – catches gazelle	(transitive action)
be	SECRETARY – – – – – could kick boss	(conditional action)

In all these subscales, the items are preceded by an appropriate representational instruction. There is one additional subscale, which is called the *cross-modal scale*, because in it items are preceded by representational instructions inappropriate to the mode characteristic of the structure involved. For example, in

see	WEASEL – – – – – easel

the association involves a rhyming response, which is characteristically verbal, but the instruction is visual. Someone following instructions should give this a low rating as it would make a poor visual association. A high rating indicates the operation of response bias effects. These may derive from a number of sources, such as carelessness in following instructions, or wanting to appear imaginative, or simple yea-saying. The cross-modal scale was included in the MOTQ because both the Betts Questionnaire upon Mental Imagery (DiVesta, Ingersoll and Sunshine, 1971; but see Ashton and White, 1980) and Marks's Vividness of Visual Imagery Questionnaire (Berger and Gaunitz, 1977) have been shown to be contaminated by response bias effects, notably social desirability.

. The MOTQ itself can be found in appendix C, along with reliability and standardization data.

The MOTQ does not seek to divide people into verbal, visual and enactive types, but assumes that each person uses all three forms of representation, with the balance varying between individuals. The three ways of thinking are not wholly independent of one another; in particular the visual scales relate to both verbal and enactive in a rough mirroring of the triptych arrangement of the three semantic domains of chapter 3, where visual imagery also occupied a conceptually central position.

A reliable instrument for measuring cognitive biases opens a number of doors. It becomes possible to look at differences between men and women, to explore differences between people following different careers, and to look at the cognitive correlates of the three ways of thinking. The following sections review some of the findings for each mode of thought in turn. The technical data on which these discussions are based are given in appendices C and D.

Inner speech: a style for commerce

One of the traditional places to look for cognitive style differences has been in different careers, or, more usually, in schoolchildren or students who are aspirants to different careers. It is assumed that different jobs make different kinds of intellectual demands, and thus attract people with different cognitive biases. For example, Hudson (1966, 1968) looked at the differing subject choices in convergent and divergent schoolboys: he found that, roughly speaking, the convergers opted to specialize in sciences, with the divergers tending to go for arts subjects. Witkin (1976) has also found different career patterns in field-dependent and field-independent people. Field-dependent people, those whose perceptual and social judgments are sensitive to, or influenced by, the perceptual or social environment, tend to go into socially orientated vocations such as clinical psychology and nursing. Field-independent people, who separate perceptual or social figures from their respective grounds, are more likely to be found in the natural sciences, engineering and mathematics.

The work of standardizing the MOTQ involved students studying a variety of subjects. Of these groups there was a pronounced bias towards inner speech only in the commerce students, indexed by their relatively high score on the MOTQ verbal scale. These are students who are aiming for careers in business, where the organization and management of other people will usually be an important responsibility. A verbal bias can be taken to be an advantage here, because it is largely through speech that people persuade, negotiate, request or order the others with whom they interact in their commercial and administrative trans-actions.

Other evidence would support this interpretation of the MOTQ results. Harrell and Harrell (in a technical report cited by Pilkonis and Zimbardo, 1979) showed that verbal fluency is the single best predictor of whether a Master in Business Administration will achieve success in the business world. Certainly high verbal fluency and a self-confident delivery are important in persuading others towards the speaker's viewpoint in decision-making situations, and this is independent of the content of the speech (Scherer, 1979).

The MOTQ scale which best reflects the fluency of ordinary speech is the phrase completion subscale. The fact that this scale correlates with a broad vocabulary (on the General Aptitude Test Battery or GATB) suggests that people with a pronounced verbal bias have refined their speech to be a powerful and effective social tool. Those who use inner speech a lot also apparently tend to use it rather well.

It is unclear whether a verbal bias predisposes a person towards a business career, or whether a career choice directs the person's thinking into a particular cognitive channel. Developmental data on field dependence indicate reciprocal effects (Witkin, Dyk, Faterson, Goodenough and Karp, 1962) and the same might reasonably be expected for other cognitive styles.

Visual imagery: a style for the arts and social sciences

Galton's (1880) assertion that women have a greater power of visualizing than men has generally been confirmed in work on imagery vividness (White, Ashton and Brown, 1977; but see Ashton and White, 1980). The MOTQ findings point in the same direction: here too women show a general bias towards visualizing, which is particularly strong on one of the visual subscales, that concerned with object–attribute relationships. In terms of career choice, visualizing is associated with the arts and social sciences (see also Diehl and England, 1958). These are of course the kinds of subjects which attract many women, at least at undergraduate level, and it is significant here that male arts and social-science students showed a much weaker visual bias than did the women.[1]

There are two important cognitive correlates of a visual bias: the first is the kind of conceptual flexibility measured by the Pettigrew (1958) test of category width; and the second is vividness of imagery.

Category width is concerned with a person's ability or willingness to acknowledge that some objects may deviate markedly from their category norm. For example, the average window might be 34 inches wide, but could there possibly also exist windows only 1 inch wide? Somebody with narrow categories will say no; somebody with wide ones, and this includes visualizers, will say *yes*. Richardson (1977b) also found a relationship between visualizing (assessed by vividness) and category width, though only for women.

The relationship between visualizing assessed on the MOTQ, and imagery vividness as measured on the Betts Questionnaire of Mental Imagery (Sheehan, 1967), is interesting partly because the Betts has been so widely used in individual differences research. All the MOTQ visual subscales show some relationship with imagery vividness, with the visual attributes subscale showing the strongest relationship. This correlation between imagery vividness and the appreciation of object–attribute structures is an interesting one. It may arise for a very simple reason: that *vividness is itself an attribute*. To say of an image that it is vivid is to use an object–attribute structure. Furthermore, many of the features for which *vivid* is an appropriate adjective are themselves attributes of objects. For example, colours may be vivid, and talk about *colourful objects* or even *colourful images* uses object–attribute relationships. Vividness is, as it were, an attribute of attributes.

It can be conjectured that these two major correlates of visualizing, broad categories and vivid imagery, meet some of the cognitive requirements of being a social scientist (and this typically meant training as a social worker), or being an arts student. The conceptual tolerance indicated by wide categories, and the potential for imaginativeness and sensitivity indicated by vivid imagery, would have general usefulness in both areas of endeavour.

Enactive imagery: a style for engineering

Enactive imagery as assessed by the MOTQ involves two main kinds of cognitive structures, those concerned with action, and those concerned with feeling. Men tend to be biased towards enactive imagery generally, though at the level of specific structures this bias is evident only for the action-oriented aspects (especially transitive action and physical consequences). For one of the affective subscales (affective consequences of action) women in fact show higher scores than men.

In terms of career aspirations, a bias towards enactive imagery is evident in engineering students. Interestingly, this is equally strong for engineers of both sexes, showing that other factors, presumably including interest and training, can override the more general sex differences here.

One of the cognitive abilities taken to be useful in engineering is spatial flexibility, the ability to manipulate mentally three-dimensional objects in space. Spatial flexibility tasks typically involve giving the person a picture of a two-dimensional shape, and in effect asking: if this shape were transformed in some way (folded up, or reoriented), which of the following test figures would it then match? Men are normally better at these tasks than women (Maccoby and Jacklin, 1974; McGee, 1979).

The fact that enactive representations are important in engineering, and for men, points towards a relationship between enactive imagery and spatial flexibility. The MOTQ data support this suggestion, with the particular enactive subscales of importance being the two which involve imagined action (transitive action and conditional action subscales). These findings make the same point for adults as Piaget and Inhelder's work (1971) makes for children: that transformational imagery requires internalized action, not just internalized perception.

The general relationship between spatial flexibility and enactive imagery supports the suggestion mooted in chapter 3, that the transitive interactions of enactive imagery constitute a relative and therefore a more flexible form of spatiality than the static and environmental space of visual imagery.

An important rider must, however, be added: the relationship between spatial flexibility and enactive imagery holds only for men. Women show a pattern that is difficult to interpret, and which, if anything, suggests that whereas men are using internal action, women are using their famous intuition. For women spatial flexibility shows positive correlations with primary-process kinds of thinking

(MOTQ affective and rhyme subscales), and negative correlations with rational, conceptually organized thought (the superordinate subscale).

These sex differences suggest that the frequently reported male superiority for spatial tasks may be a quantitative difference which has qualitative underpinnings, resting on the use of different cognitive strategies.[2]

The possibility of strategy differences between men and women indicates that we need to look more closely at what people are actually doing when they are trying to solve spatial-flexibility problems. There is some relevant work by Ashton, McFarland, Walsh and White (1978) which shows that people may possess an imagery ability which they do not necessarily use in spatial tasks unless they are explicitly instructed to do so, and J. T. E. Richardson (1978) draws a related distinction for learning situations between coding *ability* and coding *preference*. The relatively low correlations between enactive imagery and spatial flexibility may be partly a result of some people possessing an enactive ability which they prefer not to use.[3] The work on idle thoughts indicates that enactive imagery is the most emotionally traumatic of the three forms of representation, so it may be that some people prefer to avoid using it.

In summary

The Modes of Thought Questionnaire, which assesses cognitive biases on the basis of characteristic structural features, provides a way of looking both at general differences in mode of representation, and at more specific differences in the use of particular cognitive structures. There are general differences between men and women, with men showing an enactive bias and women a visual one; and there are also representational differences between students studying different subjects, which may override the general sex differences. Commerce students, both men and women, tend towards inner speech; arts and social-science students (especially if they are women) show a bias towards visual imagery; and engineers of both sexes show a bias towards enactive imagery.

Each mode of thought is related to specific cognitive abilities which may interact positively with career choice: a verbal bias is related to an extensive vocabulary, useful in the persuasive verbal fluency of those going into business and management; a visual bias is related to the broad categories and the vividness of imagery which may be useful in the arts and social sciences; and an enactive bias is related to the spatial flexibility important in engineering.

These findings lay a general foundation for the studies of the next chapter, which extend the work on individual differences to the general area of personality.

6

Aspects of identity

William James (1892) noted that consciousness is in constant change, consisting of a stream of thought in which no state ever recurs or is identical with what preceded it. It is easy to overlook how natural and effortless this continual changing is, and to assume, in theory at least, that the stream of consciousness consists basically of static entities ('thoughts'), to which a dynamic component must then somehow be added. In practice (as distinct from theory), what is difficult is not making thought go; this is effortless. The real difficulty is rather in making it stop. If one tries to hold an idea static in the mind, it rarely lasts for more than about a second and then manages to turn itself into something else. There are in fact special exercises, called meditation exercises, for making thought stop; but nobody needs exercises to make thought go: it does it by itself.[1]

On what makes thought go

A survey of psychological theorizing indicates three possible kinds of explanation of what makes thought go. There are, as it were, three *prototype* accounts, not necessarily held in their pure form by any one theorist, but permeating much of the general theorizing about dynamic aspects of psychology.

First of all, there are *energy accounts*, which add energy (instinctual, psychic, drive, or spreading activation) to what are otherwise static constituents. Freud is an energy theorist, though of a very sophisticated kind. Spreading-activation theories of memory are also energy accounts.

Secondly, there are *structural-tension accounts*, which get round the problem of an extrinsic energy source by assuming that it is the structural tension within the cognitive representations themselves that provides the motive force for change. Most *Gestalt* theorists held some version of this view.

Thirdly, there are what can be called *transformational or metabolic accounts*, where it is process that is seen as fundamental rather than stability. Apter's (1982) view of motivation as intrinsically unstable, or the idea of a procedural semantics, approach such an account.

To use an analogy: the question of what makes a car go can be answered at the first level by reference to the petrol added to it as an extrinsic source of energy. It can be answered at the second level by reference to the torsions in the innards (or something of the sort); and it can be answered at the third level by reference to the explosive oxidation of hydrocarbons. The different kinds of account are useful for different purposes, as each emphasizes a different aspect of what is after all a complex process.

The three kinds of account of what makes thought go can be used to give three different interpretations of the relationship between structure and energy in the thought process. These interpretations contribute towards an understanding of the notion of cognitive style, in which the relationship between structure and energy is a central concept.

Structure and energy in cognitive style

In the conception of cognitive styles formulated by the Menninger group (e.g.: Klein, 1958; Gardner, Holzman, Klein, Linton and Spence, 1959), these styles are seen as underlain by sets of cognitive structures, responsible both for representing reality (thought), and for channelling the discharge of instinctual energy (emotions and personality). The cognitive structures thus provide the interface between thought and personality, with their mark being visible in both.

For example, the cognitive style of field dependence has both cognitive and personality aspects: a field-dependent person has difficulty both in picking out embedded figures from their visual context; and in separating themselves from their social context, being therefore easily swayed by the opinions of others. There is clearly a structural isomorphism between the cognitive and personality domains here. What is not so clear is precisely what it means to say that the same structures underlie both the cognitive and personality characteristics. This is where the three different accounts of 'what makes thought go' can be brought into play. They give rise to three rather different conceptions of this structural connection.

The energy account of what makes thought go would see the static structures underlying cognitive styles as conduits or sluices for controlling the flow of originally instinctual energy. This is roughly the account given by David Rapaport (1959) in his attempt to systematize psychoanalytic theory. The energy of the id is seen as basic, with all else derived from it. The structures themselves would then be regarded as a bound form of the originally free energies of the libido. The structures are indeed only able to control the discharge of libidinal energy because they are themselves a bound form of that energy. The disadvantage of this account, as David Foulkes (1978) has pointed out, is that it involves an unnecessary duplication of conduits and drives: the bound energies of the structures only duplicate the originally free energies of the libido.

A number of cognitive-style theorists have preferred a structural-tension model which avoids this duplication. Here the energy necessary to drive the system is seen as a tension or force intrinsic to the cognitive structures themselves (e.g.: Klein, 1967; Rubinstein, 1967; Gardner, 1969; Schafer, 1975). The intrinsically energetic structures function as a kind of mental clockwork, with tension in the wound-up spring serving as a propulsive force. This account too runs into problems, this time over the ontological status of the structures involved. These are in fact the same general problems as those encountered in the section in chapter 3, which discussed the notion of structures in cognitive psychology ('Some thoughts on "structure"'). The mind is not a tangible mechanism with tangible structures, even if the brain is. The structures underlying cognitive styles cannot therefore be actual things, only metaphorical ones. Borrowing the structural tension model from the world of real phenomena leads to smuggling in the specious assumption that mind, like the real world, has spatial extension, and may be occupied by quasi-objects, such as structures.

This was one of the problems encountered in chapter 3, where it was suggested that the notion of cognitive structures could best be interpreted in yet a third way: as descriptions of the kinds of transitions made between one thought and the next in the stream of consciousness; in other words as descriptions of essentially temporal patterns. This interpretation ties in with the third account of what makes thought go, the 'metabolic' account. Thought is metabolic in the sense that one thought naturally changes into the next in the stream of consciousness, just as in a metabolic system one biochemical entity changes into another, or in the car engine the hydrocarbons of petroleum change into water vapour and carbon monoxide gas in a vigorous oxidation reaction. 'Cognitive structures' amount to the 'equations' describing the kinds of changes that occur between one thought and the next, just as chemical equations describe the changes that occur in the chemical reactions which transform one kind of molecule into another.

The metabolic account of the nature of cognitive structures – as descriptions of patterns of cognitive change – allows a reinterpretation of the notion of cognitive style. It leads to an essentially *attentional* account of cognitive-style differences. Different modes of thought afford different kinds of transition in the stream of consciousness between one idea and the next and thus result in the shifting of attention in characteristic ways. Even starting from the same focus of attention, internal or external, each mode of thought will lead attention off down different pathways, through different cognitive transitions or transformations.

This general perspective allows the following initial interpretation of the personality differences which accompany particular cognitive styles: how people attend to the world is one of the marks of their personality. Different people normally select different things to attend to, but even if they attend to the same thing they do so in different ways, and thus end up making different kinds of sense of it. This was seen in the free-association studies where, for verbal representation, making sense included finding what category a thing belonged to; for visual imagery, it included what the thing looked like, and where it was; for enactive imagery, it included what it could do. That similar patterns of meaning might emerge when people are thinking about themselves is suggested both by the idle-thoughts study and by the finding that different career choices are associated with different cognitive styles.

These findings do not say anything directly about the personality traits associated with different cognitive biases, though they do encourage some speculations in that direction. The two empirical studies which follow look in detail at these relationships between thought and personality.

The first study is concerned with gathering initial impressions of the kind of personality characteristics which people with a verbal, visual or enactive bias in their thinking are likely to have. The evidence here is not particularly formal, and uses an adjective rating-scale technique to generate impressionistic and intuitively graspable 'portraits' of the three personality styles. This loose work is then followed up by the more conventional psychometric work of the second study. In both studies the Modes of Thought Questionnaire is used to allow particular personality traits to be related to the cognitive structures characteristic of the three ways of thinking.

Initial impressions of identity: the portraits study

The portraits study involved the use of the MOTQ together with an adjective rating scale (see appendix E). The correlates of the three mode scales sketch in the initial outlines of the portraits, and are shown in table 6.1. The correlates of the particular subscales flesh in these outlines and are shown in table 6.2. These tables show only the positive correlates, and only those unique to particular modes or subscales. They thus exaggerate the differences between the personality portraits associated with each cognitive style, but provide very clear pictures of the distinctive character profile associated with each.

Each table includes two levels of correlation, straightforward Pearson's correlations, and partial correlations controlling for the cross-modal scores. The cross-modal scale functions as something of an existential wedge, which allows us to prise up the social veneer and peep beneath it. The correlates of the cross-modal scale itself are shown in appendix table E.1 and include *friendly*, *dutiful*, *open*, *interested*, and a number of other attributes that are socially desirable, especially for women. Controlling for the cross-modal scores bypasses this aspect of the persona, and reveals what is generally a rather darker personality beneath it.

Table 6.1 Unique correlates of personality adjectives with MOTQ mode scales*

	Verbal			Visual			Enactive		
	men	all	women	men	all	women	men	all	women
a) Controlling for cross-modal scores									
sexual		content involved	consistent generous religious	argumentative romantic thoughtful	creative curious self-aware defensive open emotional artistic	sensual	evasive	sad envious	guilty hatred jealous disgusted annoyed different inferior gullible
b) Pearson correlates									
involved		content secure relaxed independent			peaceful gentle sentimental enthusiastic understanding sensual emotional		solitary		
sexual				nostalgic thoughtful dependent		sensitive			

* The entries in the table are as in the original personality questionnaire. In the text their syntactic form is sometimes modified for grammatical reasons.

Verbal subscales

	Opposites			Phrase completions			Rhymes			Superordinates		
	men	all	women	men	all	women	men	all	women	men	all	women
cross-modal scores controlled	suspicious	content		involved sexual	superior like power	free	free	secure	independent	shame ambitious	fascinated afraid of failure	hopeless
Pearson correlates	suspicious	consistent	generous	sexual involved	popular lucky	relaxed patriotic excited superior	free		religious secretive	sociable shame	fascinated	fascinated

Visual subscales

	Environment			Attribute			Intransitive action			Part		
	men	all	women	men	all	women	men	all	women	men	all	women
cross-modal scores controlled	disappointed reliable	sympathetic nervous self-aware	empty gentle	gullible unsociable	humiliated indecisive apathetic		sentimental sense of wonder	defensive indignant	romantic rational	dependent	protective	
Pearson correlates	reliable artistic			gullible unsociable	insecure	apathetic	dreamy		sense of expectation	dependent	depressed	sociable

Enactive subscales

	Consequence			Affective consequence			Affective			Transitive action			Conditional action		
	men	all	women	men	all	women	men	all	women	men	all	women	men	all	women
cross-modal score controlled	isolated lonely interested inventive calm compassionate	serious		self-conscious critical	shy		antagonistic		solitary	annoyed stubborn	inhibited disgusted aggressive cynical suicidal		feeling of joy		depressed regretful self-indulgent
Pearson correlates	calm sad	patient dominant	vulnerable inventive	shy			antagonistic evasive	grateful like risks	inferior rational friendly		intense	inhibited		irrational	

* The entries in the table are as in the original personality questionnaire. In the text their syntactic form is sometimes modified for grammatical reasons.

Before discussing the particular structural relationships between cognitive and personality styles 'the question needs to be asked as to what these portraits are of. The analyses are correlational and thus do not divide people into pure types. Since to a certain extent we are all capable of using all three ways of thinking, these portraits can be read as descriptions of three aspects of the self, which appear in different proportions in different individuals. The verbalizer portrait taken alone, for example, is less a full description of any particular individual than an asymptotic projection of a verbal bias; and calling someone a verbalizer in what follows means not that they use *only* verbal representation, but that they use it a lot.

Verbalizers and the liking for power

The personality characteristics of verbalizers map on to their cognitive character-istics in quite precise ways, as is shown in figure 6.1. The verbalizer 'portrait' is composed of three main interconnected features, concerned with: the role of the institutional hierarchy; the use of language as a social tool; and superstition. All three relate to the central theme, which is a general concern with power.

Verbalizers make sense of the world by fitting things into hierarchically organized sets of categories. They seem to make sense of themselves in the same way. The hierarchy is now an institutional structure rather than a cognitive one, and the verbalizer defines him or herself by reference to a role within it. A social role in the bureaucratic system is the equivalent of a concept in the cognitive one.[2]

The role provides a sense of order and *consistency*, but it also allows for some vertical mobility. Verbalizers are *ambitious* to move up the hierarchy and appear to be *fascinated* by authority.

Unfortunately, where promotion is possible, so is demotion, and verbalizers are aware of threats to status in their *fear of failure, suspicion* and *shame* (men), and *hopelessness* (women).

The terms used to describe the cognitive structures are also used to describe the institutional ones. In most large organizations there are literal superordinates, people who are in authority over individuals, and in many commercial and indeed other organizations there is a literal opposition – the group or firm against whom one is competing for markets, prestige, or success of other kinds. This competitiveness provides considerable relish and a spur to achievement for many people. Its disadvantage, and all ways of thinking appear to have both boons and banes associated with them, is that competitive thinking tends to be pre-emptive, blinding the competitors to the existence of any alternative way of thinking. Kelley and Stahelski (1970) found that if naturally competitive and naturally co-operative individuals interact, the competitive definition of the situation tends to win the day, and the co-operators are also forced into taking a competitive stance.

The verbalizers' definition of situations may be a similarly influential one, partly

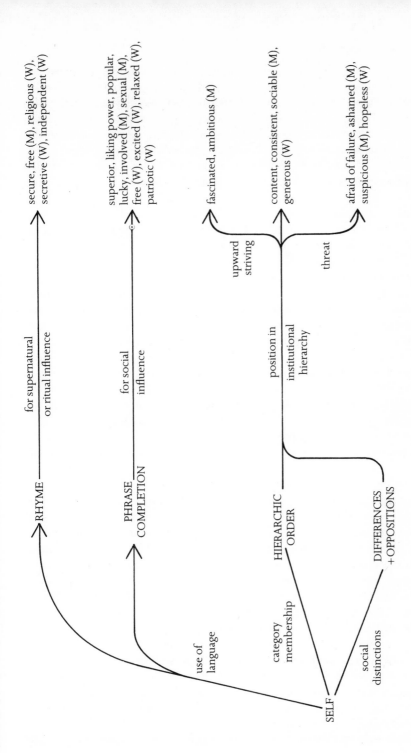

Figure 6.1 Relationships between cognitive structures and personality characteristics for verbal representation

because these people have a capacity to put their own viewpoint in a persuasive manner. The personality adjectives which correlate with the phrase completion subscale, the most speech-like of the MOTQ subscales, are all positive, reflecting a confident self-image. The spectrum of adjectives here appears to be a consequence of the fact that once loosed from its referents language becomes available for more rhetorical functions. Verbalizers appear to use language as a very effective social instrument, adapting it to the business of making friends and influencing people. In addition to their *sense of superiority* and *liking for power*, verbalizers describe themselves as both *popular* and *lucky*.

Barthes (1972) sees dereferentialized language as a tool of the politically conservative, who use it to preserve and bolster the status quo. There are some suggestions of conservatism in the verbalizer portrait, in the *patriotism* of the women; and perhaps also in the *sexuality* of the men, which indicates a traditional male stereotype.

The third general constellation in the verbal portrait can be interpreted, though tentatively, as relating to superstition and to attempts at supernatural influence. This interpretation is prompted by the correlation of *secure* and *religious* with the MOTQ rhyme subscale, and by the fact that rhyming structures have the non-sensical appeal of soothing mellifluence that characterizes much ritual language. Rhymes are satisfying not because they make meaningful reference to anything, but because they have a musical quality which is satisfying in its own right. Much ritual and religious language exploits this, and relies on an archaic language (as did the Church of England until recently) or an alien language (as Catholicism used Latin until recently).

Lévi-Strauss (1968) sees myth and ritual as being in cultural equilibrium. Myth, which he sees as based on oppositional structures, takes things apart: virginity and marriage, life and death; and something – ritual – is needed to put them back together again, and provide a sense of continuity. Within the verbal cognitive style the ritual rhymes may therefore be balancing the mythical and divisive opposites.

If there is one theme that permeates the verbalizer portrait it is the need for power, the need to order and control events in the world. Power can be gained and exercised in many ways. There is power of a basic kind in the ability to name something and thereby to categorize it. There is also power in criticizing those things which are difficult to categorize, as was seen in the verbal idle thoughts of chapter 4.[3] Power with a more constructive social effect derives from a person's position in the bureaucratic hierarchy, with the responsibility attached to that status for organizing other people. Status must of course be apparent to others, and according to McClelland and Winter (1971) those liking power will take care to form social alliances which enhance their prestige, and will spend money on the possessions that exhibit it. Rather more worrying is the finding of Kipnis and Vanderveer (1971) that those liking power will also give disproportionate rewards to those who ingratiatingly support them.

The exercise of power in most organizations requires the effective use of talk:

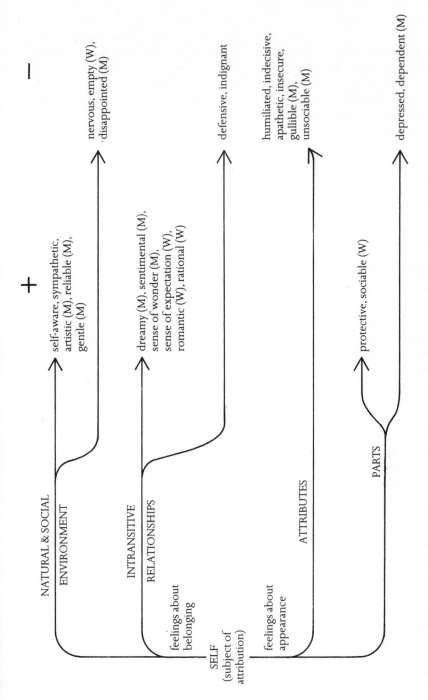

Figure 6.2 Relationships between cognitive structures and personality characteristics for visual imagery

to inform and persuade, and to participate in the polished pattern of interaction which attracts respect and popularity. The evidence suggests that people biased towards inner speech have honed their language to make it a fine tool capable of achieving these aims.

The final aspect of power may have more importance in Ireland than elsewhere. It stems from the power of ritual, especially religious ritual, to control otherwise incomprehensible events.

While Freud did not talk about cognitive styles, he did suggest that different people may invest most of their libidinal energy in one or other of the domains in the psyche. In chapter 4 it was suggested that there was a relationship between speech and the super-ego; and of Freud's descriptions of his three 'libidinal types' (1931), it is the obsessional type, dominated by the super-ego, that corresponds to the verbalizer. Freud saw such people as the upholders of civilization, for the most part in a fairly traditional spirit.

Visualizers and the need for affiliation

The relationships between personality and visual ways of cognitively construing reality are shown in figure 6.2. In the free-association studies, many of the important visual structures, when described in terms of case grammar, involved a subject of attribution, to which parts, attributes, locations and intransitive actions, could be attributed. In the visualizer portrait, the self becomes the subject of attribution (as opposed, for example, to an agent or an experiencer). This appears to involve an externalized awareness of the self, mediated through sensitivity to the environment (and especially the social environment), and has motivational consequences.

Relationships to environments are of an odd form in that one cannot do anything directly about them. At the most one can be in, and perhaps acting in, the physical environment; and, as shown by the idle-thoughts study, one can perform for the social one. If one has no hope of direct influence, a receptivity to the environment, and an ability to mould oneself, chameleon-like, to its requirements becomes useful. The self is not an agent so much as a marionette, and it is the environment that pulls the strings. The receptivity of visualizers to the environment gives the impression that they are Romantics, not in the limited, modern sense, but in the sense of the nineteenth-century artistic and social Romantic movements. Visualizers have the *artistic* emphasis of Romanticism, with its *dreaminess* and *sense of wonder*, and the *self-awareness* that such an attitude to the world reciprocally involves. They show too the humanitarian concerns of many of the social reformers of the Romantic period, being *sympathetic, gentle* and *reliable*; and there are suggestions also of some of the more maudlin aspects of Romanticism in their *sentimentality* and (small r) *romanticism*.[4]

A troublesome consequence of sensitivity to the environment is a *dependency* on it. Instead of being driven from within, as erstwhile drive theory would have it, visualizers are 'called' from without, motivated by their responsiveness to the environment. In place of an inner awareness of motives, their self-awareness appears to be external, a matter of seeing themselves from outside and of governing their behaviour from that perspective. This interpretation arises from the correlation of *self-aware* with the MOTQ environment subscale. Here, as in the visual day-dreams, people seem to see themselves from outside and then worry about their appearance. Bion (1962) refers to the developmental task confronting human beings as the 'resolution of the conflict between narcissism and social-ism' (p. 309). Visualizers seem to solve the conflict by a subtle integration of the two, through an external self-awareness which allows them to look at themselves while taking the viewpoint of other people.

The negative aspects of the visualizer's personality follow from the onus for motivation being located externally, which results in *emptiness* and *apathy*; and from the lack of direct control these individuals can exert over the environment, which results in *nervousness*, *insecurity* and *indecision*.

The negative aspects of the visualizer portrait are a consequence of the same sensitivity that underlies its positive features. Objective self-awareness is useful for affiliative purposes but it tends not to penetrate the skin, and the person is in danger of becoming an appearance with nothing inside.

The negative feelings about the self may be particularly poignant when the visualizer's dependency is ab-used and she or especially he is rejected or otherwise ostracized. Then follow *disappointment*, *defensiveness*, *humiliation* and *indignation*. The *unsociability* of male visualizers may be both a response to and an attempt to avoid this sense of social ostracism. It is not that other people do not matter, it is rather that they matter too much. One can only be really humiliated or indignant if one cares a good deal about the opinions of others. Indignant people are not being a-social; they are going off in a huff, which is different.

The visualizer portrait can be summed up as reflecting a general need for affiliation. Visualizers like other people and want to be liked by them. They have the character of Freud's erotic type, who needs to be loved and who is dependent on those who may withhold this love. The dynamics of this need of affiliation are complex, relying on an external self-awareness and an ability to mould the persona to fit in with the needs of others. It is possible that this externalized self-awareness originates in the kind of joint attention we engage in with our friends, and which we engaged in with our mothers in infancy. Joint attention involves the child following the mother's gaze, so that they are both looking at the same thing. This is a prerequisite for learning language, as words must refer to the same thing for speaker and hearer. It may be that externalized self-awareness is an extension of this phenomenon of joint attention to the situation where the gaze of the other is on the self. Following their line of regard leads to seeing oneself as they do.

The socially oriented style of the visualizer is coherent with the visual bias of the social science group of chapter 5 (psychology and social-work students), and also with the fact that women tend to show a visual bias. Conventional sex roles would see both nurturance and social dependency as acceptable for women, and would sanction the *sociability* that fulfils their affiliative needs. The same behaviour in men would not universally meet with equivalent approval, and the men, in contrast to the women, claim to be *unsociable*.

There is nothing contradictory in the fact that two opposite tendencies, sociability and unsociability, may be part of the same portrait. What this means is that the dimension of sociability is always salient for visualizers. They have what Markus (1977; Markus and Sentis, 1982) would call a 'self-schemata' of sociability, which allows them to process information relevant to social belonging and social ostracism more quickly and efficiently than people who are 'aschematic' in this regard, that is, people who do not care one way or the other. Marcel Proust was a schematic in this regard:

> In the case of the solitary, his seclusion, even where it is absolute and ends only with life itself, has often as its primary cause a disordered love of the crowd, which so far overrules every other feeling that, not being able to win, when he goes out, the admiration of the hall-porter, of the passers-by, of the cabman whom he hails, he prefers not to be seen by them at all, and with that object abandons every activity which would force him to go out of doors. (*Within a Budding Grove*, part 2, p. 123)

Enactive imagers and the need for self-efficacy

The portrait of the enactive imager can be divided into three broad aspects, involving the self as agent, the self as experiencer, and the self as solitary being. All three have a bearing on the dominant need of the enactive imager, the need for self-efficacy. Figure 6.3 shows the relationships between cognitive structures and personality characteristics.

The enactive portrait is of an individualist, driven to do what he or she has to do, and rather heedless of what anyone else thinks about the matter. The strong motivations for personal achievement are countered by equally powerful (one fears, more powerful) frustrations. All three portraits include opposite extremes, but differ in the dimensions they define. For the enactive imagers the poles are set by inventiveness at best and suicidal depression at worst.

The most positive aspects emerge when action has physical consequences (the MOTQ consequences subscale). Then people are capable of *calmness and compassion*; and show an *inventiveness* along with a number of traits that are probably its natural complements – *interest, seriousness, patience* and *dominance*.

The inventiveness of the enactive imager contrasts in interesting ways with the artistic orientation of the visualizer; and creativity appears to be important in both, though in different manifestations. (*Creative* itself is correlated with a number of visual and enactive subscales, though only with the visual mode scale. Visualizers may be interested in whether something is creative in the sense of aesthetically

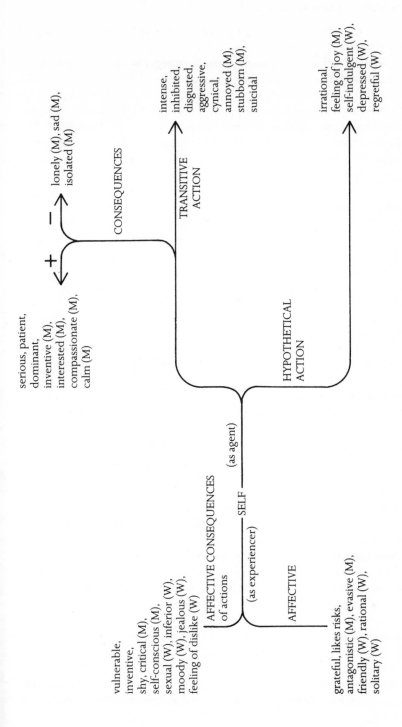

Figure 6.3   Relationships between cognitive structures and personality characteristics for enactive imagery

pleasing; enactive imagers in whether something is creative in the sense of working effectively.)

The darkest side of the enactive personality emerges in connection with the MOTQ transitive action subscale. The best possibility here is intensity, which is probably a very positive attribute for its possessors, though it may not be everybody else's social cup of tea. All the other correlating adjectives are negative, ranging from inhibited, through disgusted, aggressive and cynical, to suicidal. This suggests either that action is often frustrated by others, with the consequent anger being directed both towards others and towards the self; or that enactive imagers have strong impulses which they have difficulty in controlling; or, more likely, both.

The MOTQ conditional action subscale can be interpreted as reflecting attitudes to the future and to what could be. Its correlates range from the feeling of joy which can be derived from idle or whimsical (irrational) speculation, to the regretful feeling engendered by the realization that the hypothetical is not easily translated into the actual. Taking conditional and transitive subscales together there is some basis for arguing that men can more easily distinguish between the hypothetical and the actual, and that when frustrated in attempts to achieve some personal goal they turn their anger outwards and dig their toes in determinedly, becoming stubborn and annoyed; whereas women turn their anger inwards and become regretful, self-indulgent and depressed. This may or may not be any more than a reflection of society's tolerance of some kinds of aggressiveness in men that are not normally acceptable in women.

The two MOTQ subscales which are concerned with affectivity, the affective subscale itself, and the affective consequences subscale, show attitudes to the self as an experiencer. The affective subscale generally provides a more positive picture than the affective consequences, which reveal a painful vulnerability. The difference is something like that between simply feeling, and feeling in response to interaction with others.

When simply feeling, enactive imagers show themselves to be grateful and to show liking for risks; this indicates some zest for living. They also show something more difficult to interpret within the context of an affective scale, and that is rationality. Since a similar relationship recurs in the psychometric work reported later (where the affective subscale correlates with emotional stability on Cattell's 16PF) it is worth assuming that this is no accident. One interpretation is that it is only unacknowledged feelings that subvert rationality. Acknowledged ones are incorporated into a kind of rationality in which feeling is important; in wisdom rather than stark logic.

When the enactive imager is responding to interactions with others, the zestful and hopeful picture disappears, and is replaced by vulnerability and victimhood. Men describe themselves as self-conscious and critical, and women feel themselves to be inferior, moody, jealous, and capable of feelings of dislike. Sexual, for women, relates to this group, and provides a contrast to its correlation with the verbal phrase completions for men. Sexuality relates to vulnerability for women and to power for men.

One personality characteristic which is not confined to a particular MOTQ subscale, but which colours the entire enactive portrait, is an evident solitariness. Many of the other traits of enactive imagers suggest an interest in things rather than people, and their social needs are probably better met by a few strong one-to-one relationships than through general sociability. Enactive imagers are capable of *patience, compassion* (men) and *friendliness* (women), indicating that they value some closeness with others, but beyond this they appear to be natural loners: they are *solitary, shy, isolated,* and *lonely.*

A number of factors appear to contribute to this. Intensity tends not to make for easy social relationships, let alone aggressiveness, whether directed outwardly or inwardly. Furthermore, invention of most kinds tends to be a solitary if not a positively lonely activity, as of its nature it implies going beyond the opinions of other people and into a realm where consensus fails and one is sustained by a sheer and possibly bloody-minded faith that what one is doing is right. Innovation and social awareness rarely coincide with any ease, and to preserve the one it may be necessary to forfeit the other. Indeed the role played by other people in the life of the enactive imager seems to be a predominantly negative one, as they are probably the source of most of the frustrations and inhibitions which stand in the way of personal fulfilment.

What enactive imagers need has been described under a number of headings. Bandura (1977) talks about 'self-efficacy', de Charms (1968) refers to 'personal causation', and White (1959) uses the term 'competence'. The active and inventive aspect, which is to say roughly the positive and masculine aspect, of the enactive portrait, is appropriate to the engineers of chapter 5, who were biased towards this way of thinking.[5] Emotions play a motivational role in the need for action but they may also have some importance in their own right. Whether the predomin-antly tortured emotional tone of the enactive portrait reflects an emotional openness without need of repression, or an anguish much in need of it, is unclear. The morbid tenor of the enactive day-dreams indicates at least some openness here, and enactive imagers may have an ability to make use of strong emotional experiences as a powerful component in their psychic functioning. This ability may eventually be channelled into their motivation and constructive action. On the negative side, Plutchik (1954) noted that chronic muscle tension, resulting from a blocking of action, is a feature of most forms of maladjustment.

Freud's remarks on the third of his libidinal types, which he calls the narcissistic, are relevant to the enactive imager. These are people with a proneness to action and a weak super-ego. They are independent and not easily overawed. During periods of cultural change they may become leaders, but, he says, they are liable, if frustrated, to psychosis and criminality. Strong stuff.

Conclusion to the portraits

The portraits study shows how it is possible to relate particular aspects of personality to particular ways of thinking.

Each mode of thought emerges as a cognitive style in the true sense, a life style as well as a way of thinking. Each focuses the person's attention on the world in a particular way and leads to different ways of making sense of it and living in it.[6]

Each mode of thought has a way of being a success and a way of being a failure, and both are specific to the mode of thought and rather irrelevant outside it. Verbalizers are concerned with power, status and order, and therefore necessarily also worried about failures of power, losses of status, and their associated chaos. None of this is very important to the enactive imager. The enactive imager is concerned with invention and despair, both of which probably look like self-indulgence to the verbalizer. The visualizer has concerns midway between the extremes, and worries about affiliation and rejection. Padgett and Wolosin (1980) have shown better dyadic communication in those who are cognitively similar, as both verbalizers and enactive imagers are to visualizers; and the two extreme groups may need the social mediation of the visualizers just as, at a semantic level, verbal and enactive structures needed the semantic mediation of the visual in the triptych arrangement described in chapter 3.

A second approach to identity: the psychometric study

The adjective rating scale of the portraits study was effective in giving general impressions of the personality characteristics associated with the three cognitive styles. This section discusses some more formal work carried out with Sean Hammond and Elizabeth Dunne, which was aimed at treating the same phenomena in a different way. This psychometric work again used the MOTQ, along with the following tests: Wilson-Patterson Attitude Inventory (WPAI), Rotter's Internal–External Locus of Control Scale (IE), the Marlowe-Crowne Social Desirability Scale, the Eysenck Personality Questionnaire (EPQ), the Personal Orientation Inventory (POI), Cattell's 16PF, and the Couch Keniston measure of Acquiescence. The technical details for this work are given in appendix E, along with the results upon which the following discussion is based.

As a general description of the results it is useful to borrow some terms from David Riesman's *The Lonely Crowd* (1950). He was concerned with the importance of different personality types at different stages in cultural evolution, and talked about *tradition-directed people*, who have power during times of stability; *other-directed people*, important during periods of cultural decline when social values dominate over those of personal achievement; and *inner-directed people*, who are important as trailblazers during periods of social transition, when old structures have broken down. These terms can be lifted from Riesman's work to provide useful and cogent labels for the three cognitive styles: the verbalizers are tradition-directed, the visualizers are other-directed, and the enactive imagers are inner-directed.

Tradition-directed verbalizers

The portraits study indicated that verbalizers are interested in power. Power requires to be exercised and tends to polarize the world into the haves, those who have it, and the others, the have-nots, over whom it is exercised.

The psychometric data indicate that women tend to be the have-nots, finding self-esteem in becoming the guardians of traditional morality. They show a *religion-puritanism* which, in general confirmation of the portraits data, correlates with the MOTQ rhyme subscale. They also believe in the efficacy of force, shown in their *militarism-punitiveness*. This correlates with the MOTQ opposites subscale, and can be interpreted as a physical counterpart of the verbal criticisms found in the idle thoughts. In both cases admonishment is deemed to be deserved by those violating conventions. These characteristics combined with their *conscientiousness, external locus of control, humility* and *apprehensiveness* portray the traditional woman, subservient to a man but wielding considerable moral power of her own.

The men, though less clearly, occupy the traditionally dominant position. The unclarity arises from an asymmetry in the power relation: underdogs have no reason to look for extra people to be subservient to. One boss is enough. Top dogs, however, do want to extend their suzerainty. For the men this quest is furthered by *forthrightness* and *spontaneity* in expressing themselves and by their *internal locus of control*, all of which are presumably harnessed to their persuasive powers. Phares (1965) has shown that people with an internal locus of control are more effective than those with an external locus in getting others to change their attitudes, even when adhering to a script. Interestingly men who claim to find verbalizing easy or enjoyable (on the questions at the end of the MOTQ) show a strong *extraversion*, which would fit this persuasive and perhaps argumentative picture. There is some evidence that the verbalizer may sometimes be hoist by his own persuasive petard, as *acquiescence* (yea-saying) correlates with the MOTQ phrase completions subscale.

The general theme of the verbal correlates is a traditional one, of women who stay at home as moral guardians, while men go out and are assertive. The traditional picture is not necessarily a conservative one (in the authoritarian sense measured by the WPAI), though verbalizers do have a number of traits associated with authoritarianism. There are positive correlations of WPAI *conservatism* with the MOTQ questions about the ease and enjoyment of verbalizing, and it may therefore be that verbalizers are not typically authoritarian, but that authoritarian-ism represents one of the dangers to which verbalizers are prone.

Other-directed visualizers

Visualizers have a *constructive view of human nature, do not accept aggression* and are not *ethnocentric.* This indicates a general tender-mindedness which is supported by negative correlations with EPQ *psychoticism* and WPAI *realism.* Women also show an *anti-hedonism,* which is less a purely visualizer characteristic than something typical of women of all sorts (perhaps because a number of the WPAI items are concerned with a sexual hedonism which tends to exploit women).

The converse of this positive, tender-hearted view of others is that visualizers (and women more strongly than men) also want to be liked by others, and are willing to present themselves in such a way as to encourage this. *Social desirability* and the EPQ *lie scale* correlate most strongly with the MOTQ visual scales, and sufficiently strongly in relation to the environmental subscale to survive the partialling out of the cross-modal score, which itself correlates with social desirability. The pattern revealed by the environment subscale is telling. It also correlates with *external locus of control* and *lack of spontaneity.* These can be interpreted, along the lines of the visualizer portrait, in terms of an ability to see oneself as others do, and to define oneself from that viewpoint.

Not only do visualizers want to be liked, they probably are liked. They have the kind of unabrasive personality that makes them easy to get along with; they are *relaxed, self-assured, happy-go-lucky, controlled* (men), and *emotionally stable* (women). They may also have the great social skill of actually remembering social information, as Swann and Miller (1982) found for their vivid imagers.

The picture of the visualizer is of someone who is sensitive to and interested in others, and who is socially aware rather than socially boisterous. Men in particular show a strong *introversion,* paralleling their *unsociability* in the portraits data.

The literature on imagery and extraversion is confused. A number of other studies have also found a relationship between visualizing (assessed in various ways) and introversion, for example Huckabee (1974); Gralton, Hayes and Richardson (1979); Riding and Dyer (1980); and Stricklin and Penk (1980, though only for stable people). Others have found visual imagery to relate to extraversion, for example Gale, Morris, Lucas and Richardson (1972, though only if they used inappropriate statistics); and Stricklin and Penk (1980, for neurotics).

The root of this confusion may be that the EPQ, like most psychometric instruments, confounds saliency with polarity. It assumes the dimensions of introversion and extraversion to be equally salient for all, and then proceeds to position everyone somewhere between the two poles. This fails to take account of the complexity of the visualizer's social concerns. Visualizers face a conflict in both needing the good opinion of others and resenting their dependence on them. The women probably find this conflict easier to resolve than men, perhaps because the nurturing visualizer role is a more effective and less problematic source of self-esteem for women. Women are the *self-sufficient* ones here, and turn to others with something to offer in exchange for social approval. Men cannot enter into quite the same bargain.

Inner-directed enactive imagers

Riesman describes inner-directed people as important during times of social transition, when new problems arise which need new solutions. At other times they are misfits, at best tolerated, or, in traditional societies, institutionalized in such roles as that of the shaman. Freud, in his description of the activity-orientated narcissistic type, refers to a similarly extreme blend of charisma, psychosis and criminality.

The personality correlates of the MOTQ enactive scales indicate that enactive imagers in current Irish society are irked by conventions, but are generally powerless, in the absence of the appropriate *Zeitgeist*, to do much about them.

Enactive imagers show a muted version of the humanitarianism of the visualizers, though the *capacity for intimate contact* shown by the men suggests that their relationships with others may be more personal than nurturing. The enactive imagers' rebelliousness and non-conformity are uniquely their own. These show up in an *anti-religion-puritanism* (mostly for women: this has more significance in Ireland than it might have elsewhere) and a *lack of acquiescence* (mostly for men). As in the portraits data it is the transitive action subscale that most strongly reveals the frustrations encountered in being an enactive imager, correlating with a *lack of spontaneity*, a low *self-acceptance* and a low *self-regard*.

The women (though not the men) show a distinct aloofness, being *self-sufficient*, *reserved*, and *shy*. This may be partly a matter of preference, as solitariness would allow them to pursue the dictates of their own inner-directedness; and partly forced on them, as their *undisciplined self-conflict* is unlikely to make for comfortable interactions. The positive side of the enactive imager emerges most strongly with the affective subscale, which suggests that if people can acknowledge their strong feelings and see them as good and useful rather than the source of *Angst* and frustration, they can emerge to a relative *emotional stability*.

Conclusion and transition to part two

The findings of the portraits and psychometric studies strongly support one another, and between them richly reveal the personality traits associated with particular cognitive biases: the verbalizer's traditional orientation and need for power; the visualizer's general orientation towards others and need for social affiliation; and the enactive imager's inner-directedness and need for self-efficacy.

Within the overall modes, particular features of cognition can be related to specific features of personality. To have a particular way of thinking is to attend to and make sense of objects, events and people, in particular ways. These ways of attending determine the salient constructs in the person's life world, and have concomitants (with no claims about which comes first) in how they see themselves, and in the general structure of their social world.

Mischel (1968) has shown that how people see themselves, as assessed on personality questionnaires, does not necessarily bear any strong relationship to actual behaviour. This is not to dismiss these accounts of personality as irrelevant. In its natural context a 'personality' is as important as a vehicle for communicating and being convivial with one's fellow humans as it is for predicting behaviour.

The two studies of this chapter, in looking at how people construe their own personalities, have taken an essentially cognitive approach to personality. They have none the less provided a good deal of information about the kinds of values and feelings important to each cognitive bias: the value on power and control in verbal representation, the value on social affiliation in visual imagery, and the emotional intensity and value on being an agent of one's own destiny in enactive imagery. These feelings and values clearly match the cognitive structures associated with the three forms of representation; and yet this very matching, this very isomorphy, arouses suspicion. It is possible that instead of touching the affective elements themselves, the work so far has only looked at *construals* of them, filtered through the now familiar cognitive structures. The chapters of part two therefore look in greater detail at some of the evaluations and feelings important in each of the three modes of thought.

Part 2

Particular evaluative issues

7

Values in inner speech: preference for categorical clarity

Evidence from the preceding chapters indicates that an important evaluative domain for verbal representation derives from its categorical and hierarchical structuring. In the idle-thoughts study the negative aspect of these evaluations was evident, with criticisms being directed towards the misfits, the entities which were atypical within the conventional order. In the portraits study it emerged that self-evaluations may use the same principle, with verbalizers evaluating themselves within the context of what is now an institutional hierarchy. High self-esteem arises from two things: the security of knowing one's role; and the status of having a higher one.

Horizontal and vertical dimensions of categorizing

The two kinds of evaluation important to verbalizers mirror what Rosch (1978) described as the two dimensions of categorizing, the horizontal and the vertical.

The vertical dimension is defined by superordinacy. It is the dimension along which rockers belong to the category of chairs, which belong to the category of furniture (in the conceptual order); and schoolchildren are subordinate to teachers who are subordinate to head teachers (in the institutional one). The horizontal dimension is marked by relations of opposition, or more broadly, differentiation. It is the dimension along which chairs differ from tables, and form 2A differs from form 2B.

The quintessence of the order which these two dimensions impose on phenomena is caught in the notion of prototypes. The prototype of a category is that which maximizes both similarities within the group and differences between groups (Rosch, 1975b; Rosch and Mervis, 1975). Prototypicality, the degree to which an object resembles the prototype at the category centre, has a number of important consequences for cognition; all of which suggest that typical instances are more easily and better processed than atypical ones. Prototypical items are more easily learnt, more speedily classified as belonging to the category, and more likely to be generated in response to the category label than atypical ones (Rosch, Simpson and Miller, 1976). Furthermore, in memory, prototypes exert a systematic bias such that, once categorized, objects are remembered as more typical than they really are (Cantor and Mischel, 1977, 1979; Tsujimoto, 1978). It has also been suggested that categories themselves are represented cognitively in terms of their most typical exemplars (Anderson and McGaw, 1973; Anderson, Pichert, Goetz, Schallert, Stevens and Trollip, 1976; Robbins, Barresi, Compton, Furst, Russo and Smith, 1978) though there is disagreement here (Gumenik, 1979).

The empirical work in this chapter is concerned specifically with the evaluative aspects of categorizing. The first two studies look at whether prototypicality is also an evaluative yardstick, as is suggested by several features of verbal representation. It seems unlikely that prototypicality is the only yardstick here, and the first study sets prototypicality considerations in perspective by looking at people's general ways of evaluating things. It looks at what people think and feel about members of the animal kingdom.

Favourite creatures

The study of favourite creatures asked for both quantitative and qualitative data on how people felt about animals. For each of twenty four animals, ranging from donkey to seagull and pig to spider, people were asked first of all to rate how they felt about the animal (on a seven-point scale); then to describe how they felt (interest, revulsion, or whatever); and then to give the reasons for feeling as they did. The reasons were content-analysed and the kinds of reasons were related to the evaluative ratings (regardless of the particular animal). Procedural details and information on feelings about specific animals may be found in appendix F, and more general results are given in table 7.1

People clearly use many criteria for evaluating animals, and most of these are themselves intrinsically evaluative. The locus of the value is often merely projected from the eye of the beholder to the corpus of the animal (from 'I like it' to 'it is nice'). People explain their subjective liking for donkeys by reference to their objective likeableness, which is evidenced by their possession of intrinsically positive properties such as beauty, gentleness and a tolerance for children. In contrast, flies, vultures and rats are ugly, slimy scoundrels, and of course people dislike them.

Equally self-evident is that people should value a number of farm animals for

Table 7.1 Evaluations: relationships between ratings and reasons

Reason* and example	Spearman's rho†‡	p
Nice body part – – it has a nice face	+.75	.001
attribute – – a beautiful creature/the right size	+.58	.01
action – – graceful/wonderfully fast	+.51	.02
character – – I admire its cunning/its gentleness	+.86	.001
environment – – it lives by the sea and I love the sea		
other (eulogies for other/unspecified reasons)	+.37	
total (any of the above)	+.80	.001
Nasty part – – it's got an ugly face	–.29	
attribute – – it's slimy, I hate slimy things	–.75	.001
action – – it wriggles horribly	–.71	.001
character – – it's selfish and vicious	–.23	
environment – – it lives in a squalid place		
other (dislikes for other/unspecified reasons)	–.69	.001
total (any of the above)	–.77	.001
Dissonant part – – too much hair/no face	–.32	
attribute – – too big	–.34	
action – – moves too close to the ground	–.28	
other – – weird/outlandish	–.11	
total (any of the above)	–.54	.01
Understandable to people – – I pity them/very affectionate	+.71	.001
Not understandable – – you can't talk to a goldfish	–.20	
Useful to humans – – I love rashers	+.45	.05
Not useful – – useless creatures/can't see why they exist		
Familiar – – see them everyday	+.27	
Not familiar – – – never seen one	–.23	
Symbolic, non-human – – scorpion is a zodiac sign	+.20	
human – – reminds me of my boyfriend	+.33	
Really harmful – – it bites your toes/kills people	–.61	.01
Phobic – – it gives me the shivers up my spine	–.49	.02
Superordinate – – it's a bird/insect	–.46	.05

* Interjudge agreement, taking categories as subjects, Spearman's r_s = .96.
† Analyses using animals as subjects, N = 24.
‡ Absence of an r_s value indicates too little data.

their utility in providing rashers, wool or haulage energy, though utility appears to be a second-rate evaluative criterion. Only those who are not beautiful need to be useful.

People also use a 'social' perspective which measures animals for their fitness to engage in social intercourse with humans. It is important to people to be able to 'read' animals for their intention and character, just as we read one another. This is possible for medium-sized creatures with faces, and preferably big brown eyes, through which window the animal soul can be glimpsed and responded to. Stray dogs capitalize most effectively on this:

> *stray dog* (affection +3) Because he is hungry, lost, and because he has been abandoned by someone.

> *stray dog* (pity him +3) He is experiencing sorrow, and that's all there is for him to face.

> *stray dog* (I love stray dogs +3) Their eyes are so pathetic. They are faithful – they will follow you around.

Where animals cannot be read from their faces, people use the more molar criterion of action. The capacity to do harm by biting, stinging or infecting with disease, reduces an animal's likeableness; and some harmless actions may become .suspect if interpreted in human terms: touching the human person without permission is particularly ill regarded. Even purely intransitive actions, where humans are only spectators, are construed in evaluative terms. Rapid scuttling, rarely innocent when done by humans, is seen as being equivalently furtive when done by lizards, spiders and rats. Indeed references to such nasty actions were among the strongest predictors of negative evaluations, and tended to be evoked by the same set of animals that reaped the phobic responses of 'the creeps' or 'the shivers':

> *rat* (hate them −3) Because of their abrupt and quick run for whatever they want.

> *spider* (hate and am afraid of them −3) 'Cos of their legs and how fast they can move, and even when crushed they can sometimes get up again – ugh!

Weerts and Lang's (1978) work on small-animal phobias also shows movement to be an important trigger of phobic responses.

Being nasty on conceptual grounds

One fairly small group of evaluative reasons differs from all the others in making no appeal to characteristics which are themselves intrinsically evaluative. These are the references to dissonant qualities.

A characteristic was taken to be dissonant when it was not intrinsically evaluative, but became so when displayed by an animal. Smallness, for example, or hairlessness, is no reason to dislike a matchbox or a teaspoon, but diminutive size is a reason for some people disliking rats, and hairlessness a reason for some disliking pigs. Conversely hairiness is fine for donkeys and bulldogs but odd on gorillas; apparently because people assimilate them to a human category ('reminds me of my boyfriend'), where biologically, if not culturally, the norm is nakedness. Crabs are so dissonant one wonders how they manage to form a *Gestalt* at all:

crab (hate them −3) Horrible appearance, no real face, no apparent feelings.

crab (I don't like them −2) They move on the ground totally. I like animals that are off the ground, like dogs, horses.

crab (hate their eyes −3) Eyes on stalks, and 'sideways' walk – horrible – ugh.

The negative evaluations justified by these dissonant or incongruous character-istics presuppose that there is an animal norm, which is good, and animal deviance from the norm, which is bad. The norm is apparently (and as Rosch supposed) a mammal, and the use of other superordinate labels (such as insect, reptile or bird) carries negative evaluations.

While references to dissonant characteristics are relatively rare, they are im-portant in cracking the façade of incorrigibility presented by other kinds of justification: they explain evaluations by reference to something that is not itself an evaluation. In some cases conceptual considerations may underlie the more self-evident evaluative truths. For example, something without a face cannot engage in (highly valued) social intercourse, and is thus doomed on sociability grounds. This is not to say that values on the basis of social intercourse can be *reduced* to the possession of a face (etc.), only that possession of a face may *afford* social intercourse.

The first study has served its purpose of showing that conceptual criteria are sometimes important in evaluating animals, even though these considerations may be buried by, or less important than, criteria of other kinds. The next study focuses particularly on prototypicality considerations.

Typicality and liking: eulogizing the typical

Here the same twenty four animals used in the study of favourite creatures were presented to another group of people, this time with a request that they rate them for prototypicality, and give reasons for their ratings. Having done this, they were then asked for ratings of liking (see appendix F). It is then possible to look at the relationship between prototypicality ratings and the kinds of reasons given; and at the relationship between ratings of prototypicality and ratings of liking. Results are shown in table 7.2.

It is interesting that in her instructions for rating typicality, Rosch (1975b) specifically differentiated it from liking, as if to counter some confusion between the two. There turns out not to be a confusion but a strong relationship; and one that makes good sense. In valuing the typical, people are valuing what is most meaningful within the taxonomic system. Taking this semantic domain alone, it has to be the case that *in general* we prefer the norm. To prefer the atypical would be to value chaos over order. We could not do that and survive.[1]

Of course matters are never quite that simple. Within the general association of typicality and liking for all animals, there are complications introduced by the

Table 7.2   Typicality: relationships between ratings and reasons

Reason* and example	Spearman's rho†‡	p
Appropriate§ part – – 4 legs	+.88	.001
attribute – – it's a good size	+.78	.001
action – – it walks (on all fours)	+.83	.001
character – – it's gentle and intelligent	+.84	.001
environment – – it lives on land	+.53	.01
evaluation – – I admire it, and real animals should be admirable	+.27	
total (any of the above)	+.86	.001
Inappropriate part – – it hasn't got any legs	−.67	.001
attribute – – pigs are nude	−.67	.001
action – – it walks upright/wriggles	−.75	.001
character – – it is vicious, animals aren't	+.21	
environment – – it lives in the sea	+.39	
evaluation – – I hate rats but like animals	−.54	.01
total (any of the above)	−.89	.001
Understandable to people – – very affectionate pets	+.80	.001
Not understandable – – no communication with a fly	−.63	.001
Useful to humans – – provides wool/domesticated	+.62	.01
Not useful – – pest, useless/wild	+.53	.01
Familiar – – often see them	+.68	.001
Not familiar – – never seen one	+.17	
Symbolic, non-human – – stands for evil in my mind	+.34	
human – – reminds me of relatives waiting for someone to die	+.34	
Really harmful – – they kill people	+.11	
Phobic – – they give me the creeps		
Superordinate categories – – it's a bird	−.67	.001
A real animal – – my idea of what a real animal should be	+.88	.001
Not an animal at all – – (it's a fish) and not an animal	−.64	.001
Relation of typicality to evaluation		
Correlation between typicality and liking (both from this study)	+.71	.001
Correlation between typicality (this study) and evaluation (previous study)	+.69	.001
Correlation between liking (this study) and evaluation (previous study)	+.95	.001

* Interjudge agreement, taking categories as subjects, Spearman's r_s = .79.
† Analyses use animals as subjects, N = 24.
‡ Absence of an r_s value indicates too little data.
§ What counted as appropriate sometimes depended on the person – in particular, some thought animals should be cunning, others that they should not be.

VALUES IN INNER SPEECH

existence of subordinate categories of animals: which is to say that the organization of the animal kingdom is represented by a taxonomy and not by a list.

The folk taxonomy

Figure 7.1 shows the taxonomy implicit in the typicality ratings. It shows that naïve
zoologists (many having done no nature study at school) make the same kinds
of distinctions as sophisticated ones, though in different terms. It may take a
specialist to recognize an *exoskeleton*, but anyone can manage *crunchy, hard*, and *it's
got a shell* (for crab).[2]

Even where people expressed zoologically aberrant beliefs, they made intelligent errors, and generally confused phylogenetic neighbours; for example,
believing that crabs are insects; less surprisingly, that spiders are; that spiders can
fly; that lizards have six legs rather than four; that snakes really do have legs and are
only hiding them.

The folk taxonomy, like the zoological one, descends from the prototypical
mammals, through birds (warm-blooded but non-mammals), reptiles (verte-
brates but cold-blooded), with various arthropods (with exoskeletons) at the
bottom. At the top are:

stallion +3 Stronger and more able than man. Four legs, hairy body, tail,
friendly nature, yet not cowardly or weak.

stray dog +3 Because standard animal for me = four-legged – reasonable size.
Stray dog – four legs – reasonable height, would be visible – noticeable.

tiger +3 Big + wild, four legs, strong, etc.

donkey +3 Bigger and stronger than man, ears, hairy body, four legs, tail.

Criteria for prototypicality include appropriate appearance, character,[3] behaviour and environment, all of which a zoologist would understand; also
familiarity, comprehensibility, utility and the zoologically dubious whether-the-
person-liked-them. Animals at the bottom of the taxonomy fail on many of these
criteria:

fly −2 Too insignificant when placed in comparison to man. Only weak little
legs. No tail.

spider −3 Too small. Not lovable.

goldfish −3 Fish aren't like animals. Cold, scaly, cruel eyes.

crab −2 Marine animal. . . . Shell instead of hair. . . . Too many arms and legs!

Often sets of atypical characteristics are encapsulated by reference to a relevant
superordinate category such as *bird*, *reptile*, or *insect*. These categories stand in a
somewhat ambiguous relationship to *animal*, which sometimes includes them

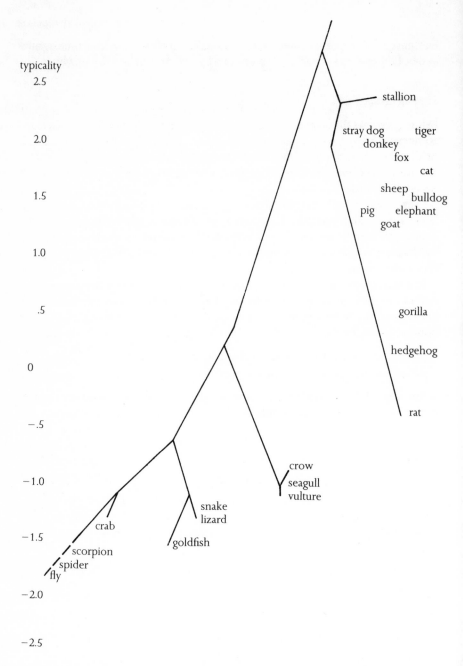

Figure 7.1   The folk taxonomy

and sometimes serves as a contrast set at the same level of categorization. For example:

vulture −3 A vulture is an ornithological specimen.

seagull −2 Even though a bird is an animal, in my subconscious I'm always sure to differentiate between bird and animal.

lizard −2 Consider it a 'reptile'.

spider −2 Insect class.

The evaluative taxonomy

If we combine the results of the two studies, and superimpose the evaluations from table 7.2 on the folk taxonomy, we get the evaluative taxonomy shown in figure 7.2.

This shows that the evaluations within each taxonomic category have overlapping ranges. In general, mammals are favoured, but the least favourite animal, rat, is also a mammal. The most liked bird, seagull, is nicer than fox and much nicer than gorilla, which are both mammals; and even creepy things like spiders are better than vulture, which is the worst bird. This suggests that something of low value as an animal may be of high value within its own category.[4]

Conversely, animals can be of low value within their own category; and to be a bad exemplar of a good category is to be very nasty indeed. This is not confined to animal categories. Higgins and Rholes (1976) also found that extreme negative evaluations accrue to atypical instances of positively valued categories. *Casual surgeons* and *immoral priests* are true rotters. Storms (1979) reports similar evidence on sexual stereotypes. In the current data rats suffer from being bad (atypical) exemplars of the good (and typical) mammals. This produced quite a conflict for some people:

rat −2 Being an animal lover, I like to consider all standard animals as being pleasant. Thus I'm very reluctant to admit the rat as a member of the animal kingdom at all.

rat −2 Horrible, dirty, more like a reptile.

rat −3 I have an intense hatred of these creatures who don't deserve to be called animals.

rat −2 Don't think of it as an animal, just with abhorrence.

Small-animal phobias

It may be possible to discuss *some* small-animal phobias in categorical terms: spiders, followed by lizards, snakes, rats and cats evoke phobic comments in the

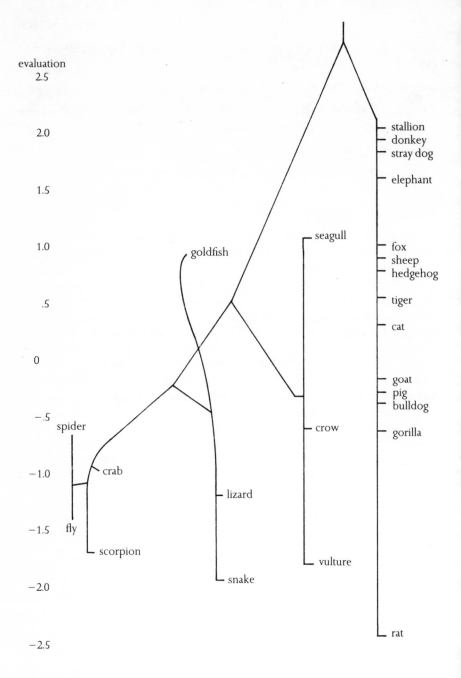

Figure 7.2 The evaluative taxonomy

first study, and most of them appear in some form in standard lists of phobias (Geer, 1965; Wolpe and Lang, 1964). All these are atypical either within the general category of animals, or within a more specific sub-category. Cats have fur (rather than hair), funny eyes, and 'seem to have no backbone'. Rats are too small, have naked tails, and crawl along the ground. Both are thus atypical mammals. Lizards and snakes have suspect ways of moving about, snakes have no legs, and both are dry skinned but remind people of water, which makes them atypical land animals. Spiders are classified by most people as insects, though strictly they are arachnids, with eight legs and no wings. It is possible that they would be less creepy – literally – if they had wings and were even typical insects, which they are not. They also touch people without asking permission, which seems to violate a fundamental propriety.

One consequence of being a very nasty thing is that people will avoid it altogether if they possibly can. This leads to a vicious circle in which people avoid even thinking about the misfits which threaten the conceptual system; and this avoidance ensures that the conceptual system remains too impoverished to accommodate them; which ensures that they will continue to be misfits. Landau's (1980) work on animal phobias shows that people do indeed avoid the very knowledge about the phobic animal that might reduce their fear. Wolpe (1978a) claims that phobias are not mediated by cognition. Perhaps in some cases they are mediated by lack of cognition.[5]

Superordinacy and evaluation

In summary, the two studies together support the view that the semantic relationship of category membership defines a perspective of preferences within the region structured by the category. Within the general category of animals, typical members are preferred to atypical ones: thus tigers are preferred to crows. Furthermore, more typical subgroups of animals are preferred to less typical subgroups: thus mammals are preferred to birds and birds are preferred to arthropods. This relates to the fact that the properties attributed to the super-ordinate category of animals-in-general are those of its more prototypical and preferred subgroup: we tend to assume that in general animals should have mammal properties rather than reptile or arthropod properties.[6] However, some complications arise when considering entities which are bad members of good subgroups, such as the hated rat which belongs to the generally favoured mammal group.

In other words: in general we favour typical members of categories, but in detail complications arise because categories contain sub-categories which may have different prototypicality and evaluative profiles. When we rate a seagull a poor animal but a good bird we are legitimately shifting both conceptual and evaluative frameworks. And the conceptual system is organized in such a way that it is easy to do this. In order to see how this may be, it is necessary to look at the second kind of cognitive structure which is important in the organization of conceptual hierarchies: the relation of opposition.

Opposition and stereotypy

Identity, within the categorical system, is defined by who one is against as well as who one is with. In Rosch's terms, prototypes maximize the differences between categories as well as the similarities within them.

Oppositions become particularly important in the case of categories which occur in natural pairs, and where the two poles are defined in opposition to one another: nature and nurture, arts and sciences, men and women, them and us. Here differences are exaggerated, even to the extent of mud slinging between adherents of the poles, and the dichotomous judgments which Hayakawa (1965) and Frenkel-Brunswik (1948, 1949) identify with authoritarian thinking. The exaggeration of differences is part of a normal cognitive process, apparent even in dealing with emotionally neutral stimuli. Tajfel and Wilkes (1963) had people making judgments about lengths of lines. As soon as the longer lines were given one category label and the shorter lines another, people's judgments showed an accentuation of differences between the two groups. Only somewhat later did they also show an accentuation of similarities within groups. A similar accentuation of differences occurs in social group situations on minimal pretexts (e.g. Tajfel and Billig, 1974). Members will even sacrifice their own profit in order to preserve intergroup discrimination, and will be particularly zealous where the distinctions are salient to the definition of group identity (Turner, Brown and Tajfel, 1979).

This evidence suggests that the tendency to exaggerate differences will push the prototypes of opposed categories away from their category centres. Instead of prototypes which represent the typical, we get caricatures or stereotypes which represent the most extreme.[7] Within this system, preferences should attach less to the typical than to the stereotypical, to those things which maximize differences.

One way of exploring this hypothesis is through the medium of popular fiction. Pulp fiction is a wonderful repository of stereotypes, and deserves psychological attention, even if only on the grounds of its immense popularity. Cawelti (1976) classifies 'formula stories' into a small number of distinct types: Adventure, Mystery, Melodrama, Alien Beings and, the particular focus here, Romance. Like mythologies and folk-tales of other eras this literature is familiar and comforting. It projects a vision of order which has little regard for the troublesome complexities of the actual, and which tells us a good deal about what a mind would get up to if it didn't have a world to tame it. Or, more alarming, if it were inattentive to that world.

Stereotypes in romantic fiction

The following discussion is based on a sample of thirty romantic novels of the kind marketed through newsagents, supermarkets and corner shops in the summers of 1979 and 1980.

Two characters are essential to the romantic plot: heroine and hero. Two others are frequent but optional extras: the other woman and the other man. The most important relationship within this quartet is of course between heroine and hero, and is one of opposition. This opposition covers appearance, kinship ties, personality, hair colour and eye colour. Some of the more quantifiable attributes are shown in table 7.3.

The typical hero has dark or black hair and either grey eyes with metallic modifiers (iron, steel, silvery, crystal, gunmetal) or blue eyes with cold ones (cool, cold, icy). He is about 34 years old, scion of a dynasty, either aristocratic or commercial, and has a Rolls or Mercedes to prove it. He is arrogant, incisive, ruthless, and, of course, uncompromisingly masculine.

The typical heroine has blonde hair and green eyes. She is about 23 years old, and an orphan, who at best drives a Mini. She is fine boned and delicately moulded, kindhearted, and fragile at the ankles if not elsewhere.

The exaggeration of differences here is sufficient to override social normality entirely, and even to disregard a number of well-known genetic principles

Table 7.3   Characters in romantic fiction
(Figures are percentages of novels containing characters with the attributes specified. No. of novels = 30)

Characteristic	Girl	Man	Other woman	Other man
Hair colour				
dark/black	10	51	30	11
brown	17	17	0	15
blond/e	37	14	44	22
red	20	0	4	0
Eye colour				
grey	10	34	0	0
blue	13	29	33	19
black/dark	0	7	11	8
yellow/ish	3	7	0	0
green/hazel	23	4	0	8
brown	20	0	7	8
violet	7	0	7	0
Heir/ess	3	60	19	15
Orphan	43	3	0	0
Average age	23 yrs	34 yrs	27 yrs	28 yrs
Transport	public or Mini	Mercedes or Rolls	?	Cortina or Chev.
General	fine boned, delicately moulded, kindhearted.	arrogant, incisive, ruthless, uncompromisingly masculine.	beautiful, sophisticated, calculating, possessive.	undemanding, immature, lacking air of mastery.

relating hair and eye colour. The definition of male and female in opposition to one another requires that they have as little as possible in common. In none of the thirty novels did man and girl have either the same hair colour or the same eye colour. Borgida, Locksley and Brekke's (1981) assumption that stereotypes reflect popular beliefs about base-rate distributions of characteristics within social groups is clearly not upheld here. Man and girl are certainly stereotypes, but neither, thank goodness, represents a norm, or even popular beliefs about norms.

Subsidiary characters lack the conceptual purity of man and girl, and are both contaminated with the traits of the other sex. The other woman is strikingly female in physique, and she is often blonde. The discerning heroine, however, is swift to note that the blondness may be artificial, and mask a masculine darkness that is her true colour. Moreover, like the man, the other woman is older than the heroine, her eyes are a ruthless blue, and she is arrogant, calculating, and may suffer from riches.

The other man makes fewer appearances, but when he does he is revealed as prone to the feminine traits of youth and blondness, and lacking in the air of mastery which marks true males.

Defining main characters through opposition to one another has important consequences for the plot. The heroine may be friendly with the other man, on the basis of the fact that they have something in common. Between heroine and hero there is nothing in common. Denied the more usual commerce of interest and affection, they must relate magically, through the sexual magnetism that has her quivering at his touch, or, for particularly potent males, at his glance.[8] The magic is countered by misunderstanding until the final denouement. Then opposites coalesce, a variety of celestial events occur, and the heroine is absorbed into the dynasty.

Characterization and plot together clearly indicate that conceptual opposition is A Good Thing. To man and girl, as different as human beings can be, is given the reward of transcendental bliss and happiness ever after. Sexually blurred others are rewarded at best with mere friendship, and at worst by being abandoned on the wedding morning.[9]

Opposition, like superordinacy, defines a dimension of evaluation. In this case preference goes to what is most opposite, as shown both by the rewards allocated within the fiction, and by the popularity of the fiction itself.[10]

Value conflict in taxonomic systems

The evidence on prototypicality and opposition, taken together, shows that it is better to be a typical category instance than an atypical one; and that it is better to be more different from contrast categories than to be less different.

The two kinds of values can sometimes be in conflict, because within the taxonomic system, what are opposed categories at one level belong to the same category at a superordinate level.

In the gender system for example, different criteria are used for evaluating men and women. Men should be strong and assertive and women soft and nurturing. Both happen to be human beings, and one set of values therefore has to give way in the superordinate category. The work of Broverman and her colleagues (Broverman, Broverman, Clarkson, Rosencrantz and Vogel, 1970) on criteria for mental health in men, women, and human beings, shows that criteria for healthy human beings are overwhelmingly male. To be a healthy man is to be a healthy human being. To be a healthy woman is to be an unhealthy human being.

Doise (1978) has shown that social-class membership can give rise to a similar conflict in the working class. Apprentices are torn between the working-class values of their own group and the middle-class values of society at large.

These conflicts arise because what is variety at one level of categorization must become unity at the more superordinate level. The conceptual structure simply suppresses one pole of a dichotomy and uses the other to stand for both; as *man* stands for people of both sexes, and, apparently, as *mammal* stands for animals of all types.

This suppression is possible because opposites are never in fact equal. The asymmetry is clearly seen in linguistics, where, for each pair of polar opposites, one is cognitively simpler and more highly valued, and the other is defined relative to it (Deese, 1973). *Good* is cognitively simple and highly valued; *bad* is defined relatively, as *opposite-of-good*. *Tall* is better and simpler than *short*, which is *opposite-of-tall*. *Male* is better and simpler than *female*, which is *opposite-of-male*.

The requirements of compressing subordinate variety into superordinate unity leads to a suppression of those lower-level categories whose identities are defined relatively. This results in a conflict of values for members of the suppressed categories, who become atypical at the superordinate level. It must be said that this conceptual resolution is extremely neat. It becomes a source of anguish, however, for the human beings who belong to the suppressed categories.

Individual differences in preference for the typical

We must in general prefer meaning to chaos. Within the taxonomic domain this involves preference for that which maximizes within-group similarities and between-group differences. Though stereotyping distorts the pattern for polarized categories, it is generally the lot of the prototype to fulfil both these requirements. It follows that people who rely on taxonomic structures (superordinacy and opposition) to make sense of their cognitive world, should also rely on them in their evaluations, and should thus show a stronger predilection for the typical than other people do. This hypothesis was confirmed in a small-scale study using the MOTQ, in which people were simply asked to write down their two favourite animals. All the animals mentioned were then given to a panel of fifteen judges who rated each for its prototypicality, using a seven-point scale. Mean ratings for each animal were used to calculate a preference for typicality score (summed over the two favourite animals) for each person in the study. Preference for the typical correlated significantly with only two of the MOTQ subscales: opposites and superordinates (controlling for cross-modal scores, $r = +.27$ and $r = +.30$ respectively, $df = 60$, $p < .05$). These are precisely the scales which tap the two dimensions of taxonomic structuring. The people who like to categorize, to put things in pigeon-holes, are the people who prefer the typical.[11]

Summary

This chapter has looked at the values afforded by the characteristically verbal relationships of superordinacy and opposition. Within the dimension of superordinacy, preference goes to that which maximizes within-group similarities. Along the dimension marked by opposition, preference goes to that which maximizes between-group differences.

Generally, prototypical members of categories are those which maximize both similarities within groups and differences between groups, and they thus benefit from both kinds of evaluation: for example, the prototypical stallion sums up both what most mammals have in common, and also how mammals differ from other kinds of creatures, such as birds or reptiles.

However, sometimes an emphasis on opposition may lead to the most favoured category members being more extremely polarized than the prototype: as for example in romantic fiction, where the highly favoured hero and heroine are maximally different from one another, and do not at all represent the typical in terms of actual men and women.

Where two categories are opposed, one is typically defined relative to the other: fe-male is opposite of male; non-mammal is opposite of mammal. This allows the relatively defined category, fe-male, or non-mammal, to be suppressed at the superordinate level; while the other, male, or mammal, moves forward and is used to stand for both. The members of the relatively defined category become atypical and of lower value at this superordinate level.

8

Visualizing, the environment and the sentiments of self

One of the most important semantic structures in visual imagery is the relationship between object and environment. This takes the form of a relationship between the *self* and the environment in the visual personality portrait of chapter 6. The relationship to the environment may take various forms, and each has implications for personality and affective life. For example, the apprehension of the natural beauty of the environment is an aspect of the artistic sensitivity and sense of wonder which emerged in the visualizer portrait. This sensitivity is extended also to the social environment, where visualizers show understanding and sympathy for other people. Here new options arise, and sensitivity to other people has as a corollary the possibility that they may serve as mirrors in which one sees oneself reflected. When visualizers, in the portraits study, claimed to be *self-aware*, it appeared to be this reflected or externalized kind of self-awareness that was at issue – the ability to see the self from outside, as others do.

This externalized awareness confronts the person with their persona, the appearance by which they are known to others, and which acts as the emissary of their inner self in encounters in the social world. The externalized perspective on the self allows the person to modify the behaviour of this emissary and to direct it into socially desirable channels. The visual day-dreams indicate that these socially desirable channels include being beautiful, friendly, famous, very good at something, or much admired by others.

The drawback of the externalized perspective is that from it one sees only an appearance, with the inner self seeming impoverished, hollow and empty. In being sensitive to others and to the world, one becomes dependent on those others and that world, a dependency which may sometimes be irksome, especially for men.

This chapter looks in more detail at the affective importance of some of the relationships a person may have with the environment. The empirical work focuses on two kinds of experiences which appear to mark important poles in the visualizer's affective life: firstly, experiences of seeing the self from outside, where people seem to be using the environment as a mirror in which they see their social reflection; secondly, experiences of being at one with the environment and especially with nature, which appear to be part of the Romanticism and sense of wonder of the visualizer portrait.

Objective self-awareness

We are both individuals and social beings, both an I who initiates actions and a me who is the recipient of the actions of others. Much of the theorizing about the me has come from sociology. This is because the ability to apprehend ourselves from the outside, as the me that others encounter, is fundamental to our sociability.

Mead (1934) uses the example of a small boy reaching for the biscuit tin, who treats himself as his parents would, and slaps his own hand. In playing the role of the parent, he is seeing himself from their viewpoint, as an object, a me who can be the target of actions by other people. This aspect of the self is publicly constituted – in this case as naughty boy – and liable to public reprimand. At its most rigid this publicly constituted self is the face or public appearance that must be worked on, kept up, and not lost (Goffman, 1955, 1956). The importance of appearance in this public self is stressed in Cooley's (1902) reference to the 'looking glass self', and in Lacan's (1977) reference to the origin of this self as being in the 'mirror stage'.

The existence of two more or less distinct aspects of the self is not easy to deal with, either practically (as in adolescence) or theoretically. Sociology has tended to concentrate on the public self, and on the socially constructed reality in which it is a participant. Existential philosophy and psychiatry treat the distinction as a moral and indeed pathogenic one. Bad faith (Sartre, 1957) or schizophrenia (Laing, 1959) are seen as resulting from collusion with the views of others about who one is, and thus living as a me that has lost touch with and suppressed its I.

Within mainstream social psychology, the existence of a public aspect of the self is tacit in such notions as social desirability, conformity, or peer-group pressure, all of which presuppose at least a zone of selfhood which is socially malleable; but it took some cross-fertilization from sociology before psychologists looked explicitly at this public aspect of the self.

Stimulated by G. H. Mead's ideas, Duval and Wicklund (1972; Wicklund, 1975, 1978, 1979) found that people could be made acutely sensitive to their public self by being subjected to states of 'objective self-awareness'. Such states can be produced in a number of ways: by the presence of an audience or a television camera, by the use of a tape recording of the person's voice, and most powerfully by the use of a mirror.[1] In objective self-awareness, people become concerned about being evaluated, and tend to show an increased conformity to the social norms or standards governing the situation.

Experiences of seeing the self from outside

Much of the psychological work has concentrated either on experimental manipulations of self-awareness, or on the measurement of self-awareness as a personality trait. The following study looks at the experiential aspects of naturally occurring episodes of objective self-awareness.

The study involved the following instructions:

> Most of the time we are implicitly aware of ourselves from 'the inside'. However, there are moments when we suddenly seem to become aware of ourselves as it were 'from the outside'. These moments are important for an understanding of the self and of self-awareness, but at the moment we know rather little about them, beyond the fact that they seem to show great variety, being sometimes pleasant and sometimes not, sometimes significant and sometimes trivial.

> Choose an episode from your own experience where you were aware of yourself 'from the outside' and describe in as much detail as you can what happened, both in terms of what was going on objectively, and in terms of how you experienced it and felt about it.

Eighty people (fifty-eight women and twenty-two men, all psychology students) wrote descriptions of their experiences. The major themes of the descriptions are shown in table 8.1.

The typical experience of seeing the self from outside takes place in a group of people, either friends or strangers, and in a social setting (pubs and discos rather than mountain tops). It involves what is often a sudden switch of attention in which the person becomes aware of a split between two aspects of the self. The experience is often unpleasant, involving embarrassment and a sense of rejection. Sometimes the experience is less traumatic, with people using objective self-awareness as a way of monitoring their own performance when they are uncertain about how to behave. Sometimes the experience is pleasant, with people feeling considerable satisfaction at a newly constituted social self. A final, small group involves the avoidance of physical or mental pain, and these perhaps come closest to being genuine out-of-body experiences.

With the exception of this final group, all the experiences involve other people, and vary depending on how well one knows these others. At their least known, the others are strangers. At their best, friends and relatives.

Being noticed, the body and embarrassment

William James (1892) commented that no more fiendish punishment could be devised than that of being turned loose in a society in which we remained absolutely unnoticed. First days at university probably come as close to the fiendish as is possible:

> I sat for a moment and gazed intently at the faces – so many people I do not know. My look came full circle around the lecture hall and finally I was face to face with my best friend – myself. Suddenly I became aware of an intense fear

Table 8.1 Experiences of seeing the self from outside

Constituent of the experience*	% of people mentioning
Context	
with a group of people	42.5
people involved were friends or relatives	32.5
built environment, e.g. pub, disco, school	30.0
people involved were strangers	23.8
sudden† – – experience involved a sudden switch of awareness	20.0
with one other person	17.5
alone – – person was alone when the experience occurred	12.5
natural environment – – outside, natural setting	5.0
Varieties of outsideness	
seeing self from outside, non-literally	30.0
taking viewpoint of particular other(s)	22.5
true out of body experience, literally seeing the self from outside	12.5
seeing the self from the viewpoint of generalized other	12.5
view mediated, e.g. by a mirror, or writing	12.5
result of introjection of another's comments	8.8
Social aspects	
conformity to other's view of self	23.8
refusal to conform	6.3
Personal complements	
bad feelings – – embarrassment, fear, loneliness, guilt	40.0
aware of split between inner and outer selves	38.8
self-knowledge† – – learning something about oneself	37.5
good feelings – – pleasure and joy	22.5
self-critical about the self one sees	21.3
uninvolved – – feeling calm and detached from the situation	18.8
'not me' – – feeling that the seen self is not really me	13.8
being objective about oneself	11.3
pain avoidance – – avoiding physical or mental pain	10.0
surprise at the experience or at what one sees	7.5

* Interjudge reliability assessed using Spearman's rho with categories as subjects, $r_s = .86$. Average agreement per category 96.0%, the lowest, 90.0%.
† Mentioned in the introductory instructions.

within me – such a strong feeling of insignificance – I have nothing to show that I am an individual any more – the lecturer looks on me as 'one more' – I am nobody here.

Without the attention of others we are nobody and nothing. We have no social self. To be noticed is a minimal requirement for constituting a social self. The first steps in the construction process are those which may be done by strangers: we acquire the body by which we are known to others, and the rudiments of an appearance upon which all else will be hung. An important part of this early stage is being seen as a body of a particular sex. This is probably so familiar that we notice it only when something novel happens:

> We got out to a gay club which was a very select gay club. I for the first time realized how a female felt to be 'sized' up with interest.
> The club was almost all male with old men and young alike. They were all in little clusters and we walked in. Suddenly I felt like stepping back in fear and horror. All eyes turned on me. Suddenly I began to realize they were all looking at me with interest. Whilst there I became aware of my self as a point of interest and tried to avoid all eye contact with the people there. I felt myself become defensive and shy whilst at the same time somewhere I thought how flattering all these people flocking round to try and talk to me. . . . The experience had a very crowding and smothering effect as I was the only straight person there and seen as a challenge by these people. I cut the night short by refusing invitations to four parties.

To be noticed is a minimal requirement for constituting a social self. It gives one a body, a basic appearance, and one can then begin to worry about the details. Sometimes people use objective states of awareness as a way of monitoring their appearance and allaying social anxiety. People watch how others are behaving, and from the same perspective they watch themselves and then try to fit in, behave correctly, use the right knife and fork. Here objective self-awareness serves a regulative function. It is a way of blending in and identifying as a member of the group, albeit a new one:

> It was important for me to establish a good relationship with the Staff and especially the boys. As I was from Belfast and almost everyone else was from the south I found it very hard to settle in and be 'myself'. I kept observing other people and how they coped with situations, and then noticed that I became an observer of myself! . . . I tried to observe myself without consciously altering my actions – this I could do for a while but once I really became aware of myself I sometimes altered my course.

Once a persona has a little belonging and a little self-esteem under its belt, it becomes liable to new hazards, notably embarrassment. There is no better route to embarrassment than making a fool of yourself in front of someone whose esteem you seek:

> In the company of three friends and one new acquaintance I related a piece of graffiti I'd seen. . . .
>
> The newcomer, whom I'd been unconsciously trying to impress, burst out laughing and the others laughed also. Between laughs he choked out that he didn't 'get it', and then asked: 'Do you get it?'
>
> I stopped laughing and experienced the 'outside', detached view of myself blushing and feeling generally uncomfortable at having been caught out as a pseudo intellectual and thought 'How can I save face?'
>
> The conversation continued along other lines but for a while I was aware of myself being subdued and feeling self-conscious. I had to shake myself out of it by consciously applying myself to the conversation and interjecting what felt like trivial little comments.

It is only the self-confident who manage to continue making even trivial contributions to the conversation under such circumstances. Others shut up, get out, or find an excuse to go to the loo. The painful thing in these situations is a disgraceful disloyalty. People become somehow detached from their self, and side self-critically with a generalized or specific other against it:

> It was at that moment I came to realize myself from the 'outside'. I listened to myself talk and I felt I was a really thick person, clumsy and awkward. Before I was never like this, and with most people I am not, but it happened. I left him after a while and I sat in the toilet for the rest of the night!

Sociological analyses of embarrassment (e.g.: Sattler, 1965; Gross and Stone, 1964; Weinberg, 1968; Modigliani, 1968, 1971) show that it arises when a person is caught between two incompatible roles, or, more in line with the current data, when a projected self-image is suddenly rent and a very different person revealed through the gaps.

Psychological theorists, while differing in detailed interpretation (Duval and Wicklund, 1972; Carver and Scheier, 1981), assume that once objective self-awareness has revealed such a discrepancy of selves, the person will normally try to reduce it. There is, however, a sense in which such efforts are too late. One has already slipped on the banana skin or zipped the table-cloth into one's trousers, and absolutely nothing can be done about that. Mechanisms of discrepancy reduction are designed to avoid embarrassment, not to cope with it when it happens. What one needs then is not discrepancy reduction but panache or divine intervention. Or failing either of those, one can magically hide by avoiding eye contact, feeling very small, and wishing that the very earth would open up and annihilate the self along with its horrid predicament. Sociologists (Goffman, 1956; Garfinkel, 1955–6) see these pieces of magical thinking as self-protective, head-in-the-sand techniques, which, in avoiding the eyes of the audience attempt to pretend away the existence of the *me* that caused all the problems in the first place. They are tactics designed to declare the situation 'unreal'. The more polite class of audience may decently collude, showing what Goffman terms 'civil inattention'.

Shame and embarrassment have long been seen as socializing agents (e.g.: Tomkins, 1963; Lewis, 1979), and Wicklund (1982) claims that objective self-awareness is as well. He points out that it may backfire, producing very nice and polite but uninventive beings in a culture that needs a bit of idiosyncrasy. Pilkonis and Zimbardo (1979) take this concern further. Extrapolating from their work on shyness, they suggest that those who are excessively vulnerable to what others think of them may constitute the silent majority liable to be trampled over by oppressive political regimes.

Acquiring social membership

Not all objective self-awareness is awful. After a bit of practice at running a persona, there are rewards to be had:

> I had to give a dinner party for about twelve people. I was quite nervous about it. However much to my own surprise I was doing it and very confidently at that. To the guests I was the efficient hostess. I saw myself capable and confident – a self I was not aware of. I had to laugh at myself at this, as it were fake image.
> 'If they only knew what I was really like.'
> So I realized that I was a little more confident than I normally gave myself credit for.

These experiences of being seen in some valued social role are often joyful, particularly if the new role involves ritually marked status passage:

> I have just had a baby girl recently. This is our first child and obviously I had expected that there would have to be changes not only in our daily lives . . . but also in my own personal feelings about myself as I now had another dimension to my make-up – I was now a mother.
> However, this realization did not occur to me until quite a few weeks after her birth – at the baptism ceremony.
> The text of the ceremony was quite beautiful – it said that I had brought a child into the world, that she would be dependent on me initially for all her needs, that I would be her first educator. As I listened and participated for about 20 mins, I was indeed very much overwhelmed by what I had done, that I was now to be something or somebody other than I had been all my life until now. It was a very frightening thought that I was now a mother and would be for the rest of my life. It was also a joyous feeling.

'Being an efficient hostess' is not quite the same thing as being an efficient hostess; and becoming a 'mother' is not quite the same thing as becoming a mother. One of the features of these realized social identities is that they confer a new set of expectations, both for the person herself and for others. People use this aspect of social identity to license new behaviour for themselves. For example, the fledgeling schoolteacher can now give orders to schoolchildren, whereas before she or he wouldn't have been 'allowed' to. New social identities thus allow and promote new kinds of relationships with the social world, and afford new opportunities for self esteem.

Abdicating the self to avoid pain

The kinds of externalized self-awareness considered so far are all fundamentally social in character. The final type is not obviously so. In this relatively small group of experiences, when something truly horrible is about to happen, or is happening, people psychically flee from their body and observe it detachedly from outside. This sometimes occurs in situations of intolerable mental distress which, if felt, would swamp any ability to cope with the situation; and it sometimes occurs when life is physically under threat:

> I was behind the wheel of the car, when a dog ran out, and there would have been no possibility of avoiding him except to swerve, which I did, sharply. I suddenly seemed to be travelling in the direction of someone's 'residential' brick wall, and thought a bit clinically that I was sitting in a car completely out of control, and time seemed to reverse itself, then go full forward again the way reels of film can be speeded up, but movements are slow.
>
> Before the impact everything (sense impressions) slowed down and I had a detached uncomfortable feeling as of an observer of the incident.
>
> My only feelings now of it, are that I became aware of a body (mine) in danger, and mentally objectified myself, analogous to rolling up in a ball, to protect myself from pain.

Though these experiences are not obviously social, they may depend upon prior social experience. The body that the ejected consciousness sees is the body that others see, and is presumably constituted originally as a social entity. Many of the socially provoked experiences of objective self-awareness involve some sense of detachment from the self (simultaneously with an awareness that it – rather than I – is feeling acute embarrassment), and the instances of pain avoidance appear to be an extreme form of the same phenomenon. They also represent an extreme form of the sense of emptiness mentioned as a hazard for visualizers in the portraits study. These episodes of ejecting consciousness from the body may also be seen as similar in some ways to the near-death experiences described by Raymond Moody (1976), where one commonly reported early phase consists of just such an externalized view of the self.

Constituting a persona

The data from the study as a whole shows that most of the experiences of objective self-awareness are generally concerned with how we are constituted in the eyes of others, as the social entities that are part of a public and intersubjective domain. Precisely how we see our self through the eyes of others, and how we feel about that self, depend on the others. Strangers are understood as construing only the basics: noticeability or insignificance, sex, and probably other features of physical appearance. With people a little closer, and whom we want to like us, the construals go a little deeper, to include our being seen as clumsy or as a pseudo intellectual. Embarrassment becomes a possibility here. With those even closer, the physical evidence becomes less important and the social meaning of that evidence more important. Motherhood does require the physical evidence of a baby, but its meaning far transcends the existence of that evidence. Here the social group may support the sense of enhanced self-esteem derived from being seen to have a new social role.

Even the experiences of objective self-awareness which are motivated by the avoidance of pain may be grounded in social experience, as the body we see here is the body that others see.

All these experiences usually involve attention first to the environment, and particularly to one or more of a group of people, and then the reflection of that attention back on the self. Experiences of objective self-awareness may be grounded in the phenomenon of joint attention, which is important from earliest infancy in the social constitution of reality (Bruner, 1975, 1981). Even young infants are very good at following the line of regard of their minders, and mothers will use a number of strategies to encourage the child to follow her glance and pay attention to what she is looking at. Only when such joint attention is achieved can the child begin to learn about the intersubjective world, including learning about the meanings of words.

With a long training in following the line of regard of others it may become natural to continue doing so when we ourselves are the object of regard. When others look at us we see not them but ourselves through their eyes; and this constitutes us as social objects, as beings with a social appearance, a social persona.

The metaphors *seeing through the eyes of the other*, and *reflected in the eyes of the other*, are presumably based on the fact that the eye of the other may *optically* reflect the world or even ourselves. In use, however, such expressions have more than just this optical reference.

One interpretation of what more is referred to is to say that the other serves as an instrument through whom we know the intersubjective social world, just as physical instruments, such as telescopes and spirit levels, are the instruments through which we know the physical world.

An instrument is both an object in its own right, and a 'medium' transparent to a reality of a different order. Michael Polanyi (1958), one of the few philosophers of science who talks about the importance of instruments, uses the example of the stick used by a blind man. The stick is an object in its own right, but through its tapping the blind man comes to know the world. The unskilled user of an instrument confronts it as an opaque object, and part of learning the skill of being a user is that the instrument becomes transparent, allowing access to the reality beyond itself, and which it merely transmits. Unskilled users of sticks are aware of the stick in the hand and of its tapping; skilled users apprehend a world through the stick.

The primary 'instruments' through which we know the social world are those who cohabit that world with us. At one level they are physical objects – bodies – objects in their own right, but they also show us how the world is, by showing us how they attend to it and behave in it. The behaviour of their physical person is transparent in showing us what the important cues are in this intersubjective world, and how we should respond to them.

In the exercises of joint attention at our mother's knee, we were seeing the intersubjective world through her. In responding to it as she did, initially perhaps simply by imitating her, we were coming to inhabit her world. She was the first instrument through whom we apprehended the social world, and in whose eyes we saw the world reflected.

As adults too we engage in joint attention with those we are close to, seeing the world as they see it, responding to the same cues in the same ways, and expressing appreciation for the same things. People negotiate the definition of their social world by watching one another's behaviour, and 'reading' it for its social meaning.

In experiences of external self-awareness people can also read their own behaviour for its social meaning. The experiences can be considered as aligned along a continuum of what might be called social transparency. At one end the experience presents the person as opaque, as an object, a body, and as socially insignificant. The first indications of transparency are heavily dependent on the body; as when the recognition of sexual identity opens a window on a world of possible social interactions coloured by that identity. To those who know us well, our behaviour is transparent to a wider range of social meanings, and friends may read many aspects of the nature of the social world through one another's behaviour. When things go wrong, this semiological character of behaviour collapses, and it ceases to signify a shared social world. Our actions become opaque, and their social intention vanishes; and there we are as a body, making meaningless gestures, embarrassing because they suddenly fail to open the door to anything beyond themselves. When someone refuses to laugh at our jokes, our definition of a joint reality deflates and we feel rejected. When we lose our way in a speech, we cease to be the vehicle of the message which flows through us, and become a mere blushing, ridiculous body.

These experiences of seeing the self from outside shed some light on the nature of what has until now been a problematic construct in the description of the visualizer's world: the notion of the 'social environment', and how it can apparently be coextensive with the physical one. What makes a physical environment a social environment is the presence of someone else – real or imaginary – in it, through whom we may apprehend it. The social environment is an environment of values and strategies for interaction, overlaid on a physical environment of bruter objects. It is the behaviour of others that informs us about these values and these strategies. We see the environment through them.

The visualizers' need to belong, or need for affiliation, apparent in the portraits study, and their need to appear socially desirable, apparent in the psychometric study, are rooted in this way of reading the environment through others, and the corresponding desire to have others see the world through them. People not only treat others semiologically, as signs of the world they inhabit, but also wish to be used themselves in the same way. To be socially desirable is to provide a clear vision for others of how things are. This is why social desirability, in terms of idle thoughts, is not a simple matter of conformity or collusion; it is singing the beautiful song that speaks for everyone, or becoming the TV personality whose definition of social events is widely accepted by others, or, on a smaller scale, becoming the schoolteacher whose definition of the world is adopted by the children in her class.

On holiday from the persona

The social environment is not the only environment that we inhabit, though it may be the most important one. We also have a relationship to the natural environment which is less fraught with complex social meanings. The business of tending to a persona and of keeping a watchful eye on how we are reflected in the eyes of others, may occasionally be gratifying, but it requires a good deal of effort. We are like classical Greek actors, one hand always occupied by clutching the mask. Sometimes it is good to put the thing down. Interestingly, situations in which people forget about their persona, like those in which they are aware of it, are experiences where the environment plays an important role. This time however the environment is typically natural rather than social, and affords experiences of being at one with nature. The importance of this kind of relationship with the environment emerged in a study on 'what people like'.

The study was simple, and involved asking a group of people (thirty-nine women and twenty-one men) first to write down ten things that they liked (with anything at all being permissible as 'a thing'); and then to pick one of them and describe it and why they liked it.[2] The results of the content analysis of the descriptions are shown in table 8.2.

The experiences fall into a major and a minor group. The majority concern being at one with nature. This includes a feeling of closeness to nature, an awareness of its visual beauty, a sense of peace, relaxation, freedom and timelessness. Physical activity may be involved, or the person might just sit, watch, day-dream, or find in nature symbols of his or her own life.

A smaller group of experiences are sociable, often involving eating and drinking with a group of friends. Some social experiences have a quality of

Table 8.2   Constituents of liking

Constituent*	% of people mentioning†
environment – – mention of	25.0
freedom, e.g. from restraint or coercion	23.3
sharing information or activity with another person	21.7
close to nature – – at one with the environment	21.7
sensual vision – – beauty; visual parts and attributes	21.7
peace and relaxation	20.0
physical exertion – – typically sports	18.3
symbolic of something else, as trees may symbolize life	15.0
enjoyment, pleasure	15.0
thinking to oneself – – allowing thoughts to wander, day-dreaming	13.3
being valued by others, having their attention or support	13.3
amusement and fun, being cheered up	13.3
social group – – being part of a group	11.7
eating and drinking	11.7
timelessness – – sense that this is going on or could go on for ever	10.0
change – – that things grow, develop	10.0
touch of wind, sun, other people	10.0

* Interjudge agreement assessed using categories as subjects, Spearman's r_s = .97. Mean agreement per category = 95%.
† Percentages are low because many people wrote only one or two sentences.

absorption in the social environment which parallels the experiences of being at one with nature. Here music, dancing and alcohol are usually involved.

Being at one with nature

In experiences of closeness to nature people link themselves to the cosmos in a number of ways. First and most importantly, they attend closely to the environment, which then reveals its manifold richness. It is possible to give one's attention unreservedly because nature, unlike human beings, does not ask for anything in return. Sometimes these experiences of being at one with nature are shared with others; indeed this may be part of their special delight, but the others are not looking at us and not making us aware of ourselves as complex social stimuli. The absence of being socially construed and socially constrained gives people a great sense of freedom:

Nature
Nature is like magic for me. I like it for many reasons. Nature is natural beauty and it only goes through its own life cycle. Peace, calmness, sincerity, beauty, joy are just some of the emotions I feel when surrounded by nature. . . . Nature

offers me freedom and I find it very relaxing. Nature gives me so much and asks for nothing in return so it is easy to like it.

One of the things that it may give is a sense of timelessness. Nature provides the metaphors which link human temporality to that of the natural world:

Sea-sides
On a sunny day you sit by the sea and watch the ebb and flow of the tide – it symbolizes time, life and eternity. Large stones becoming sand, one's life becoming meaningless.

People do not only sit in nature, looking at it and paying attention. They also run about in it, cycle through it, scuffle its leaves, and sail on it. These activities too are relaxing, and are probably an important aid to the sense of communion:

Sailing
I like sailing because when you're sailing you feel relaxed, and totally away from everyone. It's as if you're totally isolated, and you can feel a great sense of freedom, it also seems to blow all your troubles away. . . . It also enables me to get close with nature. I like it because when you're sailing you make full use of nature, i.e. water and wind.

What seems to be important about these relaxing activities is that they are essentially responsive, drawn out of us by the environment calling to us to respond to it. They typically involve intransitive actions, actions like running, sailing and cycling, which serve to relate person to environment in an experience of absorption.

Csikszentmihalyi (1975) would describe this absorption as an experience of flow. He was interested in why people should undertake such activities as climbing or rock (=disco) dancing. A sense of flowing with the experience seemed to describe what these activities, at their best, offered. According to Csikszentmihalyi's analysis, in the flow experience there is a merging of action and awareness so that the right action happens of itself, without need of prior and separate deliberation. There is a concomitant centring of attention and a living in the moment, without thought of the past or of any goals that the activity might, almost coincidentally, have; and there is a loss of ego and of self-consciousness, and a transcendence of individuality.

Some social experiences afford a similar sense of merging or flow, only this time it is an environment of music and movers:

Music and dancing
I love nice music (Neil Young) and I also love going out and dancing even though I am not a very good dancer but I love being among a number of 'movers'. There is a sense of belonging, enjoyment and acceptance and everybody throws away their inhibitions and 'freaks out'.

Diener (1977, 1979; Diener, Lusk, DeFour and Flax, 1980) discusses some similar social phenomena under the heading of 'deindividuation'. This is facilitated by being in a large group, preferably of similar people, and without the onlookers that would precipitate objective self-awareness. Early fears about the low morality of the mob mind have not been supported, and it seems that what the mob gets up to depends on whether pro-social or anti-social cues are provided (Johnson and Downing, 1979); in either case, however, there does tend to be a general uninhibitedness, lack of planning, and a lack of concern about what others think. The enjoyment of all this can be ruined by objective self-awareness. In the study on seeing the self from outside, one person described a festival atmosphere in which, drunk and dancing upon a table, she caught the eye of a sober acquaintance, and realized with horror that she was not behaving as her convent education had taught. She forced this objective view from her mind to prevent it spoiling the rest of the night. Very sensible.

There is a mental equivalent to physical and social flow, which one writer referred to as 'thinking to myself'. It involves aimless or day-dreamy drifting, as if thought too were on holiday:

Lying in the swimming pool
I become totally separated from everything else and even myself – I can feel myself but I'm not really in control (physically). Mentally I just drift from thought to thought like sand falling through a series of sifts gradually getting smaller.

Seeing and seers

Experiences of being at one with nature are magical, cleansing and relaxing. They 'take you out of yourself'. In Csikszentmihalyi's terms they are experiences of flow, in Maslow's (1968) they are small-scale peak experiences.

As rational, workday beings we do not have them; as weekend beings, free to follow a less intellectual wisdom, we may. They appear to be the peaceful, relaxed and frequent form of a type of self-transcendent experience whose more ecstatic and rarer version is mysticism.

According to Laski (1961), mystical experiences are often triggered by nature, particularly mountains and sea, and sometimes by physical exercise. They nearly always involve a sense of unity (which Zaehner, 1957, sees as the distinguishing mark of mystical experiences); and in them, even if one is active, the will is in abeyance (James, 1902).

Zaehner differentiates nature mysticism from true experiences of God, and there may be good reason for this. Certainly the need for experiences of self-transcendence continues while particular gods come and go. For Lévy-Bruhl's (1965) 'primitive' the need was met by mystical participation; for the drug culture of the 1960s it was met by getting stoned and achieving cosmic consciousness; for some Christians it is met by charismatic renewal or Molt-mann's (1972) theology of play.

In traditional societies special days were set aside to satisfy this need. Then they were called holy days. Now they are called holidays. Now, as then, there may be feasts, dancing, intoxication and a general obliteration of ordinary consciousness in favour of a consciousness of the self as part of a wider group or cosmic unity.

It is worth underscoring the dependence of experiences of unity with nature on characteristically visual patterns of thought.

The chief alchemist in transforming an agitated ego-driven weekday person into a relaxed, self-transcending, weekend one is the environment. It is the repository of complex and beautiful things to look at, and some of these serve as the natural symbols that link human rhythms to those of the cosmos. The environment is also the locus in the intransitive actions which physically relate person to place. The timelessness of these actions is the experiential counterpart of the present-continuous tense typical of visual imagery; these are actions with a present, but without a past or future.

Not surprisingly, images of nature scenes have been employed in psycho-therapy in a number of positive roles. Cautela (1970) uses them (among others) as covert reinforcers for covert good behaviour. Wolpe (1973) uses them in systematic desensitization to counter tension and help people relax. Leuner (1977, 1978) uses them in his guided affective imagery. Evidence from the current study suggests that these images may function by evoking the intrinsically rewarding experience of being part of something bigger than the self, with the accompanying sense of peace, freedom and relaxation.

One aspect of this relaxing effect may be simply that the person's attention is drawn away from the self. This breaks the vicious circle often involved in anxiety, where physiological signs draw attention to themselves; this forces the person into a state of objective self-awareness; which in turn exacerbates the anxiety. Wegner and Giuliano (1980) have shown that physiological arousal does increase self-focused attention, and a number of studies have shown that such attention can increase anxiety and disrupt performance (Sarason, 1972; Carver, Blaney and Scheier, 1979; Scheier, Carver and Gibbons, 1981).

However, to see nature, or even images of nature, as only having a role in distracting us from inner awfulness hardly does justice to some very powerful effects. Nature is not only a distraction, she is also The Great Mother, and this remains true whatever our science and sophistication. From her we arose, on her beneficence we ultimately depend, and to her we ultimately return. In experi-ences of being close to nature we finger the umbilicus attaching us to the natural order, and this provides us with a sense of place, of being a tiny part in a much larger whole. One way of describing the shift of consciousness that occurs in these episodes of being close to nature is to say that we move from seeing ourselves as an object in an environment, a figure isolated against its background, to seeing ourselves as a small but necessary part of a greater whole. This involves a shift from one visual structure, in which objects are located in environments, to another, in which parts are perceived in their relation to the wholes they constitute.

The sentiments of self

William James (1892) divided the self into the I, the knower, and the me, the known. The me he further divided into three: the *material self*, the *social self*, and the *spiritual self*. Roughly speaking, experiences of objective self-awareness concern the first two of these selves, and experiences of being at one with nature the third. Each of the three emerges in a particular way of relating to the environment and involves a particular set of sentiments (see figure 8.1). These are such feelings as peace, embarrassment and pride, which would not normally count as full-blown emotions, and which are, to use James's distinction, the emotions of the me rather than the I.

The spiritual self is that which gives attention to the natural environment, becomes absorbed in its beauty, and sees itself as a small part of a greater whole. The feelings involved here are a sense of wonder, freedom, peace and relaxation.

Attention to others in the social environment may be reflected back on the self in experiences of externalized self-awareness. These appear to be grounded in the joint attention with others which constitutes the intersubjective world, and which, when the look of others is turned on the self, constitutes it as an object belonging to this intersubjective domain.

Initially, we are constituted as a body, the material self which is all that strangers know of us. Those who know us better can read the behaviour of this material self for its social meaning. Desirable social behaviour affirms the social world and is transparent to it – in which case self-esteem and pride are appropriate feelings. Ineffective social behaviour may result in the persona clouding over and losing its social transparency: this is embarrassment, in which we become an opaque and ridiculous body.

The self which appeared as a subject of attribution in the visualizer portrait is clearly not a simple entity. It may be the subject of different kinds of attributions, following James's distinction between the three selves that make up the me. But in addition to being an object in the physical world, it may also be a signifier, transparent to a socially constructed reality.

If there is one general evaluative principle which covers all the feelings to which the me, the visualizer's dominant self, is prone, it would perhaps involve reference to the importance of belonging. What this belonging means depends on the situation. In relation to the natural environment it means being able to see oneself as a small part of the greater whole. In relation to the social environment it means participating in the intersubjective world, and at best reciprocally affirming the validity of that world in one's interactions with others.

Not belonging represents failure. It engenders a sense of isolation which may be manifest as feelings of insignificance, loneliness, rejection, or embarrassment.

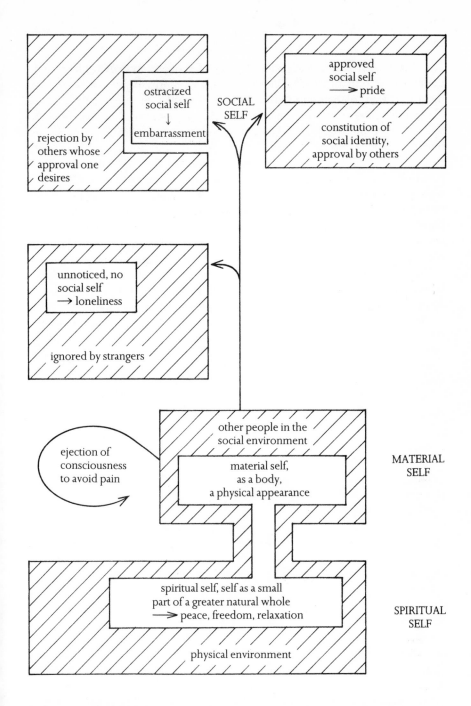

Figure 8.1   Relationships to the environment, and the sentiments of self

In conclusion

The characteristically visual relationship between object and environment has a number of important affective consequences. Attention to the natural environment may lead to absorption in it, and to experiences of oneness with nature. If the environment is social, attention to it may lead to a state of objective self-awareness in which the self is constituted first as a physical appearance, and then as a social persona. The self as the subject of attribution, important in the visualizer portrait, can here be analysed further into the spiritual, material and social selves which William James described as making up the *me*, the self as known, and which are constituted in various relationships with the environment. The emotional range of the visualizer portrait is a reflection of the vicissitudes of these selves. The feelings involved are typically not strong emotions, but milder *sentiments*, which can all be described as concerned with the importance of belonging. Belonging to, feeling at one with, the natural environment engenders feelings of peace and freedom; belonging to the social environment, being socially approved, is evident in pride and self-esteem; and failures of belonging result in such negative experiences as loneliness and embarrassment.

9

Emotions and enactive representation

Verbal, visual and enactive modes of thought all involve evaluations, but they differ in the extent to which these evaluations are accompanied by palpable episodes of feeling.

In inner speech the evaluations appear in the form of preferences, and it is the value judgment that appears to dominate over any feeling element. The evaluations may have attitudinal and behavioural consequences, in that *preferring* X means *liking* X, and therefore being inclined to favour X-related activities. It may also mean *not liking* Y, and avoiding or merely tolerating places and events where Y is to be found. However, *to prefer* X, though it clearly embodies a value judgment, is hardly to experience an episode of feeling about X. Liking and preferring are general attitudes rather than distinct occurrences in one's subjective life.

The way of being in the world that visual imagery represents has a stronger feeling component. The feelings involved are of a particular kind. William James called them the feelings of the *me*, of the 'known self'. In terms of case grammar they are the feelings of the subject of attribution. They range from the relatively quiescent feelings of peacefulness or pride, to feelings which involve distinct and episodic 'pangs', as for example in embarrassment.

The evidence from preceding chapters has indicated that the stronger emotions, where we are suddenly lifted out of the ordinary world and thrust into an emotional one, belong to enactive representation. These might be called the emotions of the I, of James's 'knower', or of the case grammatical agent and experiencer. These emotions – fear, anxiety, joy – involve an evaluation of their object, but this evaluative constituent is thoroughly embedded in an emotion which includes much more than just an evaluation.

Strong emotions are typically found in a complex conjunction with two other components of enactive imagery: transitive action, and the future towards which this action is directed. In the free association studies the emotion sometimes provided the 'push', the motivation for action, with the envisaged future goal providing the 'pull', as if transitive action were in a temporal sandwich between feeling and the future.

Action, emotion and the future are also correlated in the personality portrait of the enactive imager. These people are inner-directed, motivated towards goals of their own chosing, and at their best when allowed to pursue them. Then they are intense, patient and inventive. If this motivation is frustrated, the emotional energy goes sour, and turns to stubbornness, aggression and even thoughts of suicide.

Action and emotion also both occur in enactive day-dreams, but here they are uncoordinated, as if the clutch were out and the motivational engine idling. This may be because of the absence of the future which would add a goal orientation to what are, without it, rather impulsive actions.

This chapter further explores the relationship between emotion and enactive imagery. To prevent any notion that the connection is a simple one, it is first worth reviewing briefly some theoretical perspectives on emotion: emotions have been many things to many theorists.

Some perspectives on emotion

The diversity of views on emotion suggests that either one of them is right and an awful lot of others are wrong; or that most of them are right in a non-exclusive way, each touching on a different aspect of the phenomenon. The following are a small sample of points that have been made on the nature of emotions.

1) *In emotions we are 'moved'*. Emotions are passions. In them things happen to us and in us to which we are passive (James, 1892; de Rivera, 1977; Averill, 1980; Leventhal, 1980).

2) *Emotions are thoroughly embodied.*

a) Many emotions belong to our biological inheritance, and are grounded in instincts or innately based behaviour systems (McDougall, 1928; Rapaport, 1953; Plutchik, 1980; Scott, 1980).

b) There are consistent, pan-cultural, and even pan-species facial expressions for particular emotions (Darwin, 1872; Tomkins, 1962, 1963; Izard, 1971, 1977; Ekman and Friesen, 1971; Ekman, 1982; Schwartz and Weinberger, 1980).

c) Many emotions involve arousal. This may be general, of the viscera, of skeletal muscles, and/or of the autonomic or central nervous systems (Duffy, 1962; Jacobson, 1938, 1970; Cannon, 1929; Gellhorn, 1964, 1968; MacLean, 1958).

d) In the absence of any explanation for general arousal, people find it aversive (Maslach, 1979a and b; Marshall and Zimbardo, 1979; despite Schacter and Singer's 1962 findings).

e) However, people are not particularly accurate in their perception of bodily changes (Shields and Stern, 1979).

f) The complexity of the relationship between the emotions and the body is exacerbated by the fact that the bodily or facial expression of emotion may *decrease* the objectively assessed physiological manifestations (Jones, 1935, 1950; Lanzetta and Kleck, 1970; Notarius and Levenson, 1979); while *increasing* subjectively experienced emotion (Laird, 1974; Lanzetta, Cartwright-Smith and Kleck, 1976).

g) The bodily component may be more important in some emotions than others. James (1892) distinguished the 'coarser' bodily emotions (anger, fear, grief, etc.) from the 'subtler' and less bodily (moral and intellectual) feelings.

h) Averill (1974) remarks that the desire to reduce emotions to the bodily level may not reflect the facts so much as our evaluation of them. We see emotions as belonging to the lower, beastly part of us (as if ratiocination could happen in a disembodied mind).

3) *There is a strong though complex relationship between emotion and action.*

a) Emotions are the experienced counterpart of instinct (McDougall, 1928).

b) Emotions are themselves motives for actions, or at least the basis for them (Leeper, 1948, 1970; McClelland, 1955; Hillman, 1970; Dahl, 1979).

c) Emotions motivate because they amplify drive signals (Tomkins, 1962, 1979, 1980).

d) Some emotions involve a particular bodily attitude, preparatory to action (Bull, 1951; Arnold, 1960).

e) Some emotions occur when action is blocked or prevented (Claparède, 1928; Dollard, Doob, Sears, Miller and Mowrer, 1939; Sartre, 1962; Dembo, 1976).

f) Some emotions 'root us to the spot', paralysing action and having a generally disorganizing influence on behaviour (Young, 1961; Suomi and Harlow, 1976).

4) *Emotions have an important cognitive component.*

a) They involve appraisals or evaluations, and are the means whereby objects, events or ideas are seen as being imbued with value or hedonic tone (James, 1902; Polanyi, 1958; Arnold, 1960; de Rivera, 1977; Schlosberg, 1954; Davitz, 1969, 1970; Lazarus, Kanner and Folkman, 1980). This is a very old idea – Arnold traces it at least as far back as Thomas Aquinas.

b) Emotions may depend on how one labels them: the same arousal may be seen as preparatory and productive excitement, or as debilitating terror (Alpert and Haber, 1960; Hollandsworth, Glazeski, Kirkland, Jones and van Norman, 1979; but see also 2d).

c) Emotions may depend on the causal attributions one has made, or on the stories one tells oneself (Weiner, Russell and Lerman, 1978, 1979; Beck, Rush, Shaw and Emery, 1979).

d) Emotion is an interrupt mechanism that allows attention to be paid to particularly pressing circumstances (Mandler, 1975, 1979; Simon, 1967; Folkman, Schaefer and Lazarus, 1979).

e) Emotion may be intrinsic to cognitive structures, particularly as tension therein (Festinger, 1957; Heider, 1958; Kelly, 1958; Klein, 1967).

f) Emotion involves consciousness: it is not just motivation, action, bodily arousal, or facial expression, but the *awareness* of them (James, 1892; McDougall, 1928; Bull, 1951; Tomkins, 1962; Scheier and Carver, 1977).

g) Similarly, emotion words refer to *experiences* (Davitz, 1970; Leventhal, 1980).

h) Emotions leave nothing ùntouched, and may transform our entire world (Heidegger, 1967; Sartre, 1962; Dembo, 1976).

5) *However, emotions may not be dependent on prior cognition.*

a) Emotional responses sometimes precede cognitive ones, at least phenomenologically, and may sometimes be independent of them (Zajonc, 1980; Zajonc, Pietromonaco and Bargh, 1982).

b) Some affective disorders remain intransigent to efforts at cognitive manipulation (Wolpe, 1978a and b; Ledwidge, 1978).

6) *There may be some emotional primitives.* Despite the vast number of different emotion words in everyday language, there exists a belief that at a theoretical level these can be reduced:

a) To a small number of distinct fundamental emotions – including joy, anger and fear, but not avarice or humility (Izard, 1977; Leventhal, 1980).

b) Or to a small number of usually bipolar fundamental dimensions – e.g. pleasant–unpleasant, and calm–excitement (Wundt, 1907; Schlosberg, 1954; Davitz, 1969; Frijda, 1970; Russell, 1978, 1979).

c) Combining (a) and (b), pairs of fundamental emotions are sometimes seen as structurally related – e.g. joy and sorrow are opposed, and do not occur together; love and security are reciprocally related, in so far as security is being-loved (de Rivera, 1977; Wolpe, 1973; Solomon and Corbit, 1974; Plutchik, 1970; Schwartz and Weinberger, 1980).

d) Some complex emotions (e.g. depression) are combinations either of fundamental emotions or of emotions with other processes (Izard, 1977; Arieti, 1970; Arnold, 1960).

7) *Emotions carry social information.*

a) The large amount of work on facial expressions (see also 2b) shows how emotions convey important social meanings, some of which human beings share with animals (Darwin, 1872; Eibl-Eibesfeldt, 1980).

b) Emotions themselves can be considered as transitory social roles (Averill, 1980).

8) *Despite their complexity, emotions are seen as unitary phenomena.*

a) They are organized as *Gestalts* (Leeper, 1948, 1970), in which the physiological, cognitive, behavioural and other features form an integrated package (Izard, 1977; Young, 1961; Leventhal, 1980; Lazarus, Kanner and Folkman, 1980).

b) However, the connections between the constituents in the package may be loose, allowing for different individuals to show biases in their emotional response systems (Lang, 1968; Odom, Nelson and Wein, 1978; Borkovec, 1976; Musante and Anker, 1974).

9) *Emotions have been a frequent moral and theological concern.* Either some passions are to be transcended, as hatred in Christianity; or all passions are to be transcended, as in Zen Buddhism, where even love may lead to attachment.

From even this very brief survey of the literature on emotions it is evident that they are complex; and that though the literature is extensive, psychological knowledge remains confused. On some aspects the evidence is plain, and definite statements can be made; for example, on the fact that the facial expressions of emotion convey important information to members of our own species, and in some cases also to members of other species. On other aspects things are less clear, and while it is apparent that there is a general relationship between emotions and action, or cognition, or bodily activation, the precise direction and nature of the relationship is not clear. Does emotion motivate action or only occur when action is blocked? Does emotion precede or follow cognitive processes? Is the bodily arousal the same in anger and euphoria and only the cognitive component different, or not? Part of the complexity here may be that beyond a certain point it is probably not very helpful to talk about emotions in general, and it becomes necessary to look more closely at the specific properties of particular emotions. Another problem may be that there is a natural tendency to view emotions as entities, like other objects, which can be analysed into constituent parts and dimensions, just as real things can be analysed. This may be an inappropriate way of looking at them.

A number of writers, especially Buytendijk (1950) and Fell (1977) have called for phenomenological studies of emotions as a way of coming to grips with the subjective core of emotional experience, which tends to be lost in many studies on separate aspects or dimensions of emotionality. Experiential research is the bedrock to which psychology can turn or return when more sophisticated techniques have brought us to the kind of bewildered impasse where we find ourselves saying, 'But what is an emotion, really?'

Emotion sequences and commitment scripts

The study on the phenomenology of emotions involved people writing descriptions of emotional experiences in response to the following instructions:

> This is a piece of descriptive and introspective research on 'where emotions come from'. Think of a *particular* occasion where you experienced fairly strong feelings of emotion. Choose an episode which is recent enough (or strong enough) for you to remember fairly clearly: it does not matter what kind of feelings were involved. Describe in as much detail as you can, using whatever

words come naturally, what led up to the experience, the experience itself, and the 'come-down' period, if any. Try to re-live the experience mentally, and write as you go through it.

The responses to this request provided complex and often poignant data, the important components of which are given in full in appendix G. The descriptions show how people construe the term 'emotion' when they are relatively free from the trained psychologist's preconceptions.

An emotional experience has the character of a traditional novel, with beginning, middle and end. It may have considerable temporal extension, stretching out over minutes, days or months (and this is without the lead-up and come-down mentioned in the instructions).

Most emotional experiences contain more than one emotion (on average 2.4), and the different components are linked together in temporal sequences.

Some emotions have invariant positions in these sequences. If the experience includes surprise or shock, these are typically at the beginning, as a prelude to other feelings. If it includes joy or relief, these are typically at the end, terminating a period of anxiety or fear. Depression and guilt tend to follow the expression of anger, and betrayal requires one first to have loved.

The temporal interdependence of emotions is recognized by Tomkins (1962, 1963), and Solomon and Corbit (1974). For Tomkins some emotions are a function of the 'gradient of neural stimulation', not of its absolute level: analogically, emotion is more like acceleration than speed. Tomkins sees fear as resulting from an increase in the gradient of neural stimulation, and happiness from a decrease. In any organism with even a toehold on homeostasis, what goes up must come down. This points to the conclusion that one emotion must sooner or later be succeeded by its 'opposite' to return the person to equilibrium.

The content of an emotional experience consists of more than just the emotions themselves, however, as these arise in the context of living, without which the feelings would be meaningless.

The following example contains at least nervousness, panic, being scared, getting upset, being shaken, bursting into tears, and feeling guilty. These all fit together in the one experience by virtue of the fact that there is a world in there too, filled with bicycles, traffic lights, instructions, lovely shaking old men, and obligations to be on time, which all play their part in the existential conversation:

Last week I decided I would try to use my fairly new ten-speed racer to college – the Latin advisory session was on at 10.00 a.m. and I left at 9.15 to be sure I would get there in time. I was nervous on the roads – coming down the huge hill that leads away from the house I felt nervous in traffic. – Filled with all these sorts of emotions my adrenalin ran 90 miles to the dozen, I panicked and as a result lost my way. This made me more scared and a little upset as time was moving on. I hate being late for anything.

Somewhere in the middle of nowhere I followed two sets of instructions to get to College Road. As I was turning right (following the second person's instructions) I signalled – A man behind me in a car thought I was overtaking a nearby parked lorry and bashed into the back of my pride and joy – Silver Dream Racer. That didn't matter as much as the fact that it happened – It was too much, I burst into tears. I was very shaken though thank heavens unhurt (I was only thrown off the saddle).

The man who was, as I say for lack of a better word the culprit – was fortunately a lovely middle age/old man who was by then shaking in his boots. We were a mess, him shaking and me crying – he was so nice I felt guilty that I wasn't at fault – in fact I even apologised to him for giving him a shock. He took me home, gave me his address from a letter – he couldn't write it he was so shaken. Also he took the bike to be fixed and offered to take me to college, my original destination. Of course as soon as I got in the door I burst into tears again, delayed shock I suppose.

This episode is the story of a set of nested commitments: a physical commitment to staying alive; a personal commitment to get somewhere on time; and a social one to comfort and be comforted by the other main participant.

Virtually all the emotional episodes had the same general structure, in that they involved crises or turning-points in one or more commitments: commitments to life, threatened in accidents; commitments to loved ones, broken by death or disloyalty; commitments to a career, with hurdles like exams to pass; commitments to a social persona, under attack from unjust others. Borrowing the notion of *scripts* from Schank and Abelson (1977) we could say that emotions belong to commitment scripts, in which a particular commitment is the main character and its vicissitudes provide the story line. Figure 9.1 shows some of the relationships between commitments and the emotions which arise at their crisis points.

Some of the most important commitments are tacit, and arise simply from the fact of being alive. Being alive involves a number of clever mechanisms designed to keep us that way – for example, eating and acts of self-preservation. Being alive also involves doing something, having a *way of life*, or having some general plan for action and for what to do with one's life. Life, like consciousness, is a moving stream, which must, while it continues, flow in some channel. We are the beneficiaries of this stream, not its prime mover, but we still *are* responsible for directing it into a particular channel.

More conscious commitments also involve ways of life. Loving someone is a way of living with them; and wanting to be a social worker (or rich, or debauched) involves aspiring to a particular life style, including, among other things, a behavioural repertoire and certain sorts of action.

Becoming

Integral to most emotional experiences is an interlocking set of constituents

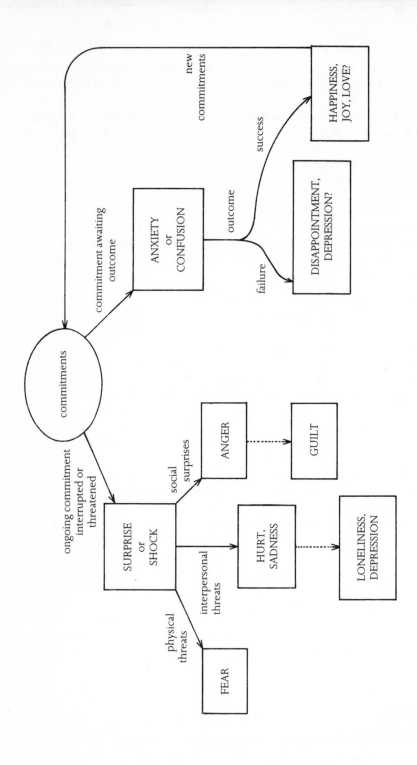

Figure 9.1 Some relationships between commitments and emotions

relating to time, and particularly to the future. A creature without a future is a dead creature; to have a future is to be alive.

Many emotions reveal the extent to which we already exist in the future, projected through plans and intentions. Becoming that future self is gratifying; being deprived of it can be agonizing or infuriating. The temporality involved is not that of clock time, in which it would be sufficient just to wait; it is the time of Allport's (1955) *becoming*, of commitment and of action. Most of the emotional experiences contained interrelated themes of: the future (realized, disrupted or lost); action (performed, desired or impossible); and the body (arousal and/or paralysis). It is convenient to discuss these in isolation, though *in vivo* they are interrelated.

The future and its emotional vicissitudes

The (non-emotional) components of emotional experiences particularly relevant to the future are: *plans* (e.g. for a career); *waiting* (e.g. for results); *thoughts about the future* (e.g. thinking what to do next, or wondering what will happen if . . .); and in a negative sense, *death* and *being betrayed* (some of the *injustices to the self* category), which cut one off from the future.

Plans involve committing oneself to a future role, job, career, or relationship, and working to realize it. For example wanting to be a social worker, to be the lover of X, or to occupy the 'hot seat' in an encounter group, and planning what to do to achieve that. People are bound by honour to their future self. Having laid claims to it they feel obliged to do the work to bring it into being.

Plans often involve an initial commitment to a future self and then a period of waiting while the future is at stake and is being worried about. The paradigm cases are taking exams or going for interviews.

Thoughts about the future, having plans, and waiting for outcomes are all high in joy and disappointment, and especially high in what typically precedes them: anxiety, where people do what Janis (1958) called 'the work of worrying'. Here is someone attempting to tame the future by imagining they have already lived through all possible versions of it anyway:

> The test started and although I knew I had a good chance I was afraid I'd make some stupid mistake. . . . I remember thinking all the time things like, what does he think, will I pass, will I fail, what will I do if I fail and all that kind of stuff.

At least during a driving test there are still things one can do to affect the outcome. After exams and while waiting for results there is nothing, any longer, that can be done. Anxiety sometimes manifests itself in a state of befuddlement or confusion, which was a relatively common emotion in the current study, though it is not one that appears on standard lists of emotions.

The future cannot in imagination be totally pre-empted, and the uncertainty endures until the last resolving moment:

On the news that I had passed I could physically feel the relief flowing over me as if a weight had been lifted off and resulting in absolute happiness.

Happiness marks both resolution of uncertainty, and success. Success means that we are allowed to become the person that in intention we already are. Failure blocks this sense of progress. Success prefigures the next step, opening a new future with new responsibilities:

'Here it goes' I thought.
A sizeable majority on the first count. I remained pretty calm but there was a surge in my stomach – hope. Tony was beside me with his calculator working out probabilities and statistics.
'Attention please, we have a result. . . .' I had won!! Delight! Then more congratulations and commiserations.
Afterwards, there was delight which was tempered by the enormity of the decision which being elected constituted in my life. Still pleased.

People seem to feel most alive when they are *engaged* in living in some such strongly committed way. This engagement has responsibilities which stretch into the future; and which may indeed be the means whereby that future is constructed.

All positive emotions project to a future full of heady potential. Of all of them, love is the most prescient:

I remember on the evening of Nov. 21 – it was a Thursday – Owen and I went for a walk. It was then he said to me that if I wanted a relationship even though he was going away in ten weeks' time, then he did too. I was ecstatic. I was over the moon. I had never felt so happy before. The thing was I was in love with Owen even before we were going out together. It didn't matter to me that Owen was going to America because the relationship would still go on even then. I could see the relationship lasting years – even after I'd finished University. I could even see myself marrying Owen.

Love fills people with a sense of fullness, of confidence, a sense that no problem is insuperable. We perhaps feel most alive in love because it is when the future appears most burgeoning, though of course the present can be pretty good too.

The notion that having a future is generally connected with being happy is supported by Wessman and Ricks's (1966) work on mood and personality, which shows a longer future time perspective in happy people than in those who are less happy. Teahan's (1958) work on optimism and academic achievement tells a similar story: optimistic people have a longer future time perspective than pessimists; and they also tend to show a higher level of scholastic success.

The importance of the future is shown in negative form in grief and betrayal. In grief fate cheats us of a loved one, cutting us off from a joint future. In betrayal it is the beloved who does the cheating, causing a deep sense of hurt sometimes akin to grief. In these cases either a person or a relationship is … DEAD, no more, finished. We, in contrast, are 'unfinished' and, like it or not, and feeling that we too have somehow died, must crawl on into a meaningless future. The morning after betrayal:

> Dave woke me at 8.00 when he had to go to work and I woke with that sick feeling of knowing something awful had happened. Everything seemed utterly futile, it was pointless that I was going home and I had to force myself to make very trivial things seem important. I came home shattered and it took months to pull myself together.

Death is one of the few circumstances which people (at least young people) do not try to anticipate. News of it is always a shock, whether the death is sudden or comes after a long illness. It is perhaps that anticipating events here would make them too concrete, which would be – while hope endures – both too painful, and too much like a kind of bad magic which reality might think to imitate.

Death and betrayal cut clean across commitments to the future. The opening phase of emotional episodes involving them is typically a sense of shock, which signals that the future has been curtailed. Simon (1967) and Mandler (1975) both discuss surprise, which is a milder form of shock, as a mechanism for interrupting ongoing activities so that particularly important information can be dealt with. In death and betrayal what is importantly interrupted is not whatever one is doing at the time the news arrives, for that only requires a normal switch of attention; but one's commitment to a future with a particular person. One can go back later to whatever one was doing when the news came, to eating the toast or reading the novel. There is no going back to a period of life that is now closed, with oneself shut out of it for ever.

Shock and surprise describe a continuum of interruptions. Shock tends to be the first stage of threatened or actual personal or interpersonal catastrophes, as surprise is of social ones.

A look across the full spectrum of emotional experiences shows that the future is important in all of them, though in different ways. In figure 9.1 the emotions are differentiated into two broad groups, depending on whether they involve the initial interruption of ongoing commitments; or an initial uncertainty because some outcome regarding one's progress along a chosen path is as yet unknown. The distinction is between the emotions whose prelude is surprise or shock, and those whose prelude is anxiety.

Generally, emotions which open the future are good, those which close it are bad. Successes prefigure a new life with new responsibilities; love projects to an infinite and rosy future. In contrast grief and hurt signal the abrupt termination of a future; and fear and anger signal threats to the future, but retain enough faith in it to hope for survival or revenge. Anxiety has an ambiguous status, as it involves both hopes and fears about what the future will be. Depression also has a special status, often occurring in the aftermath of more apocalyptic emotions, and being itself as near to emotional deadness as is possible. In depression there simply is no future.

The literature on emotions generally supports this temporal analysis, though the evidence is patchy.

In research on anxiety there is a large amount of work on the importance of expectancy, which explicitly acknowledges a future orientation; and there is also work on the general importance of uncertainty, which tacitly acknowledges a future orientation (Epstein, 1972; Lazarus and Averill, 1972).

The emotion whose temporal aspects have received most scrutiny is depression. It is evident that depressed people have a shorter future time perspective than non-depressed people (Minkowski, 1958; Dilling and Rabin, 1967; Gorman and Wessman, 1977); and Strauss (1947) even talks about the 'pathology of becoming' in depression. The following captures the general sense of nihilism:

> Depression as I experience it is almost a non-emotion and a state of non-being. I can moon for hours without realizing it and feel just dull and empty when I am feeling at all. It is a blur of other emotions none of which are definite in themselves, and it has no intensity. Periodically it breaks up into anxiety about being like this and being non-functional; and guilt because I can't do what I want/feel I should. I am guilty to myself not to others.

Some theorists use concepts which are not explicitly temporal, but which have temporal connotations. Seligman's (1975) *helplessness*, for example, suggests a person facing a future which they cannot do anything about, and this attitude is the opposite pole to the *self-efficacy* that Bandura (1977) sees as essential to psychological health.

Some depressions have social as well as individual importance. In the last economic recession, Israeli (1935) looked at the time perspective of unemployed men, and found a shortened future perspective, together with a breakdown of their constructive outlook on life. This underscores the fact that psychologically, the future does not just exist, but is constructed by individuals who are able to do something to realize it. This links in with the second major component of the emotional experiences: action.

Action in passion: moving and being moved

Interrelated with the role of the future in emotions is a group of constituents concerned with action. Action is important because it is what we can do to realize the future. Indeed it is all we can do.

The particular categories which delineate the role of action are most important-ly *action itself* (highest in fear), *wanting to act* (highest in love); *frantic behaviour* (displacement activities, most frequent in anger and disappointment); and possibly *prayer* (a kind of supernatural action for use when all else fails, and most frequent in fear and sadness). Retrospective judgments about actions may be made, for example that one's *response was out of proportion* (most frequent in anger); this is often followed by the judgment that one has *learned from the experience* (especially associated with guilt).

Action is most urgent when life is at stake. Scene: a grimy American railway station:

> There he was a knife in his hand and looking big, strong and ugly. I thought I was about to faint, I was only a few steps away from the open. . . . So close but yet so far! My heart pounded until I was sure it had fallen out. My feet were weak but I knew I had to run. I pushed him sideways not knowing how I retained my strength and made a dash.

Action is also frequent in love, guilt and anger, though here it may sometimes be inhibited by reticence, morality, or the absence of the appropriate person, and instead of actually acting, people *want to act*. Some of the wants eventuate in the actions, for example, wanting to apologize for a misdemeanour and later doing so. Others do not. Anger may want to wipe its object from the surface of the planet but in practice will settle for lesser revenge.

When the person has done all that is possible, but is still 'primed' for action, the energy tends to get released in frantic behaviour:

> I had to wait for about 10 minutes for the call to go through and during that time I had to keep busy to fight off the nervousness. I was all 'wound-up' and nowhere to release all this energy, so I cleaned the kitchen in 10 minutes.

Displacement behaviour is one way of keeping emotion under control, and features prominently in anxiety, disappointment, surprise and anger. In anger situations it may deflect aggression from the victim, and provide a way of escaping from insoluble conflict with aplomb:

> My brother, Sean, has the disgusting habit of 'burping' at regular 20-second intervals after a meal, and invariably forgets to excuse himself. This may not seem a cause for grave concern, and certainly not 'strong emotion', but it is an almost constant source of irritation in my house. . . . There we were watching the television when suddenly Sean belched, sighed, and sat there contentedly! Something in his manner really annoyed me and I fumed quietly waiting for him to say 'excuse me'! Of course he didn't, to aggravate me, and I started screaming at him, calling him a disgusting creature and other such horrible names. Then I pounded out of the room, slammed the door loudly and flounced up the stairs.

Actions of all sorts represent an optimism that, however bad the situation, something can still be done about it. In some situations no action is of any possible avail, and then there is neither action, nor the desire for it, nor tension to be channelled anywhere. The world has already caved in, and the person stands helpless, hopeless, grieving or betrayed, among the ruins. These are situations in which there is no action possible because there is no longer a future to act towards.

Sometimes people resort to prayer as the one thing they *can* do. This is of particular importance in bereavement, but sometimes also occurs in extreme fear, after exhausting actions of more conventional sorts. A prior atheism is no necessary exclusion:

> At first things were fine, the weather was still and I felt reasonably confident. Then things began to go wrong. We encountered fog and as we had no fog horn I had to sit on the bows playing a violin. The alcohol was still having an effect however as I was not able to fully comprehend the danger of running into a tanker or trawler on the river.
>
> When we were out at sea and it grew dark my fear took firm hold. I had wanted to see land at all times and I was convinced that Liam was sailing for open sea. We had a heated exchange over this while Liam denied any such thing. The blackness of the sea was the most frightening aspect of the trip and when the wind picked up and we were running into 20-foot waves which seemed to loom higher than the mast I retreated to the hold, a gibbering wreck. Most of the trip I spent securely wrapped in a life jacket clutching the distress flare to my palpitating chest. I made quite a few bargains with God and others. I even made a bargain with Sedna, an eskimo Goddess I had read about as a child, that I wouldn't try to sleep with Liam's sister if we made it.

Important for the understanding of emotional phenomena is the coexistence of action with a sense of passivity. De Rivera (1977) says that in emotion we are 'moved', although in some paradoxical way we are also the mover; and Leventhal (1980) sees emotional behaviour as involving an interplay between willed and involuntary action. The balance may depend on the particular emotion. In love and guilt, people often express a desire for action before they do it, indicating that will has some leverage in the matter. In anger, however, people often *do* have a sense of losing control. This is a lapse of will to which considerable guilt attaches, and people often make the retrospective judgment that their response was out of proportion:

> It was a football match. And as usual I took this match seriously, a bit of competitiveness was good. After a while things didn't go well for me. I made mistakes, I wasted chances, I was playing below my usual standard. I no longer enjoyed the game. I began to play dirty, I no longer cared whether it was the ball or the man I kicked. Then I picked on one person. I really went in hard, he held me down on the ground, I could not get up. I felt small and timid. He hit me. I got up and started to swing my fists. Soon the other lads stopped it. . . . I sat on the ground, feeling miserable. My anger had taken control of me, I no longer had, as I like to call it, 'I' control. What happened afterwards was painful on the

inside. I couldn't forgive myself, was it in fact a dream? I felt the need to make up. In fact I cried about it. This was something that had taken control, not for the first time. And so I apologised. I could hardly find the words to say anything. In fact all I could blurt out was 'I'm sorry'. But it was enough.

People probably learn more from letting rip and feeling guilty about it afterwards than from never letting rip in the first place. One of the most frightening (or sometimes exhilarating) aspects of emotional situations is that they have an internal logic which is incorrigible and peremptory. Freud said of the unconscious that in it there is no negation. There is no negation in some strong emotions either.

In some situations it is only 'being moved' that keeps us alive. Here conscious willing would certainly go along with instinct, even if it doesn't have time to come first:

> I come round a bend, and see too close for comfort two vehicles side by side coming towards me. A lorry and a car exactly alongside it in my lane. Some kind of assessment of chances went on very swiftly so that I knew I had to brake sharply, and the action probably coincided more or less with the thought. I must have flung my left hand across as if to protect a passenger, though there was none (I discovered I must have afterwards as all the things hadn't fallen off the seat).

As a conscious creature each of us is in fortunate symbiosis with a preconscious creature who does a lot of the work for us. It too has an epistemology, out of which grow the more detailed and familiar articulations of reason.

To see what may be going on here, consider what is a key phrase in the foregoing account: *Some kind of assessment of chances went on very swiftly so that I knew I had to brake sharply, and the action probably coincided more or less with the thought.* In order to 'assess chances' it is not necessary to know: *red Renault car, circa 1975, with a driver and two passengers travelling at about 58 m.p.h. in a northerly direction and overtaking where it shouldn't be, so that if it continues along its current trajectory and I continue along my current trajectory at the speed I am now travelling we are due for impact in about half a second.*

Such a statement is only a slight caricature of the sort of thing we normally see as being informative, because we actually have a very civilized conception of what counts as information. Information is something that is socially informative, something which describes a state of affairs in such a way that it is meaningful to others as well as ourselves, and is thus impersonally meaningful.

In emergencies we are not concerned with this kind of knowledge by description, but with direct and urgent knowledge by acquaintance. Here all the socially communicable paraphernalia is stripped off, and we are left in very basic semantic territory indeed. All we need to know initially is that there is a *thing on collision course.* This is rather too semantically attenuated a statement to be socially interesting, but it is enough for the individual experiencing it to press the panic button, start the adrenalin, slam on the brakes. Having acted to ensure survival, one then has the time to worry about the cognitive curlicues, and about all the features that civilized human beings would be interested in.

This analysis is relevant to the discussion initiated by Zajonc (1980), who questioned whether cognition needs to precede affect. As Lazarus (1982) points out, Zajonc takes a rather rational and reflective view of what constitutes cognition, as if cognition had in some way to be finished before feeling could start. This is an unnecessary assumption. In fact we never finish cognitive processing in the sense of doing it exhaustively, even when at leisure, and there is no reason to think we have to start doing so in emergencies.

In emergencies we initially do only enough cognitive processing to get us out of the emergency. This may be very little. The thing-on-collision-course analysis, for example, is probably achieved very early on in the visual system. Babies and other rudimentary beings can manage the analysis of looming, and can take appropriate evasive action, and frogs can manage something very similar by the level of the optic nerve (Lettvin, Maturana, McCulloch and Pitts, 1959), so adult humans should have no great problems here.[1]

Seligman's (1971) discussion of 'prepared fears' may relate to this kind of processing. We are biologically prepared to respond very rapidly to certain hazardous situations on the basis of extremely primitive 'cognitive' analysis. Acute sensitivity to collision course, dark, and unusual, would be sufficient to keep us out of most kinds of trouble, physical and social.

Perhaps the difficulty in talking about the necessity for 'cognitive appraisals' in emotion, as Arnold (1960), Lazarus (1981, 1982) and Mandler (1982) do, is that it encourages the belief that there is some rationally articulated activity going on, and that the person is reflectively aware that the situation they are facing is likely to be bad for them. This is the position Zajonc appears to be criticizing. It is also a position that results in the apparent paradox, that on the one hand we need to know whether something is harmful or not before we can know what to feel about it, while on the other we seem to have started doing the feeling before we even know what the thing is.

Rather than such conscious deliberations it is far more likely that any cognitive appraisal that goes on is entirely tacit, manifest in the fact that we automatically and immediately take the appropriate evasive action; and reason, because it is epistemologically sophisticated, and because it likes to talk to other people, separates out this tacit judgment as representing something called a 'cognitive appraisal'. There is a cognitive appraisal, but it is implicit in what we do, and not a separate cognitive event. Too many separate cognitive events and people would not manage to avoid the car crashes that as a matter of fact they often do manage to avoid.

'Being moved' and 'losing I control', are a reflection of the fact that the rational intellect and its language, which often can be used for the control of action (Luria, 1961), including the control of some emotional action (Novaco, 1979; Camp,

1977), may, in survival situations lag far behind it. Because cognition can sometimes be used as a cause of other behaviour, including action, we tend to think it always is. This is far from the truth. Langer (1978) has recently shown how much social interaction, previously assumed to be underlain by thought, is in fact rather mindless. This is true of other types of action as well. For much of the time we do things first, and reason scuttles along self-importantly afterwards. As conscious beings we are not prime movers, but, at best, rudders. We think we are in charge while we chug along normally, and only notice that there is an engine as well when it gives us full power.

*

To summarize the role of action in emotions, it can be said that emotions in general involve variations on the theme of action, just as they involve variations on the theme of the future, and for related reasons. It is primarily through action that our present self creates or preserves the vital relationship with its future self, the self that it is planning to become. When an area of the future self has been lost (bereavement) or usurped (betrayal) there is nothing to relate to, and action is at a minimum. While there is still hope, as in anxiety and, at least most of the time, in fear, it is still worth while to be ready to act, even if this readiness has no better activity to be channelled into than tearing one's hanky into tiny pieces or cleaning the kitchen in ten minutes. In survival situations, actions may be initiated on the basis of rudimentary processing, and we feel that we are the passive 'moved' as well as the active 'mover'.

Activation and paralysis

Emotions are perhaps second only to pain in bringing home to us the fact that we are embodied creatures. Most of the time we can get by with an assumption that a body is something we *have*, or possibly something we are *in*. Emotional experiences confront us with the unmitigable fact that we also *are* a body. This body is not the physical appearance important in visual imagery, but the body which feels. Not the subject of attribution but the experiencer.

People have a wide and colourful vocabulary in which the body is treated as a combination of substance and metaphor:

> Even though I did not give vent to my anger, at that particular time, due to the suppression of my 'true' feelings my nerves felt 'jangled' (that is the only way I can explain it).

> When the time came to go I felt my heart would break – though I laughed and joked.

> My body taut, rigid, bristling.

I was feeling sick in the pit of my stomach.

I was overcome by a perfectly happy load of tremendous brilliant sensations.

I felt that hormones rather than blood were flowing through my veins. I was electrified.

There was no obvious pattern relating different emotions to particular parts of the body or to particular patterns of bodily activation.[2] References to some kind of bodily activation were most frequent in fear, anxiety and joy, and least frequent in sadness and hurt. These findings support the hunch that it is no accident that *activation*, *active* and *action* are cognate words. Fear, where the need for action is usually urgent, shows high bodily activation; and sadness and betrayal, where there is nothing that can be done, are low on both action and bodily activation. Action itself may be less important here than the existence of a future which makes it possible. Anxiety, like fear, retains a faith in the future, and includes many references to bodily activation; although, like sadness or betrayal, it involves a situation in which there is usually nothing that can be done, and where action itself (apart from displacement activities) is relatively infrequent. Figure 9.2 attempts to summarize some of the more important interactions between bodily activation, the various possibilities for action, and the vicissitudes of the future.

Studies using objective physiological measures support the general relationship between active engagement in the situation and physiological arousal. Grossberg and Wilson (1968) found that just reading a stimulus script to a person (verbal representation) did not produce a physiological response, whereas asking the person to 'picture the scene vividly and clearly' and to 'project yourself right into the scene' (mixture of visual and enactive) did produce heart rate changes. Lang's work (1979a and b) clarifies the situation further, showing that it is not the picturing that is important, but the person's imagined physical engagement in the situation.

Two response categories which fall between bodily activation and physical action are *crying* and *laughing*. Plessner (1970) holds that both these indicate a breakdown of the existential distance from which we normally view our own body, and which allows us to say that we are more than, or different from it. Plessner's interpretation is supported by the high frequency of crying in guilt and grief. In guilt we are forced to acknowledge that we have been victims of the body's impulses; in grief we are forced to face what we can normally disregard: a dependence on the body that dooms us to physical mortality. The occurrence of laughter in fear might also fit such an interpretation, but its appearance in surprise is less easy to account for.[3]

A final important effect that emotion may have on the body is *shock*. This is both physical and mental, often including *paralysis of action* and *disbelief*. All these are relatively high in hurt and fear; and also in surprise, to which shock is itself akin. Shocks of the strong variety are typically described through metaphors of

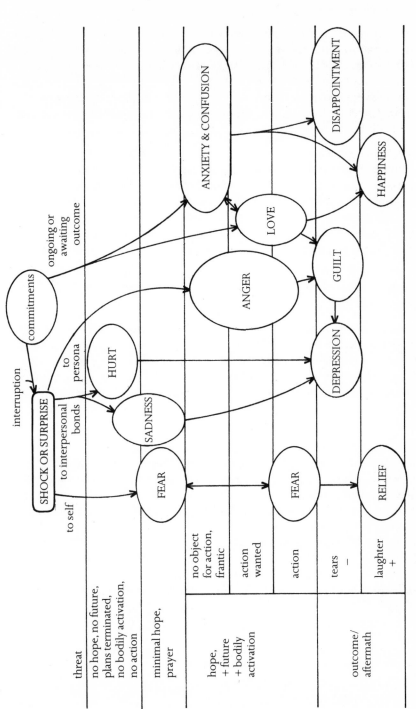

Figure 9.2 Interrelationships in emotions between the future, action and bodily activation

physical violence, such as being hit, or struck, or shattered. What people are hit with is the apprehension that the event has implications not just for the here and now but for much of life. Betrayal and threats to existence are not local events. It is difficult to take in all the implications at once, and at first there is only a sense that an abyss has opened in the foundations of life. Parkes (1972) and other writers on grief find shock to be common after bereavement. Betrayal can have the same effect. In the following, evidence has just come to light that the man may have lied:

> I began to try and find out what had been going on, and in the end I was gazing at him in horror and he was laughing at me. All I can remember is paralysing disbelief. My vision misted and my sound fuzzed and all I could see or hear was him laughing. It felt like a knock on the head or a car crash. It went on for ever. He said 'oh come on, stop kidding' and I suddenly realised that I wasn't. I've never been so utterly shocked, I felt decimated. After that I blacked out. I was talking to someone but I can't remember it at all – she told me afterwards.

Where the threat is a physical one, action has priority, and the paralysis is momentary or occurs in respites in the action. The full import of what hasn't quite happened often hits the person only afterwards:

> It is only at that point of stopped-ness, with both vehicles safely passed, that I suddenly became very tearful, quite shocked physiologically. As if after all the coping was done I could let go. Also the event sent a large surge of adrenalin or some such and it was as if that had a slightly delayed action, the effect hitting me after the event was over (it might have been disruptive at the time?)
>
> During the come-down period there were a lot of reflections on mortality, the fragility of people, physically.

The expression of fear and the experience of fear may come in many guises, which depend, among other things, on the direction of attention. Arousal narrows attention to a sharp focus (Easterbrook, 1959; Persson and Sjöberg, 1978), so it is as well to concentrate on the task of survival until the danger is over, and only then to focus on the state of the body. Self-attention tends to aggravate emotional intensity and to have a debilitating effect on action (Scheier and Carver, 1977; Carver, Blaney and Scheier, 1979).

In summary, bodily activation interacts both with the various possibilities for action, and with the vicissitudes of the future. Generally, if the future is cut off, then there is little bodily activation and little action. If the future is still open, bodily activation is high in the optimism of being able to do something about it; even if, as in anxiety, there is nothing specific that can for the moment be done.

Other modes of representation in emotion

The discussion has so far concentrated on the enactive aspects of emotional experiences. There are also verbal and visual elements that are important in rounding out the full picture. These become particularly important in the more social emotions (as opposed to what might be called personal or interpersonal ones).

News and abuse

The descriptions contain rather few references to speech, considering how much time people normally spend engaged in it. Speech enters emotional experiences in two main ways.

The first is in the announcement of the news which precipitates the emotion, usually in abrupt ritual form: 'X is dead', 'the results are out'.

The second is in abuse, which is normally given and taken in verbal form. This is not speech exactly, but yelling, screaming, the calling of names, and the use of words with venom in them. Verbal abuse may be both a substitute for fisticuffs and a way of publicly humiliating the victim, as in the revenge fantasies of the idle-thoughts study:

> To get to the point my friend arrived just after 10 o'clock. By then I had worked up a tremendous fury – enough to hit her. When she came, I verbally let loose and perhaps embarrassed her in front of the other party – but to be honest, I didn't care.

There are also occasional attempts at civilized clarification, expressions of delight, and prayers, though these are all less frequent than news or abuse.

The abuse typically occurs in retaliation for slights to the social persona, and the verbal is therefore here importantly related to the visual.

Persona

While many of the major emotions in the sample concern life, death and love, a significant group have less worthy objects. These are concerned with the survival of a persona rather than of a person, and they overlap with such self-sentiments as pride and embarrassment.

Anger in particular gets on its high horse when the persona is under threat. Occasionally, legitimate anger is provoked by genuine social injustices; but the vast majority of cases are not of this form. They are versions of the indignation of the visualizer portrait, where injustice to the self is perceived, whether it is there or not. Someone meets a friend to do her a favour and she repays it by being late; someone else tries to help an injured bird, but it refuses to co-operate and keeps frustratingly out of reach. The world should surely repay our good intentions better than this. And then the blood boils, the one person lashes out at the friend, the other abandons the stupid bird to its fate.

Apart from direct insult, which is never really satisfying because one's victim can never grovel quite enough, anger is largely an intransitive perfomance. People bluster, make noise, and talk big. These are all inflationary strategies designed to enlarge the persona. Animals do the same thing by sticking their fur out, standing on tiptoe and looking ferocious; policemen, generals and gangsters (at least in films) do it by wearing padded shoulders (see Eibl-Eibesfeldt, 1971).

Experiences of anger have an interesting relation to the embarrassment episodes of chapter 8. In both, the image that people have of themselves is shaken. In embarrassment people undermine it themselves by doing something silly, and then take the viewpoint of the generalized other against the self. In anger others are perceived as subverting the image, and its paranoid owner-occupier feels called upon to defend it; indeed, to retaliate with vigour. To switch to an objective perspective here can sometimes utterly deflate the anger, or if the switch comes later, can result in the judgment that the rage was entirely out of proportion to the event that instigated it.

Surprise is very often a prelude to anger, and signals that there is something to get angry about. Chance (1980) has recently provided a social analysis of the startle response which is enlightening here. He criticizes the normal assumption that the startle reflex occurs in response to *any* strong stimulus, and suggests instead that it has a particularly social relevance. In human and animal communities with strong dominance structures, members (and especially the underdogs) need to be on the watch for the aggressive behaviour that preserves the pecking order. In the reports of emotional experiences, surprise has all the qualities of an alerting response to what might be attempted humiliations from other members of the social group. Surprise and anger focus on those 'of my clan' and are felt towards those with whom we have reciprocal bonds of expectation. Fear is not so constrained. Those we fear are truly outsiders, though it is possible that the behaviour which, from a stranger, causes fear would only provoke anger from, for example, a lover.

Other emotions relating to the persona are loneliness, which appears to involve a lack of persona; and depression and guilt, both of which tend to follow anger and manifest the need for persona repair (though depression is also a more general 'aftermath' emotion, representing a working through of emotional crises of all sorts).

Anger, loneliness and, to a certain extent, guilt, all operate at the level of social appearances and contain elements of how others see us. They are at least as close to the social sentiments of pride and embarrassment as they are to such rawer animal emotions as fear.

Location

One final visual element which appears very frequently in the descriptions of emotional experiences is not connected with social emotions. This is the environment in which the experience occurred.

There is one trivial reason for this: all experience occurs somewhere, and reference to location is nearly always included when people describe *particular* experiences. There is more to it than this, however: episodes of love and fear both occur in environments, yet these environments are mentioned in only 10 per cent of the descriptions of love, but in 92 per cent of the descriptions of fear. The fact that elements of externalized self-awareness are also most frequent in fear suggests that people may be doing the kind of pain-avoiding psychic ejection encountered in the previous chapter, which may be mediated by attention to the environment.[4] In fear of course there are additional reasons for vigilance, as the environment is where the threats are coming from.

In situations of shock, where the news is too much to take in all at once, people seem to attend to the environment instead of thinking. Those of an appropriate vintage probably remember precisely where they were on hearing of President Kennedy's assassination. Unable to digest instantly such world shattering news, it becomes etched into our memory of where we were at the time, and we can return to the image of this environment in the following weeks and months as a way of returning to the event. Thus the import of what has happened can be gradually assimilated. The location as it were *holds* the emotional experience for us. Interestingly, emotional experiences of less intensity, such as moods, are often described in locative terms: someone may be in a depression, or in a good mood. This may be more than an interesting spatial metaphor.[5]

Agent, experiencer and time

Though verbal and visual elements make some contribution to the structure of emotional experiences, the central features belong to enactive representation. The free-association studies of chapter 3 indicated that the important cases in enactive imagery are those of agent and experiencer. The agent is the initiator of actions; and the experiencer is the subject of feelings. These two aspects of the self are intimately interconnected: agents typically do not act without any motivation, and experiencers typically do not feel outside the general context of action. In this sense, even grief occurs against a background of action, in so far as it indicates the necessity to *abandon* plans for co-action.

Agency and experience mark two different sides of the same coin. The third component of the enactive triad, the future, indicates the nature of the coin they are the two different sides of. It is through reference to a future time perspective that acting and feeling are co-ordinated.

The future here is not in clock time, but in biological time. William James noted that consciousness is forever *streaming*, but this continual movement is not unique to consciousness. It is a property of all biological systems. There is a broader *stream of life*, which includes the stream of consciousness. Living things may be able to lie down and rest for a while, but in general and in principle to be alive is to be in motion, it is to be under way. For neither the stream of life nor the stream of consciousness are we the *prime* mover, responsible for the possibility of movement itself. Of that we are the beneficiaries. In both cases, however, we can take some responsibility for the particular direction of the movements made.

We are born with some propensities for action, reflexes, which usher us towards a more conscious life, and which still underpin that life. These innately based action tendencies mean that we have, as a matter of our biological nature, commitments of particular basic kinds; for example a commitment to life itself, evident in the instinct for survival which surfaces in extreme situations. However, we also have commitments of a more conscious sort, for example, commitments to a career, to another person, or to a belief system. Commitments of both the unconscious and the conscious kinds are important in emotional experiences. Emotions arise at points of crisis for these commitments, when they are negated, or threatened, or about to move ahead.

'Having a commitment' does not mean that there is an entity in some part of the psyche which can be labelled 'a commitment'. Commitments are dynamic, they are *ways of life*. An older literature might have called at least some of them *habits*. But to call eating, or going to work, for example, habits is only to say that people do them repeatedly, and misses the essential meaning of the word.

Being alive means having to do something. It is in this sense that *becoming* is more than the 'waiting' possible to inorganic matter, which just lets time flow past. Becoming belongs to biological time and involves commitments, conscious or unconscious, general or specific, to a way or ways of life. Agency and emotion thus belong to the same ontological domain: they are manifestations of our relationship to time.

Synthesis

Figure 9.3 summarizes the work of this chapter, and also relates the stronger and more enactive emotions with the kinds of feelings involved in visual thinking, and with some of the value judgments involved in verbal thinking.

In all three modes of thought there are both positive evaluations and negative ones. The positive evaluations mark the promotion of a particular kind of meaning, and the negative ones mark the frustration or failure of that meaning.

On the positive side, the enactive emotions of joy, relief and love mark *becoming*; the visual sentiments of pride and peace mark *belonging* (to the social and the natural worlds respectively); and the verbal preferences for the prototypical and for the superordinate mark the points of maximum *order* in the conceptual system.

As regards the negative feelings, there appear to be two alternative possible manifestations of the value judgment. One is active coping, the other is passive feeling; and the difference is largely one of whether attention is focused outwards or inwards.

In some situations it appears to be possible for the person to switch from one perspective to the other, though it is probably also the case that individuals have

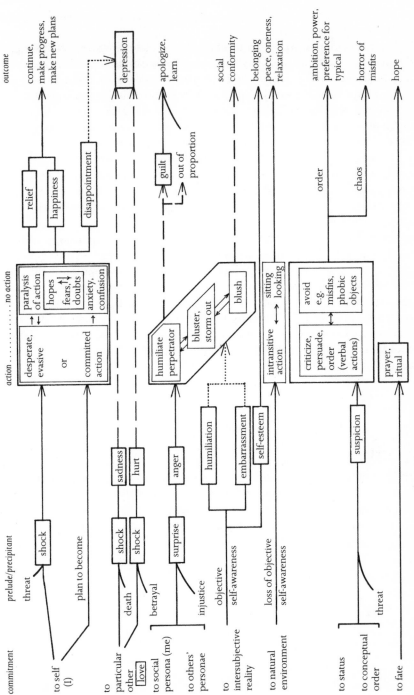

Figure 9.3 Temporal and constitutional analysis of feelings

particular attentional biases, and therefore particular styles of coping with potentially negative emotional situations.

In terror, an emotion with a strong enactive component, we can either simply feel it, usually in a moment of utter paralysis, or we can do something about it. When confronted with a charging bull one is either rooted to the spot, feeling the terror; or one runs like mad, acting it. These two manifestations appear to alternate in many fear-inducing situations. In anxiety, acting has to be done through displacement behaviours, but these *do* effectively channel the jitters that otherwise focus the person's attention uncomfortably on the body.

The visually dominated sentiments of self show a similar dynamic balance between what can be interpreted as the two faces of humiliation: the anger which focuses on the perpetrator and actively retaliates against the humiliation; and the embarrassment which focuses on the self through objective self-awareness, and passively feels the humiliation.

In the verbal realm the fact that there are two kinds of responses to misfits (criticisms in the idle thoughts and phobic reactions in chapter 7) suggests a similar organization. One can either focus outwards and contemptuously criticize what one does not like; or one can concentrate on one's own responses and feel an uncanny horror. A third possibility (suggested by the portraits study) is that people can cope with the uncanny in a ritualistic manner; and this perhaps becomes important as an active coping mechanism when the source of the feeling cannot be derided into harmlessness: in thinking about death, for example, or other eschatological matters.

*

In conclusion: this chapter began with a hypothesis that the stronger emotions might involve enactive elements. This has turned out to be the case, but the truth is inevitably rather more complex than just that. In the course of unravelling some of the complexities of the relationship between emotions and enactive factors, it has also been possible to see how the strong and enactively dominated emotions shade off into the visually dominated sentiments of self, and into the verbally based responses to the elements of the taxonomic domain.

Part 3

Integrations

10

Mind and time

This is nearly the end of the story. All the empirical evidence has been gathered in, and the two chapters of this part of the book attempt to integrate and systematize some of the findings.

The phrase 'integrate and systematize' means a number of different things. At its simplest it means drawing together the various findings thrown up by the empirical work, and summarizing the specific patterns of interrelationships between thought and feeling that characterize each of the three forms of representation. The third section of chapter 10 does this, and in effect provides a summary of the empirical content of the book.

'Integrate and systematize' has another, rather different meaning, which is explored in chapter 11. This arises from the fact that though people may show biases in their thinking, they can in fact use all three modes of representation. This provides an important kind of cognitive flexibility. Verbal, visual and enactive systems of thought construct three different versions of reality, each with its own cognitive constructs and its own set of values. They are, however, integrated into a single unified cognitive system, within which the different versions of reality can be tested against one another and so refined. Chapter 11 looks at this equilibration process, and at how it leads to a deepening understanding of the nature of reality. It focuses on one particular area of thinking: scientific thinking.

The third meaning of 'integrate and systematize' is the most abstract. It involves a re-examination of the kinds of metaphors we operate with in thinking about mind, consciousness and cognitive processes. These include both the specifically psychological metaphors, and the more general and more powerful ones embedded in ordinary language. Only through this re-examination is it possible to come to any general understanding of why thinking should proceed as it evidently does, and of why there should be the systematic relationships between thought and feeling that there evidently are. To describe patterns of relationship between thought and feeling, as the empirical work does, is not to account for how these patterns are possible. The first two sections of this chapter are concerned with some of these general issues.

Metaphors for thought

The intellect loves things. It has a tendency to reify process and quality and make them into things in their own right. This reification is seen in the dominant metaphors we use, both as psychologists and as ordinary human beings, to think about thinking.

The dominant metaphor within psychology itself has the status of a paradigm: it is the metaphor of 'information processing', implicit in which is the assumption that the cognitive processes carried out by human beings can usefully be likened to the processing carried out by computers. There can be no question that this has been both an extremely powerful and an extremely fruitful line of thought. Yet for some of us there remains a profound doubt, and a sense that however good the comparison, there are still important ways in which the minds of human beings do not function like computers.

One way in which a crack in the effectiveness of the metaphor can be explored is to look at the subtle changes that have occurred in the expression of certain mental concepts. In the old days human beings used to think. Now they process information. In some ways the difference is trivial, in other ways it is an indication of a crucial reorientation. Thinking is both process and product. It is not necessary to say that we think thoughts. It is sufficient to say only that we think. In processing information the processing and the information – the process and the product – have been taken apart, as if they could really be separated, into some stuff called information, and a set of processes which could be applied to it. Recent information processing models of memory would talk about representations or networks rather than information, but the same reification occurs. There is a network, and there are processes which act upon it, for example, which activate it, or construct new associative linkages.

The information processing model sets out with dynamic intent, as evidenced by its emphasis on processing, but it settles down into the spatialized depictions of networks; or into the convention of 'flow diagrams', in which there is in fact rarely any flow at all, but only static boxes with articulable content, linked by enigmatic arrows.

It must not be thought that this reification is a consequence of using specifically technological metaphors for thought. William James used a number of naturalistic metaphors, and they succumb to the same tendency. He likened consciousness to a stream; but here again, and despite the dynamic emphasis, it is all too tempting to assume that we are standing at the weir called *now*, capable of looking both up and downstream from it. The streaming has become *a* stream. He also referred to thinking as being like a bird's flight, with an alternation of the relatively static parts, the perchings, and the dynamic, transitive parts, the flights. This fares no better. It suggests that the perches endure in consciousness even when the bird is not sitting on them; and a trajectory has turned into a location.

In other words: infiltrating both technological and naturalistic models of mind, there is a more general and non-specialist one, which is that of mind *as a place*. In this place time has disappeared, and instead there are mental objects of various sorts, with a kind of (mental) spatial extension: memory stores, images, cognitive structures, information, representations and networks. To accuse the reification of mental entities of being the source of problems in the conceptualization of mind is not to do anything new. Ryle (1949), Pylyshyn (1973), Lakoff and Johnson (1980) and Romanyshyn (1982) have all travelled over some of the same ground. This reification causes problems because it smuggles a number of assumptions, some of them illegitimate, into psychological theorizing about mind and about cognitive processes. It assumes, for example, that mental objects, like real ones, continue to exist when we are not looking at them. We have 'learnt' about the mental world what infants in their first year of life learn about the real one: that objects are permanent. In the mental domain the unseen objects, those which are no longer in the focus of attention, still exist, but are elsewhere, stored in memory.

Furthermore, if mental objects exist, then it makes sense to talk of them having a structure, just as real objects may. These structures then become part of the mental furniture, and we are left with the problems both of the precise ontological status of the structures, and of how they relate to the content.

The empirical work of chapter 3 suggested that structures be viewed as descriptions of how thought unfolded in time rather than as entities of however abstract a sort, occupying mental space. In chapter 6 this temporal account was elaborated by likening the thought process to a biochemical process. In the metabolic pathways described by biochemistry, molecules are *transformed into* other molecules; for example sucrose is transformed into glucose and fructose; purines and pyrimidines are transformed into nucleic acids. Similar kinds of transformation occur in physical chemistry, sometimes with startling results. If a small piece of metallic sodium is placed on water, it becomes jet-propelled and rushes across the surface, getting smaller and smaller until it disappears. In this reaction the lump of sodium disappears because it has changed into something else. The changes are described by the following equation:

$$2Na + 2H_2O \longrightarrow 2NaOH + H_2$$

2Na	2H$_2$O	2NaOH	H$_2$
metallic sodium	water	sodium hydroxide	hydrogen gas

Thought involves changes as radical as those of chemical reactions. It is 'metabolic' in the sense that normally no one idea remains in consciousness for long, but evolves into the next idea. Thought must move, and the possible directions for movement are described by cognitive structures. These structures have a status equivalent to the equations describing chemical or biochemical change. In terms of mental events, a representation of a dog, say, does not itself endure in consciousness, but evolves into that of the canineness (object → superordinate), the teeth (subject of attribution → part), or the biting they may commit (agent + instrument → transitive action + patient).

In current information processing models of mind the descriptions – the reified cognitive structures – have acquired a spurious reality, and have been inserted as a functional level behind the phenomenal level. This is the equivalent of claiming that chemical equations lie behind and are the causes of the processes they in fact only describe.

This may be the point at which the conceptual requirements of artificial intelligence part company with those of natural intelligence. Certainly as a model of what human beings do, the insertion of an extra level of information processing has caused considerable problems. For example, it gives rise to such paradoxes as that involved in the claim that the cognitive structures are inaccessible to consciousness (Pylyshyn), when they were in fact discovered by people using precisely consciousness (in the form of linguistic intuition).

A model of human thinking does not need this extra level. Its introduction as the causal level of cognitive processing involves the fundamental error of mistaking a description for the thing it is a description of.[1] Descriptions, unlike real things, cannot cause one another, and so it then becomes necessary to introduce an extrinsic energy into the descriptive level in order to account for dynamic aspects of thought. As was seen in chapter 6, the integration between the descriptions, the reified structures, and the energy can never quite be achieved.

The emphasis on transformation in the metabolic metaphor gives it an advantage over James's stream or bird's flight, which emphasized only change. In transformations the mental entities are not 'conserved', and this provides a defence against the temptation to turn temporal organization into spatial extension. This brace against spatialization opens the way to a conception of mind very different from the assumption that mind is a place. This alternative view sees mind as organized in time rather than space.

Time as the form of inner sense

In The Critique of Pure Reason, written in 1781, Immanuel Kant divides experiences into two general kinds: those presented by 'outer sense', that is, experiences of objects and events in the real world; and those presented by 'inner sense', that is, mental experiences. He questions whether space and time are themselves objects of experience, and comes to the conclusion that they are not. They are rather what underlies the very possibility of experience. Space, says Kant, is the form of outer sense; and *time is the form of inner sense.*

Time being 'the form of inner sense' means that mental processes may borrow some properties from elsewhere, but their fundamental nature, what is uniquely theirs, is temporal. This essentially temporal conception of mind is the logical end-point of the interpretation of cognitive structures in dynamic terms.

Seeing mind as essentially temporal in nature has a number of far-reaching conceptual consequences.

One consequence is that it requires an intentional interpretation of memory. In a temporal view it does not make sense to assume the continued existence of memories when they are not in attention, and the best that can be said is that *we remember*, which is to say that we have some present experiences which *intend* (or point to, or refer to) a past. This makes the problem of memory a problem of intentionality or reference. The question of how one representation in current consciousness intends a real world and another a past world is one not clearly raised by most current models of memory, in which one could never in fact tell the difference.[2]

A second consequence of a temporal view of mind is that cognitive processes must be seen as being irrevocable, with no hedging of transformational bets. Having moved from the representation of the dog to the representation of its brownness, it is not then possible to return precisely to the original dog. Having gone down one mental pathway, thought is committed, and there is no way back. As James said, consciousness is a stream in which no state ever recurs.

The cognitive representations of events are not like stones, scarcely worn away at all by handling. Representations may be 'used up', translated into another form, with the original never afterwards regainable. Even as simple an operation as describing an image changes its form, as Bersted (1983) has shown, so that we can only ever find our way to similar representations, not to the original. This continual translation process may be responsible for some of the inaccuracies of memory. It may also be responsible for the fact that it is possible to 'talk things out'. This has a positive role in catharsis; but a negative one if the idea was originally the germ of a project, and it loses all its peremptoriness through being talked about.

Thoughts do not endure, to be modified while retaining their identity, they evolve into one another. As a higher-level alternative to the metabolic model, the thought stream resembles the life history of a butterfly as it goes through its various stages of development. The egg turns into the caterpillar, which turns into the chrysalis, which turns into the adult butterfly, which, by a complex route, may turn into the eggs of the next generation. From one thing a very different thing can evolve. And when it has, the original is no longer there. When there is a butterfly, there cannot also be the caterpillar from which it developed. Nature is no hoarder, clinging to the past. She is inexorable, letting nothing endure; and in this regard consciousness is not outside her authority.[3]

A third consequence of seeing mental phenomena as organized in time is that it may then be possible to relate them to neural phenomena, which are also organized in time.

For the brain, information involves the passage of impulses from neuron to neuron and from region to region. The static structures are not of themselves informative. Seeing mental phenomena as organized in time may allow connections to be seen between mental and neural levels of discourse, with both being structured in the *same* time.

This opens the possibility of matching neurological pathways to the mental pathways described by some of the cognitive structures. Evidence on the lateralization of function, with speech being subserved by the left hemisphere and spatial (and emotional) processing by the right, has general relevance here, in indicating that different kinds of cognitive pathways may be subserved by different sides of the brain. More specifically relevant is work on the separation between the neural coding of *where* something is and *what* it is. Location coding is carried out at the level of the superior colliculus, part of the midbrain, and the more sophisticated coding of visual attributes is carried out in the visual cortex (Schneider, 1969).[4] Thus two visual structures, object–environment and object–attribute, can be mapped on to specific neurological areas.

This is not intended to propose some form of reductionism, but only to acknowledge that there may be important connections between mental and neurological levels of discourse, and that they may be usefully explored by seeing mind as organized in time, just as brain functioning is.

A fourth consequence of seeing the mind as organized in time is that it makes it apparent why it is so easy to succumb to a spatial metaphor for mind. This has to do with the processes whereby an objective and stable world is constructed on the basis of changing perceptions; and with the fact that the same construction process tends to be applied in the case of changing internal perceptions.

A number of authors, including Hebb (1949) and Piaget, have emphasized the role of eye movements in co-ordinating the representation of perceived objects. It can be hypothesized that these eye movements may reflect not just spatial shifts of attention, but conceptual shifts. We move our eyes around the perceptual world in order to make sense of it, just as we move our mental attention down particular cognitive pathways in order to construe mental objects. It is therefore possible that eye movements represent semantic shifts as well as spatial ones. This would account for Loftus's (1972) finding that the number of fixations on a particular part of a picture has an effect on recall, though the duration of fixation does not.

To see how the originally shifting perceptions become converted into a stable view of an objective world, it is useful to employ an idea from McTaggart. McTaggart was one of the great philosophers of time, who in fact tried to get rid of temporal constructs altogether. He failed in this endeavour, of course, but on the way to so doing he made a useful distinction between two orders of time. There is the temporal flow represented by the time series of future-present-past, in which an event is first in the future, then becomes present, and is then in the past. Here two events are ordered in time because event A comes into experience first, and event B only arrives later. There is also an *atemporal* time series, the series represented by before-after, in which events which were originally experiences in a temporal sequence can later be coded atemporally. In this time series it is always and atemporally true that *A occurred before B.*[5]

In the stream of consciousness it is the time series of future-present-past that is dominant, with mental contents following one another in a temporally structured sequence. This time series can also be presumed to be important in the changing sequence of fixations on objects in the real world. We construct an objective and stable representation of this world by converting the information derived from the temporal flow of experience to its atemporal form.

This is a conversion which is possible for verbal and visual structures, which therefore project stable properties of an objective world. It is not so easy for enactive ones, which tend to remain part of the subjective world. For example, a temporal move from an object to one of its attributes in the flow of attention becomes incorporated into a stable atemporal construction of a reality in which the object possesses the attribute as one of its properties. Similarly, a temporal move from an object to its superordinate is taken to be a reflection of the real-world atemporal relationship in which the object is *a member of the class of*.

No such duality of time series is possible in the case of the actions of enactive imagery. Here the real-world phenomena, the actual actions, are as irreducibly temporal as their internal counterparts. And it is to this irreducible temporality, with its equivalently irreducible subjectivity, that emotions also belong.

The same process that leads to the construction of a stable objective world results in the spatialization of mind when applied to the mental world. The temporal sequence is reified into representations which are seen as imbued with an atemporal stability they do not in fact possess, and the temporal nature of mind itself is converted to the atemporal notion of mind as a place.[6]

There is one last consequence of adopting the view that mental processes and events are structured primarily in time. This is that it allows a very simple way of relating thought and feeling together. Just as emotion and action were related together as the two aspects of temporality in chapter 9, so too are their internal analogues, thought and feeling, related together as the two aspects of the temporality of mind itself.

It is of the nature of consciousness to be continually streaming. Whatever promotes or affords this process is good. Whatever impedes it is bad. Mentally as well as physically it is, simply, good to be alive. And to be alive means to be under way. Positive evaluations are no more, and no less, than an indication that the stream of consciousness is operating in accord with its essential nature. Negative evaluations indicate impediments to that natural flow.

In experiential terms the evaluative poles might be considered to be marked by insight on the positive side and depression on the negative. In insight, thoughts rush headlong after one another and we feel alive and full of energy. In depression we feel sluggish, and thoughts hardly move at all, or do so only in repetitive or incoherent ways.

In general, if attention *can* move, this is good. If it cannot, this is bad. More specifically, if it can move along one particular pathway (described by one particular cognitive structure), this is good in one way. If it can move along another pathway, this is good in a different way. For attention to be able to move from an object to its superordinate category is good in that it indicates order; if it is unable to, we are confronted with fear of the unknown. To be able to say of oneself, I belong in this social milieu, engenders self-esteem; to be unable to locate oneself socially results in loneliness. To be able to put motive or intention into action is eminently satisfying; to be prevented is infuriating or depressing.

By looking at one particular kind of cognitive pathway it is possible to speculate about the dynamics involved here. In chapter 7 it emerged that, in general, people have a preference for typical instances of categories. Furthermore, typical instances of categories are more likely to represent the category as a whole than are atypical ones. Donkeys are more typical animals than spiders or gorillas; they are preferred to spiders and gorillas; and they are more likely to be used as a representation of animals-in-general. The cognitive structure, or cognitive pathway, that is involved here is that of *object → superordinate*. The evidence suggests that some *object → superordinate* transitions are more positively evaluated than others. Specifically, *donkey → animal* is more positive than *spider → animal* or *gorilla → animal*.

These transitions do not preserve the identity of the cognitive content, but transform it into something else, just as biochemical reactions transform their original substrates into something else. In any transformation there may be some part which cannot be transformed, which is not converted into the new representation, but which remains behind as an untransformable residue. The more economical the transition, the more positive the evaluation with which it is experienced. Thus *donkey → animal* is a good transition, because donkey is a prototypical animal and its representation may therefore be easily transformed into the representation of *animal*. *Gorilla → animal* is a less economical transition because gorillas have a number of features which distinguish them from more conventional animals, and these features cannot be translated into the representation of *animal*. The existence of these cognitively untranslatable residua may be what tells us that highly atypical and uncategorizable objects are potential threats. Cognition, as it were, abstracts from reality the parts that it can accommodate, and whatever it cannot accommodate is likely to activate the body in preparation for bolder methods of coping.

Some representations are highly resistant to cognitive translation, and activate the body immediately. Others may be partly accommodated at a cognitive level, leaving less untranslatable residua which activate the body less urgently. The experience of *thing on collision course* is incompatible with the fundamental intention of staying alive, and cannot be further analysed cognitively without endangering life. It thus causes an immediate bodily response. *Ugh, it's a spider* threatens only the cognitive system, not life itself, and the bodily response here is less extreme.

It can be suggested that this transformation of the 'residua' (perhaps represented neuronally as inputs which have not eventuated in outputs), which are left behind after cognitive translations, into a bodily representation, may arise for two rather different reasons. One is that the stimulus itself at least partly eludes cognitive translation, as in the *collision course* and *spider* examples. The other is that the stimulus *can* be cognitively analysed, but the person lacks the time to do so. There would then be residua simply because of the shortage of time for the 'cognitive digestion' process that would complete this unfinished business.

The biological organism could reasonably be expected to deal with the two kinds of residua in the same way, with a bodily response resulting in both cases. This may account for such stress symptoms as the high blood pressure that is the penalty for living a very pressured life, in which there is insufficient time for 'mulling things over'. It may be that in a less pressured life, the day-dreams, fantasies and other idle thoughts of chapter 4 are the means whereby this cognitive digestion process is carried out. These idle thoughts constitute a kind of cleaning-up operation of all those things that could have been thought, but that the person did not have the time or inclination to think in their more directed thought processes.

One way of summarizing the general relationship between thought and feeling is to say that we have a natural *joie de vivre*, a joy in being alive and on the move, which is as true for mental activity as it is for physical. At the level of thought–feeling relationships, the *joie* takes different forms depending on the particular routes followed by the movements of consciousness. Efficient classification gives us a sense of order; seeing ourselves as part of the natural world brings freedom and peace; and putting our motives into action gives rise to the happy sense of becoming the person we wanted to be. Negative feelings of various kinds arise when this natural flow is impeded, interrupted, or held up in some way.

Joie de vivre could be said to be the one principle that underlies all the systematic relationships between thought and feeling that have emerged in the course of the empirical work.

Modes of thought as ways of life

To say that there is a general principle of *joie de vivre* does not say very much about specific relationships between thought and feeling. The remainder of this chapter reviews the particular associations between the different kinds of thought and the different kinds of feelings, as they have emerged in the empirical work. Table 10.1 summarizes the relevant findings.

Table 10.1 Social and evaluative worlds for the three modes of thought

	Mode of thought		
	Verbal	*Visual*	*Enactive*
cognitive structures	rhyme + phrase completion, opposite + superordinate → taxonomic structure	attribute + part, environment + intransitive action → form, location	transitive + conditional action + consequences, affective + affective consequences → action, feeling + motive
general features	dereferentialized language		
what they afford	power + status	appearance to others	self-efficacy
general social orientation	conventional, tradition-directed	social, other-directed	individual, inner-directed
how self is construed	as institutional role (≡ concept)	subject of attribution (appearance + persona + spiritual self)	agent, experiencer
significant others	superordinates, subordinates, opposition	social environment	patients, other agents + experiencers
significant entities	words	physical environment	instruments, resultants
main dimension of cognition and evaluation	ORDER (conceptual)	BELONGING (spatial)	BECOMING (future time)

Table 10.1 Social and evaluative worlds for the three modes of thought (continued)

	Mode of thought		
	Verbal	*Visual*	*Enactive*
zero value (failure to construe)	chaos, misfits	lonely, apathetic, empty	suicidal
negative value	low status	social rejection	inhibition, threats to plans
– – negative feelings	suspicion, fear of failure	embarrassment indignation	fear, anxiety
positive value	typical, superordinacy	at-one-ness (natural), social affiliation	invention, intensity, risk
– – means of achieving positive value	popularity, persuasion, criticism	external self-awareness, collusion	patience, interest, stubbornness, solitariness
– – positive feelings	feeling of superiority	peace, relaxation, pride, self-esteem	joy

It has become apparent that a mode of thought is not just a way of doing something inside the head, it is also what codifies a way of life.

Each mode of thought involves characteristic cognitive structures. These structures describe the kinds of moves attention may make, and determine how the meaning of an object will be construed. This is to say that each mode of thought can be understood as being a way, or, strictly, a co-ordinated set of ways, of attending to the world. Attending to the same object in different ways, using different forms of representation, may have quite different results. Looking at the same object one person might say, 'Yeuch, a bat'. Another might say, 'Look at its funny little claws'; and another, 'I think it's frightened'. All these represent legitimate moves from the original object and thus legitimate and meaningful construals of it: *object → category name* (verbal); *object → part* (visual); and *object → feeling* (enactive). The moves made determine how the particular object is construed, and more broadly, determine a general way of making sense of the world. This sense has both cognitive and affective aspects.

In terms of individual differences, virtually everyone makes some use of constructs from all three domains, but beyond that, individuals may rely to differing extents on one way of making sense of things and on the values that go along with it.

Being human, what we are most concerned to make sense of is ourselves and other humans, and the entries in table 10.1 reflect this. Many of the affective and evaluative complements of the ways of thinking have primary reference to a human context.

Each mode of thought involves a particular way of attending, which in turn affords a general social orientation.

Verbal representation has two important kinds of properties. Its dereferential-ized language, which can play a powerful rhetorical role in social encounters, and its hierarchical structuring. The combination provides the basis for a traditional orientation in which people worry about status and conventional values.

In visual thinking there are also two important properties: an awareness of relationships to the environment (which often has the quality of a social environment); and an ability to analyse objects into their parts and attributes. The combination of the two allows people to take an external perspective on the self and to assess their appearance (parts and attributes) from that perspective. This underlies a general orientation towards social affiliation, in which people worry about what others think of them.

In enactive imagery, action and motive underlie a sense of self-efficacy, which is the essence of the enactive imager.

Each general orientation construes the self and significant others in particular ways.

For verbal representation the self is the equivalent of a concept in a taxonomy, which is to say, a role in a social hierarchy. Relationships with others are seen in the taxonomic terms of superordinate, subordinate and opposition.

In visual imagery, the self is a subject of attribution, made up of a physical appearance, a social persona, and what William James called the spiritual self. One of the most important roles for other people is to lay a stratum of social reality over the physical reality of the environment. We share this intersubjective world with others, and through their eyes both this world and our own social being are constituted.

In enactive imagery, the self is an agent and an experiencer. The same status is probably accorded to others, who may also be the objects or patients of one's own transitive actions. Fillmore's resultant case perhaps also belongs here, representing the products of invention.

Each mode of thought has a central theme which governs both cognitive and evaluative aspects: order for verbal, belonging for visual, and becoming for enactive.

Table 10.1 picks out three values for each of the themes. These are the social equivalents of the logician's three truth values: meaningless, false and true. Meaninglessness results when an entity is not construable within the system, as taxonomic misfits violate order, loneliness signals an absence of persona, and suicidal tendencies threaten to pre-empt any possibility of becoming. If something can be construed, then it may have positive or negative value, and there are emotions appropriate to each.

Within the verbal system, positive value accrues to what is most ordered: the typical and the superordinate. Someone who fulfils these requirements in their own person feels a sense of superiority and of ambition fulfilled. Someone who does not, feels a failure. Order, and one's own status, are maintained mainly through the use of fluent and confident speech.

Within the visual system, positive value goes along with a feeling of belonging to the environment. In the case of the social environment, belonging means being transparent to social meanings, so that others may apprehend the nature of the social world through one's own behaviour. We belong to these others in the sense of being an instrument through which they may apprehend the social reality. To check their social transparency people may use an externalized self-awareness to see themselves as others do, and then mould their persona accordingly. If this process is successful, it brings social desirability and a sense of social value. The penalty for misjudging the matter may be embarrassment and social rejection. People can also feel at one with their physical environment. This involves seeing the self not as figure against ground, but as a small part of a vast and organized natural whole, and it results in a sense of peace and relaxation.

Within the enactive system, positive value attaches to what promotes becoming. People project into the future both an idea of how they themselves want to be, for example through career choices and an idea of projects they want to achieve. Whatever promotes these plans is good. Patience and interest are necessary to bring the projects to fruition, and stubbornness and solitariness may be useful to prevent other people interfering. Achievements are marked by inventiveness and joy. Inhibitions to actions, and general threats to life and its commitments, engender fear and anxiety.

Enactive imagery lives by its wits in a way in which the other two modes of thought do not. Verbal thinking provides a taxonomy as a stable backdrop to particular roles. Visual thinking provides an only occasionally fickle social environment, and, where available, a vast and infinitely accommodating natural one. Enactive thinking presents only a future, which demands of us that we make it real. It provides no ontological place where we may put our feet up and opt out of becoming for a while. This relates to the fact that enactive representations cannot be detemporalized in the way that other representations can, to form part of the construction of an objective reality.

Fortunately the three ways of thinking do not operate in isolation, and most people have some flexibility in moving from mode to mode. Exhausted by the pursuit of projects or ideals, we can turn to social pleasures, or walks in the mountains.

Sometimes shifts between modes are forced by the situation, as when acute fear or threat of pain precipitates a visually based objective self-awareness. This enables the person to look at their suffering or threatened body detachedly, from the viewpoint of the environment. And sometimes shifts between modes may occur simply because each is appropriate for making a particular kind of sense of phenomena. This is considered further in the next chapter.

In summary

This chapter sees a conclusion to the work relating thought and feeling to each other. At the specific level of the three modes of thought, each can be seen as having a major evaluative dimension, which is both an affective and a cognitive concern. Verbal representation is concerned with order, visual imagery with belonging, and enactive imagery with becoming. To account for the relationships between thought and feeling it is necessary to abandon spatial metaphors for mind, and to see mind instead as being fundamentally temporal in nature. This temporal conception has a number of far-reaching consequences. It becomes possible to see how mental events may relate to neural ones; it becomes possible to see the origin of the spatial metaphor of mind, and it becomes possible to see that the general principle relating thought and feeling is very simple: thought, like any other living process, is always on the move, transforming its representations into something else. Whatever promotes these transformations is good, and whatever impedes them is bad. Different kinds of transformation, described by the different cognitive structures, afford different kinds of evaluation.

11

The psychology of science

It has been convenient to consider the three ways of thinking, verbal, visual and enactive, as separate systems. In fact each of us uses all three, even though we may do so in different proportions. The coexistence of the three within a single coherent system is a powerful source of cognitive flexibility. Different ways of thinking construe the same thing in different ways, and the different constructions arising from the three systems can be used to refine one another.

To put it metaphorically, thinking is a creature that moves on three legs, not on one. Two legs may stand still, providing conceptual stability, while the third is lifted off the conceptual *terra firma* and reconstrues its object. This leg can then put its conceptual foot down again in a new position, allowing another leg to move in its turn.

Walking of the non-metaphorical kind is a good mode of locomotion because we have two legs rather than one, which take it in turn to hold still and to move. For this system to work the two legs must be connected, as parts of the same body, and yet operate with a sufficient degree of independence to allow each to move separately from the other.

Thinking, metaphorically speaking, has three legs rather than two, hinged together in the triptych fashion discussed in chapter 3, yet each able to operate with a degree of independence from the other two. It has already been shown that each system of thought constructs its own version of reality, with its own facts and values. While no one construction of reality can be checked against any absolute standard, it is possible to check different constructions against one another, and the discrepancies can be used to reveal how much of the constructions are of reality, and how much is contributed by the projection of human thought processes. The discrepancies can also be used to refine the overall account given of reality, by bringing the different versions into line with one another.

Instead of exploring this equilibration process within the thinking of particular individuals, this chapter explores it within the thinking of a particular community, the community of scientists, and as manifest in the productions of that community, science itself. After all, science does not happen unaided. It is conducted by human beings and marked by their thought processes and their enthusiasms.

It can be argued that it is possible to discern, within scientific activity, evidence of three epistemological strata, each marked by the constructs characteristic of one of the three systems of thought.

Each epistemological approach involves rationally articulating as the nature of reality, what in cognitive terms are the properties of thought. It is convenient to consider this articulatory process as starting with the properties of verbal representations, proceeding through visual, and thence to enactive, though this disguises the fact that the process appears to be more cyclical than linear. Science is not an enterprise that has any clear finishing point, any more than walking is an enterprise that reaches its finishing point when we have moved each leg once.

The verbal stratum: objectivity and basic entities

The scientific mind is like any other system that harvests reality. It first has to select its basic material, separate it from the rest of nature and divide it into portions of manipulable size. The articulation of verbal structures in science provides a logical foundation in which the basic entities are specified and conceptually organized. The set of basic entities defines the domain that the science is about. The basic entities of chemistry, for example, are the chemical elements; those of Darwin's evolutionary biology are the various plant and animal species.

The process of defining basic entities uses a number of constructs characteristic of verbal thought, particularly the differentiations and superordinate relationships that together define the hierarchical organization of classificatory systems.

A classical definition of identity in logic is that *everything is what it is and not another thing*. The cataloguing of 'what there is' is guided by the fact that an entity may be considered as a thing in its own right only if it is discriminably different from other things. Differences are thus important in drawing the lines around the basic entities, and segregating them from one another.

The use of differentiations in this role is clearer in psychology than in sciences where there is less controversy over the nature of the basic entities. An important aspect of the methodology of experimental psychology is that it frequently operates as if what is most real is what is most different from other things. Many experiments are organized around the comparison of experimental and control groups, in search of the grail of p<.05, which, in indicating a significant difference, also indicates a real phenomenon. There is at least one area of psychology ostensibly organized entirely around differences: that branch of personality known as *individual differences*. It is not altogether a matter of perversity that we explore our common humanity by looking at the differences between us. Seeing how we are is not simple, and differences spring to the attention much more easily than similarities do. These differences at least provide a lead into the domain of interest. There is nothing wrong with starting one's science by looking at differences. It would only be wrong to think the matter ended there.

Having made the primary segregations in reality, it becomes both necessary and possible to characterize the basic entities in terms of scientific categories, which are superordinate to the particular individual exemplars of the concept. Basic entities like *the proton*, or *ATP*, or *the nuclear family*, are types, not individuals, and they are thought of in terms of the prototypes that are closest to the category centre, and that best typify the concept.

It is at this level of articulation that social scientists normally worry about, and solve, the problem of objectivity. There is a kind of objectivity which has to do with the fact that superordinate categorizations are ways of binding together a number of individuals, which, despite their diversity, still all count as the *same thing* (Wiggins, 1967). It is this notion of *same thing* that allows one experiment to be seen as a replication of another, and thus allows science to be a communal, shared and, in that sense, objective enterprise; one safe from individual dogmatisms because other viewpoints have to be acknowledged as relevant to the same phenomena.

The definition of identity provided by this level of articulation tells us both what must be invariant and what may vary, while two situations still count as replications of each other. For something to count as a *reinforcement* it need not take precisely the same form in all experiments using it. Very diverse things can usefully be grouped under the common function 'reinforcing' without detriment to the replicability of experimental results.

In some areas the specification of identity has proved extremely elusive. For example, we cannot yet specify what counts as a stimulus for extra-sensory perception. What seem like irrelevant changes in stimulus conditions sometimes lead to unpredictable effects on results. This is an area where we cannot yet say with any confidence what the basic entities are.

The level of scientific activity at which basic entities are specified is also the level at which a nomenclature is generated. This nomenclature has its main reference to the prototype instances of the basic categories. It thus institutionalizes the initial cuts made across reality, and exaggerates the differentiations made between the basic entities. The account of reality at this level tends towards the atomistic, simply because we must chop up nature into symbolically portable chunks in order to get started at all. Once started, we can begin to worry about the aesthetics and the details of the chunks.

Naming brings order to its referents both by shifting objects towards the typical, and by relating them to one another through locating each within the abstract taxonomy of basic concepts. The danger of insensitive nomenclatures is that they, like other forms of dereferentialized language, are prone to ab-use. This is not typically a current problem with the physical sciences, which have, as it were, passed beyond their philosopher's stone and phlogiston stage. Psychology still does have some problems with anchoring its concepts in reality, and in consequence its language is sometimes in danger of degenerating into mere jargon, reliant on interverbal associations for meaning, and occasionally better for displaying expertise to outsiders than for actually doing science. Concerns about the use of diagnostic labels indicate that there may also be ethical problems with a poorly grounded nomenclature.

Though differentiation, categorizing and their attendant language may occasionally lead to rigidity, they do provide a foundation for subsequent developments. Other epistemological approaches may mitigate the crudities of the initial view, but some such primary segregation is always necessary.[1]

The visual stratum: constitution and metaphor

The stratum of knowledge stemming from the articulation of visual structures is interdependent with the level at which basic entities are specified. These entities are now analysed constitutionally in terms of their parts and attributes. This in turn generates a new level of description, as the parts of the original entities may serve as entities in their own right, which are themselves susceptible to the kind of abstract and taxonomic ordering promoted by verbal thinking.

In chemistry Mendeleev produced a taxonomic ordering of the elements on the basis of the physical and chemical properties known at the time. This ordering was the *periodic table of the elements*. The subsequent analysis of atomic structure achieved two things. It provided a structural underpinning for the organization of the periodic table, in terms of the numbers of various subatomic particles constituting the atoms of each element. It also generated a new level of basic entities to be conceptually organized, this time consisting of the subatomic particles rather than chemical elements.[2]

There is always the possibility that the constitutional analysis, instead of supporting the taxonomic analysis, might conflict with it. In psychology, having postulated the existence of three memory stores (sensory-information storage, short-term memory, long-term memory), further analysis of the properties of each (or strictly the properties of the information stored in them), began to suggest that the initial segregation was perhaps not the most useful one, but only an artefact of the methodologies used (see Craik and Lockhart, 1972). The possibility of such conflicts between different levels of construing is important in so far as they may lead to theoretical or practical advances.

Visual imagery also contributes an appreciation of metaphors, from which spring the models used to aid constitutional analysis. A metaphor asserts the similarity of two things in regard to one characteristic, and invites the prospect that there may be other similarities. The investigation of these may lead to a theoretical elaboration of the phenomena. Poetic metaphors operate the same way, using resemblances in one respect, 'Shall I compare thee to a summer's day?', as a springboard for a frequently exuberant exploration of others: 'Thou art more lovely and more temperate'.

All metaphors have limits of appropriateness beyond which they may become absurd. Kekulé's vision of a snake biting its own tail, as a metaphor for the structure of benzene, is limited in so far as snake and molecule share nothing more than circularity. J. J. Thompson's plum-pudding model of the atom was also an essentially spatial metaphor, conceptualizing the atom as a large mass of positive charge in which the negatively charged electrons were embedded as the plums. This was not just a quixotic notion, as it allowed predictions to be made about the spatial relationships between the components of real atoms. These predictions turned out to be wrong, and the plum pudding was dropped in favour of a planetary model; but the virtue of such models is not to be right for all time, only to be useful for some of it.[3]

Some models retain their fecundity over wide areas and considerable time spans, and acquire the status of what Kuhn (1970) called scientific paradigms: the telephone switchboard model of the brain, for example, or the current computer model.

Model making is an essentially playful activity; resembling the make-believe play of children, wherein a cardboard box, through superficial resemblances, may become a boat, a castle, a table or an island. Scientists as much as children get caught up in their metaphors and sometimes find it difficult to see outside them. For example, 'human information processing' concentrates on what human and computer processing have in common. Because computers (typically) have no arms, legs, hunger pangs or love affairs, the significant contribution of actions and appetites to human thinking is largely occluded from the information processing paradigm.

An important aspect of many scientific metaphors is their spatiality. This may be useful in attempting to mirror the spatiality of real objects (as in plum-pudding and planetary models of the atom). However, it may in some cases be misleading, as was seen in the case of the spatialized models of mental processes discussed in chapter 10. For example, it is (or was) convenient to conceive of sensory-information storage, short-term memory and long-term memory as occupying separate boxes in a linear arrangement. In the information flow diagrams used to illustrate this organization, the spatialization of time, though at least explicit, is still misleading. The spatialized format suggests that information is passed along a production line where at each stage something is added, or an interrogation conducted, by extrinsic agents (sets of analysers, executive programs, etc.). Information becomes a kind of inert matter, not in fact informative at all, as all the informativeness is added from without.

Space is an important metaphor in areas other than information processing. In factor analytic techniques, for example, factors are drawn out of the data as dimensions and depicted graphically, though the space here is clearly a metaphoric one.

Spatialization is part of a general propensity, within the visual stratum, to make the abstract concrete. Abstract attributes are conceptually excised from their context, and turned into things in their own right. What is in reality *structured something* is taken apart, as if there could be structures as entities existing independently and alongside the somethings.

Powerful methods of analysis have powerful hazards. Such reifications are probably the natural complement of the constitutional analyses which are achieved within the visual stratum and are its special epistemological contribution.

The enactive stratum: process and the subversion of identity

The temporality which is contracted into the static present and spatialized in the visual stratum is here allowed to stretch out as process. This involves a number of problematic notions which centre on the theme of change.

The ability to represent change itself (rather than its static end-points) develops rather slowly in children (Piaget and Inhelder, 1971); and adults also, from conservatives to philosophers, find change problematic.

Change is, of its nature, subversive of identity. It subverts both the facts and the values of the status quo; and it even subverts the use of language, because the identities and names of objects may change. Yet the theoretical description of change presupposes the very identities which it subverts. We must be able to identify what it is that is changing, and what it is changing to, but we must not worry too much about what we call the entities half-way between.

Change, looked at through the wrong spectacles, may be threatening, incomprehensible, impossible or a paradox.

Rather than accepting the existence of gradual change for which there is evidence, many people apparently prefer to believe in an essentially static universe where change is sudden and magical. Witness the (to my mind disturbing) demand in some parts of the United States for 'creationism' as an educational alternative to the theory of evolution. In evolution the identity, *ape*, is assumed to have gradually given rise to the identity, *human being*. The continuity of this transition is seen by some human beings as subversive of their identity *qua* human. Such continuities violate the sense of moral and conceptual tidiness to be gained from the drawing of firm distinctions between the angelic us and the beastly them.

There is a much discussed philosophical problem of whether the stocking which has been so much mended that no original thread remains is 'the same' stocking. And of more ancient provenance there is Zeno's paradox about how change of another kind – movement – could never occur at all.

Science does not usually get caught up in these essentially philosophical puzzles. Instead, it seeks to elucidate just what underlies the transitions that evidently do occur and which bring about changes of identity. Some aspects of this elucidation have to do with another philosophically problematic notion, that of causality.

One of the themes of Tolstoy's *War and Peace* is a debate over whether historical change is caused by abstract historical forces or by the actions of particular individuals. Tolstoy concludes that it is not a matter of either–or, but of both. The individual is the instrument of the historical forces. The relationship is similar to that between my hands and me when I (or they) plant the cabbages. My hands are the instrument of an action of which I am the agent. A similar arrangement appears to characterize interactions at a physical level, with parts serving as the instruments of interactions which produce changes in the whole. These changes in the whole may include changes of identity.

In chemical reactions, the identity of chemical substances is lost, though the identity of their constituent parts, atoms, remains unaltered. Thus metallic sodium disappears if put on water and an inflammable gas is produced 'instead'. This is not magic, but simply a matter of:

$$2Na + 2H_2O \longrightarrow 2NaOH + H_2 \uparrow$$

| sodium | water | sodium hydroxide | hydrogen gas |

The changes which subvert identity at one level are accounted for in terms of an underlying level of discourse in which entities endure, but become rearranged. In the chemical reaction which consumes metallic sodium and releases hydrogen, the ions (roughly the atoms) remain unchanged, but are shuffled around in new electron-sharing combinations.

Radioactive decay provides another example. Some atoms change their identity through a process known as K-capture. In this a positively charged proton from the nucleus 'captures' a negatively charged electron from the inner or K shell, and changes into a neutron (with the emission of a massless neutrino). Thus an isotope of beryllium (atomic weight 7, atomic number 4) changes to an isotope of lithium (also atomic weight 7, but atomic number 3). Here there is a change of identity at the taxonomic level of elements (from beryllium to lithium) brought about by dynamic interactions among the constituent parts.[4]

In psychology there may be special problems in accounting for change, because here it is typically necessary to deal with constructs and meanings rather than with tangible things. It is also tempting to ask ultimate and probably unanswerable why questions rather than the smaller-scale how questions that would lead to useful theorizing. Why questions of the sort, why do we do what we do? tend to invoke answers which refer to an originating set of instincts, or an original psychic energy, or both. There is then the problem mentioned in chapter 6, of how the active motivating force and the otherwise static substance of our psychic being manage to come together.

The utility of the smaller-scale approach which asks how change occurs, can be seen in more local theorizing, as for example in cognitive psychology, in Neisser's (1967) analysis by synthesis theory of attention. This concerns itself with the process whereby information stored preattentively, in sensory information storage, is recoded through attention into a form with greater semantic content. The lines and angles, which constitute written words at one level of analysis, serve as the basis for the construction of a hypothesis about the nature of the word at another level of analysis. In terms of the conventional segmentations made at the time Neisser was writing, analysis by synthesis was the process whereby information changed from one identity (physical information) to another (words). Interestingly, this change of identity was often seen metaphorically, in terms of a change of location – from sensory information storage to short-term memory – as if visual structures continued to dominate.

The recent appearance of such ideas as that meaning may be represented in terms of procedures (Winograd, 1972; Miller and Johnson-Laird, 1976), or that motivation may be inherently unstable (Apter, 1982), suggest that there may be an increasing trend within psychology towards the constructs of the enactive domain. The interpretation of cognitive structures in chapter 3 as describing temporal organization, and the speculations of chapter 10 suggesting that mind itself be seen in terms of temporality, may also be seen as part of such a trend.

The constructs from the enactive level can feed back into the verbal, so closing the circle. This may be because an effect is noted at one level of discourse, which leads to the definition of some entity as its cause at another level of discourse. For example, it has been observed that if the plasma of hibernating woodchucks is injected into non-hibernating ones, the latter also fall into hibernation. To explain this effect, Peter Oeltgen has recently proposed that there is, in the plasma, a molecule which acts as a 'hibernation-induction trigger' – HIT for short (Baker, 1984; Oeltgen, Walsh, Hamann, Randall, Spurrier and Myers, 1982). Here an effect noticed at the level of the whole animal, hibernation, is used to define the existence of a causal agent, HIT, at another level, the biochemical. In terms of the three cognitive systems, a construct from the enactive domain, causality, is used to operationally pick out an important entity – HIT – which can then be further refined in terms of both verbal and visual constructs.

Equilibration versus cognitive mythology

Articulating the structures involved in the different modes of thought provides three interlocking accounts of reality: *that every thing is what it is and not another thing* (verbal); *that every thing is what it is made up of* (visual); and *that every thing may interact with or even turn into another thing by virtue of what it is made up of* (enactive).

Science is non-dogmatic, in Popper's terms (1945), partly because it makes use of the conflicts between the different accounts to rearticulate one or more levels, and so refine the overall theory.

In accounts given in areas other than science this equilibration does not occur, either because there is not enough evidence to promote it, or because the vested interests in the values of a particular account are too strong to allow it. (Of course even science shows periods of lop-sidedness, when, probably for the same reasons, particular accounts dominate.)

In *The Golden Bough* (1922), Frazer comments that mythological, magical or primitive thinking uses the same cognitive principles as scientific, rational or modern thinking, but involves a misapplication of those principles. It is in fact perhaps less a misapplication than an application that is not balanced by other ways of making sense of the same thing.

Scientific thinking and mythological thinking both use oppositional structures to get their theorizing started. In science the oppositional description is later modified by accounts of other kinds. In mythological thinking the values presented by the oppositional account may be so attractive as to resist any change; also, the evidence that might promote the change may be hard to come by.

When faced with chaos, the first thing that the human mind apparently tries to do is to divide it down the middle into polar opposites. When faced with the problem of cosmogenesis, many systems of thought have seen the primal chaos as being initially organized through the separation of opposites: day and night, earth and sky, sea and land, good and evil, male and female. While the precise constructs vary, the theme is extremely widespread, occurring in ancient Greek, Maori, Hindu, Buddhist, Taoist and Judaeo-Christian traditions (Kirk and Raven, 1966; Eliade, 1976; Hesiod; Lao Tzu; Reed, 1946). It is only these primordial separations that make possible life for what the *Tao Te Ching* calls the 'myriad creatures'. The necessity of the separation is particularly poignant in Maori and Greek myths, where the cosmic progenitors, earth and sky, have to be forcibly separated in order to allow space for their numerous human and other offspring.

This image is remarkable from a psychological viewpoint, since it is indeed only when the two poles are separated and the dimension between them stretched out, that there is the possibility of individuality and multiplicity, since only then does infinite variation (along the dimension) become possible. There is a sense in which nothing could exist prior to these segregations. Faced with the problem of the creation of something out of nothing, or order out of chaos, the extraction of polar opposites provides a perfect beginning.

The difference between a mythological account and a scientific one does not lie in the constructs being used, but in what happens afterwards; in whether the account is amenable to equilibration by other constructs, or remains a projection of cognitive structures, insensitive to the evidence.

Stereotypes are a social version of the mythologizing aspect of oppositional structures. They project a crude version of how things 'should be', according to a primitive oppositional aesthetic. Their power is that they *are* an account of reality at one level, seen through the spectacles which define identity in terms of differences. What they do not do is show sensitivity to the other levels of reality embodied in the same things.

Visual thinking has also projected some culturally important myths.

The visually based capacities for analysing objects into attributes, and for instantiating attributes in objects, have sometimes operated in such a way that what are, in reality, but aspects of a single entity are extracted and reinstantiated in a series of separate other entities. Thus a variety of human emotions and abilities have received celestial embodiments in the pantheons of ancient Greek, Egyptian and Hindu thought. The celestial beings are furthermore supplied with a particular location – a heaven – in which to dwell. This way of thinking survives to some extent in many conventional religions, and forms an important aspect of what is a strong undercurrent to conventional religious thinking, being found, for example, in astrology, and in the mysticism of thinkers such as Rudolf Steiner (1979).

The same sort of mythologizing occurs in psychological claims about *entities* in the psyche (structures, traits, the super-ego, short-term memory, and so on), and in conceptions which see the mind as a *place*, with sufficient spatial extension to accommodate all the entities. The difference between these claims and those of mythology proper is that the scientific ethos values the disputes that alter its conception of reality.[5]

Finally, the enactive myths: at the cosmological level, enactive thinking can be seen as responsible for the notion of a prime mover, the first cause or creator who put the original energy into the universe and started it on its career.

Equivalent prime movers occur in psychology in the form of the instincts or drives that have been employed to account for dynamic aspects of the psyche. Action, for enactive thought, is structured between a motive and a goal. The articulation of such structures as theories of psychological processes may occlude the fact that many of these processes will continue anyway, regardless of particular motives and particular goals. Thought, for example, proceeds as long as we are conscious. We may direct it into particular channels, but we do not need to motivate it or aim it at goals for it to occur. It will happen anyway.

A more personal enactive myth is that where there appears to be a motive, manifest in arousal, there is an automatic need for action. In stressful situations people often feel the need to do something and, within limits, anything, to cope with their emotion. It is conceivable that the proper choice, in at least some of these situations, may not be one particular course of action rather than another, but the choice between acting and the more difficult course of not acting. The argument here is not that the doctrine of quiescence always dictates either the rationally expedient or the morally correct choice, but that in some situations it is worth trying to disentangle the sheer pressure of 'I must do something' from more rational and ethical considerations.

The projection of cognitive processes as mythical systems differs from their articulation in scientific ones, only because in science different versions of reality are accountable to one another, and conflict has a positive value. To the extent that scientific accounting may show particular cognitive biases at one time or another, it too may contain mythological elements.

Cognitive mythologies are not avoidable pitfalls. They are manifestations of the ways in which people make sense of their world, one another, and themselves. It may indeed only be possible to see these mythologizing aspects of thought as pitfalls from the perspective of 'afterwards' or 'from the other side'; and that perspective is not reached by circumnavigation, but only by culturally or individually tumbling in.

Appendices

Appendix A
The third free association study

Participants
One hundred and fourteen students from University College, Cork, fifty seven men and fifty seven women, divided equally into three encoding groups.

Materials
There were forty eight stimulus words as follows: twenty one concrete words representing six large animals (e.g. *lion*), three birds (e.g. *parrot*), three lower animals (e.g. *octopus*), three kinship roles (e.g. *uncle*), three professional roles (e.g. *psychiatrist*), and three blue-collar roles (e.g. *mechanic*); twenty seven abstract words made up of three representing colours (e.g. *green*), three senses (e.g. *taste*), three ideals (e.g. *truth*), three cognitive attributes (e.g. *intelligent*), three emotions (e.g. *jealous*), three months (e.g. *April*), three actions (e.g. *jump*), three sizes (e.g. *wide*), and three non-visual sensory attributes (e.g. *soft*).

Procedure
Students were recruited from the general college population. Each person was given a booklet of which the first page explained that the study involved a free association task. Then followed sixteen practice words with a request for single word or at most short phrase associations. On the second page was a request to use a particular form of representation for the rest of the study:

> *verbal representation* – say each word to yourself under your breath one or more times
> *visual imagery* – get a picture in your mind's eye of what each word refers to
> *enactive imagery* – try to imagine that you *are* whatever each word refers to

All subjects were asked to write whatever came into mind first after they had represented the word as requested. They were asked to try to follow the instructions even if they found them unnatural or tiring. Then followed two presentations of the forty eight stimulus words in different random orders.

Results

The free associations were analysed according to a set of categories generated in response to the data. Table A.1 shows the association types that significantly differentiated between the modes of thought. There were fifty one coding categories in all, only a handful of which differentiated between the three modes. Something over 50 per cent of the associations are 'wasted' here.

Table A.1 Association types in the third free-association study

Association type[1]	Mean associations per person			Mann-Whitney
	Verbal (R)	Visual (V)	Enactive (E)	
rhyme	3.5	0.4	0.5	$R > V^{**}, R > E^*$
phrase completion	4.7	2.3	2.9	$R > V^{**}, R > E^*$
reciprocal role	2.6	1.6	2.9	$E > V^{**}, R > V^*$
superordinate	3.5	2.7	2.0	$R > E^*$
polar opposite	3.3	2.0	2.3	$R > V^*, R > E^*$
environment	3.2	5.3	3.2	$V > R^{**}, V > E^{**}$
attribute	2.8	4.4	2.9	$V > R^*, V > E^*$
part	4.5	5.8	3.9	
instantiation				
– in object	6.9	9.1	6.2	$V > E^{**}, V > R^*$
– in person	2.0	4.0	2.5	$V > R^*$
action	3.5	3.5	6.4	$E > R^{**}, E > V^{**}$
personality/emotion	2.7	3.1	5.7	$E > R^{**}, E > V^{**}$
consequences of action				
– affective	1.0	0.7	2.0	$E > V^{**}, E > R^*$
– physical	1.5	1.3	2.2	$E > V^{**}, E > R^*$

1 Inter-judge agreement 89.5%.
* $p < .05$; ** $p < .01$; N1 = N2 = 38, all tests two-tailed.

Appendix B
The idle thoughts study

Participants
Twenty one people, eleven women and ten men. These were not a random sample but people who expressed an interest in the project. Many were involved in some area of creativity, especially writing. The age range was from late teens to the forties.

Instructions
The Journal of Idle Thoughts asked people to record each idle thought in as much detail as they could, and to include if possible: 1) a note on the form or forms of representation used, and 2) the emotions felt, including both those intrinsic to the idle thought itself and those evoked by the idle thought as a whole (e.g. an enjoyable wallow in an intrinsically pleasurable romantic fantasy might evoke a subsequent sense of shame).

Analysis
A total of 292 idle thoughts was produced (averaging 13.9 per person, range 5 to 31). Of interest here were differences between representational types, not differences between people, and the first step was therefore to divide the total corpus by form of representation. This was done on the basis of both what the person said, and some structural criteria from chapter 3 (references to environments, parts and attributes for visual imagery; transitive actions for enactive imagery). Content categories to describe the emotional and other themes were then generated, and themes related to form of representation as shown in table B.1.

Table B.1 Analysis of idle thoughts

| | Representational type[1] | | | | Composites | | |
| | Pure modes | | | | | | |
Coding categories[2]	Verbal (R)	Visual (V)	Enactive (E)	Combined S tests[3]	Ver–Vis (RV)	Vis–Enact (VE)	Combined S tests
Number of idle thoughts	44	100	29		34	50	
Percentage of total sample	15.1	34.3	9.9		11.6	17.1	
Number of participants producing	17	20	14		18	18	
Context in which idle thought occurred							
dozing	4.6[4]	8.0	0		8.8	18.0	(VE>E)
listening to music	0	8.0	3.5		0	8.0	
studying, at lectures	15.9	7.0	13.8		14.7	12.0	
travelling, in vehicles, incl. driving	4.6	12.0	3.5		5.9	6.0	
walking	11.4	13.0	3.5		14.7	16.0	
Time orientation							
memory	22.7	28.0	3.5	V>E*, R>E*	41.2	18.0	(RV>E)
present	47.7	55.0	79.3	E>R*, E>V*	29.4	62.0	E>RV***, E>VE**, V>RV*
future	11.4	14.0	3.5		11.8	8.0	

Table B.1 Analysis of idle thoughts (continued)

Coding categories[2]	Representational type[1]				Composites		
	Pure modes						
	Verbal (R)	Visual (V)	Enactive (E)	Combined S tests[3]	Ver–Vis (RV)	Vis–Enact (VE)	Combined S tests
Simple/compensatory							
simple, just sparked off by something	52.3	62.0	82.8	E > R**, (E > V)	44.1	72.0	E > RV*
compensating for unpleasant event	15.9	5.0	0	R > E*	32.4	6.0	(RV > E), RV > V*
Contents							
people, one or an enumerable few	29.6	40.0	44.8		58.8	58.0	(VE > R)
groups or crowds	2.3	27.0	0	V > R***, V > E***	35.3	18.0	RV > R*, RV > E**
objects	11.4	28.0	41.4	E > R***	38.2	42.0	VE > R**, (RV > R)
environments[5]	0	49.0	0	V > R***, V > E***	41.2	58.0	{ RV > R***, RV > E* ; VE > R***, VE > E***
Affective themes							
power; physical or social	18.2	18.0	13.8		61.8	34.0	RV > E*, RV > R*, VE > E*
pride; success, self-aggrandizement	13.6	14.0	3.5	(R > E)	44.1	20.0	RV > E*, (RV > V), VE > E*
criticism, belitting self or others	68.2	4.0	0	R > V***, R > E***	61.8	2.0	RV > V***, RV > E***, R > VE***
others views of the self	18.2	30.0	6.9	V > E*	38.2	28.0	RV > E*, VE > E*
– positive; being loved, famous	6.8	20.0	6.9	(V > R)	29.4	26.0	VE > R*
– negative; humiliated, ashamed	6.8	13.0	3.5		14.7	4.0	
– neutral; wondering what others think	4.6	5.0	0		0	2.0	
secrets; kept or revealed	6.8	8.0	3.5		23.5	0	

Table B.1 Analysis of idle thoughts (continued)

| | Representational type[1] | | | | | | |
| | Pure modes | | | | Composites | | |
Coding categories[2]	Verbal (R)	Visual (V)	Enactive (E)	Combined S tests[3]	Ver–Vis (RV)	Vis–Enact (VE)	Combined S tests
morbidity; physical or emotional pain	2.3	15.0	37.9	E>R*	26.5	18.0	RV>R*, VE>R*
sex and romance	11.4	27.0	27.6	V>R**, (E>R)	20.6	38.0	VE>R**
bad language and scatological themes	9.1	5.0	0		14.7	2.0	
feelings	31.8	42.0	65.5	E>V**, (E>R)	47.1	64.0	VE>R**, VE>V***
(a) positive	11.4	28.0	41.4	E>R**	14.7	48.0	VE>R***, VE>V***
– moods, e.g. happy	11.4	19.0	24.1	(E>R)	14.7	42.0	VE>V*, (VE>R)
– towards others, e.g. loving them	4.6	8.0	17.2		2.9	10.0	
(b) negative	22.7	17.0	37.9	E>V*	38.2	16.0	RV>R*
– moods, e.g. depressed	9.1	10.0	27.6	E>V*	20.6	14.0	
– towards others, e.g. hating them	13.6	5.0	10.3		26.5	4.0	RV>V*, RV>E*
human identification; empathy[5]	0	0	31.0	E>R***, E>V***	0	32.0	VE>R***, VE>V***, E>RV***
mythological; supernatural happenings	0	7.0	37.9	E>V***, E>R**	0	28.0	VE>R***, VE>V***, E>RV**
Evoked feelings							
alienation; not my thought	31.8	4.0	6.9	R>V***, R>E*	8.8	2.0	R>RV*, R>VE***
positive; enjoyment	11.4	22.0	10.3		35.3	22.0	
negative; depressed, guilty	15.9	12.0	20.7		5.9	16.0	

* p < .05; ** p < .01; *** p < .001; ( ) p < .1; all tests two-tailed.

1 Idle thought types not analysed in the table were as follows: 2 verbal–enactive composites (0.7% of the total, deriving from two people); 16 verbal–visual–enactive composites (5.5% of the total, from 11 people); and 17 'others' (5.8% of the total, from 10 people).

2 All categories were scored from the viewpoint of the ego. On the reliability of coding categories: two independent judges scored random samples of 50 idle thoughts each. Agreement on particular categories averaged 96% and 94% for each judge with the author, with lowest values 88% and 82%. Taking categories as subjects' gave values for Spearman's r_s of .98 and .97.

3 From Leach (1979).

4 Figures in the main body of the table show what overall percentage of a particular representational type contained each theme. The unit of analysis is the idle thought, not the number of occurrences of theme. This accounts for the non-additivity in the figures; e.g. if an idle thought contained both positive and negative feelings it was still only scored once in the superordinate feelings category.

5 Environments also served as a visual criterion; identifying with other entities (the human identification category, and some instances of mythological themes) also served as enactive criteria. Figures are included here as they are still of thematic interest.

Appendix C
The Modes of Thought Questionnaire (MOTQ)

When we try to hold an idea in our minds we usually find that it naturally leads to some other associated idea. This questionnaire is on such associations between ideas, and in particular looks at whether thinking about the same idea in different ways will lead to different associations.

The experiment consists of pairs of items; for each pair you are asked to think about the first item in one of three ways – either (i) to *see* a picture in your mind's eye; (ii) to *say* the word or words to yourself under your breath; or (iii) to *be* the thing – to imagine that you are who or whatever the idea expresses. You are then asked to assess the likelihood of the second idea coming along sooner or later in association to the first.

Here are three practice pairs, with explanations of what to do:

(A)   *see*   TRAIN – – – – – station . . .   (   )

Get a picture in your mind's eye of a *train*, allow ideas to come to mind in association with it, and then assess the likelihood of *station* being among them. The rating scale to use is as follows:

(1) no likelihood – wouldn't have thought of the second idea at all if it hadn't been suggested.
(2) unlikely – but it would perhaps come along in the end.
(3) eventually – not immediate but it would come along after some thought.
(4) likely – it would be in the first few ideas.
(5) certain – it would be the first idea that would come to mind.

Enter a number from 1 to 5 in the brackets following *station* to indicate your choice. These ratings are purely personal – there are no 'right' or 'wrong' answers, so just trust your intuition.

(B) *be*   SCIENTIST – – – – – apparatus . . .   (   )

Imagine that you are a *scientist*, allow ideas to come to mind in association with this imagined role play; then rate *apparatus* for its likelihood of being among them.

(C) *say*   TABLE – – – – – chair . . .   (   )

Say the word *table* to yourself under your breath, allow ideas to come to mind in association with it, and then rate *chair* for its likelihood of being among them.

Since the experiment is on different ways of thinking, it is important that you do your best to follow the instructions about saying, seeing and being, even if you sometimes find it difficult. You may find that it helps to close your eyes to think about each pair of ideas.

Here are three more practice pairs:

(D) *be*   CLOWN – – – – – laughter . . .   (   )
(E) *say*   LUGGAGE – – – – – baggage . . .   (   )
(F) *see*   BUS – – – – – bus stop . . .   (   )

You should now be ready to go on to the main questionnaire.

PLEASE TRY NOT TO MISS ANY PAIRS OF ITEMS OUT.

Many thanks for your help.

THE SCALE:

no	unlikely	eventually	likely	certain
(1)	(2)	(3)	(4)	(5)

For the first group *say* the first item of each pair

1) *say*   SCARLET – – – – – fever . . .   (   )
2) *say*   IN – – – – – out . . .   (   )
3) *say*   FLOPPY – – – – – rag doll . . .   (   )
4) *say*   HAPPY – – – – – sad . . .   (   )
5) *say* ⋅ LEAP – – – – – year . . .   (   )
6) *say*   FAT – – – – – thin . . .   (   )
7) *say*   CORPORAL – – – – – punishment . . .   (   )
8) *say*   SOFT – – – – – hard . . .   (   )

For the next group *see* the first item in each pair

9)   *see*   TRUCK – – – – – reversing . . .   (   )
10) *see*   REINDEER – – – – – forest . . .   (   )

11)	*see*	BOWL – – – – – round . . .	(	)
12)	*see*	DANCER – – – – – pirouetting . . .	(	)
13)	*see*	LLAMA – – – – – woolly . . .	(	)
14)	*see*	ROLLING – – – – – stone . . .	(	)
15)	*see*	GALLEON – – – – – sailing . . .	(	)
16)	*see*	GLASS – – – – – transparent . . .	(	)

For the next group *be* the first item in each pair

17)	*be*	GREEDY – – – – – tummy ache . . .	(	)
18)	*be*	FOX – – – – – calculating . . .	(	)
19)	*be*	CLIMBING – – – – – fall . . .	(	)
20)	*be*	OSTRICH – – – – – foolish . . .	(	)
21)	*be*	WAVES – – – – – erosion . . .	(	)
22)	*be*	COCKROACH – – – – – dark . . .	(	)
23)	*be*	SECRETARY – – – – – could kick boss . . .	(	)
24)	*be*	VULTURE – – – – – culture . . .	(	)

For the next group *see* the first item in each pair

25)	*see*	BOAT – – – – – mast . . .	(	)
26)	*see*	CAT – – – – – stretching . . .	(	)
27)	*see*	LAMP-POST – – – – – street . . .	(	)
28)	*see*	GOBLET – – – – – doublet . . .	(	)
29)	*see*	PENSIONER – – – – – strolling . . .	(	)
30)	*see*	ARMCHAIR – – – – – living room . . .	(	)
31)	*see*	HAIRBRUSH – – – – – bristles . . .	(	)
32)	*see*	ELEPHANT – – – – – grey . . .	(	)

For the next group *say* the first item in each pair

33)	*say*	SPIDER – – – – – insect . . .	(	)
34)	*say*	WIDE – – – – – narrow . . .	(	)
35)	*say*	WHALE – – – – – blow-hole . . .	(	)
36)	*say*	BIG – – – – – small . . .	(	)
37)	*say*	HOUR – – – – – time . . .	(	)
38)	*say*	UP – – – – – down . . .	(	)
39)	*say*	SCHOOLCHILD – – – – – fights friend . . .	(	)
40)	*say*	GROCER – – – – – green . . .	(	)

For the next group *be* the first item in each pair

41)	*be*	WIDOWER – – – – – lost . . .	(	)
42)	*be*	CRUMPLED – – – – – litter . . .	(	)
43)	*be*	DROPPING SOMETHING – – – – – broken . . .	(	)
44)	*be*	GARDENER – – – – – gentle . . .	(	)

45) *be*   TASTING – – – – pleasure . . .   ( )
46) *be*   SQUID – – – – – could strangle prey . . .   ( )
47) *be*   STUMBLING – – – – – embarrassment . . .   ( )
48) *be*   SWAN – – – – – defends nest . . .   ( )

For the next group *say* the first item in each pair

49) *say* COCKROACH – – – – – beetle . . .   ( )
50) *say* FAST – – – – – slow . . .   ( )
51) *say* SOFT – – – – – cushion . . .   ( )
52) *say* WINTER – – – – – tale . . .   ( )
53) *say* ABSTRACT – – – – – concrete . . .   ( )
54) *say* NIECE – – – – – piece . . .   ( )
55) *say* GOLDFISH – – – – – fish . . .   ( )
56) *say* NICE – – – – – nasty . . .   ( )

For the next group *be* the first item in each pair

57) *be*   LUNATIC – – – – – suspicious . . .   ( )
58) *be*   CAUGHT – – – – – guilty . . .   ( )
59) *be*   WORKMAN – – – – – trudging . . .   ( )
60) *be*   SPIDER – – – – – industrious . . .   ( )
61) *be*   SPOTTY – – – – – shyness . . .   ( )
62) *be*   POURING – – – – – full . . .   ( )
63) *be*   ALLIGATOR – – – – – malevolent . . .   ( )
64) *be*   LION – – – – – stalks antelope . . .   ( )

For the next group *see* the first item in each pair

65) *see* POLICEMAN – – – – – patrolling . . .   ( )
66) *see* PAINTING – – – – – gallery . . .   ( )
67) *see* VULTURE – – – – – swooping . . .   ( )
68) *see* TIGER – – – – – cat . . .   ( )
69) *see* METAL – – – – – shiny . . .   ( )
70) *see* FLANNEL – – – – – basin . . .   ( )
71) *see* LINER – – – – – funnel . . .   ( )
72) *see* LEAVES – – – – – fluttering . . .   ( )

For the next group *say* the first item in each pair

73) *say* BLUE – – – – – blooded . . .   ( )
74) *say* JULY – – – – – summer . . .   ( )
75) *say* FLEET – – – – – meet . . .   ( )
76) *say* NORTH – – – – – south . . .   ( )
77) *say* GRIN – – – – – bear it . . .   ( )
78) *say* FATHER – – – – – could carry daughter . . .   ( )

79) *say* ALUMINIUM ----- metal ...   (   )
80) *say* FUTURE ----- past ...   (   )

For the next group *see* the first item in each pair

81) *see* COTTONWOOL ----- fluffy ...   (   )
82) *see* FACE ----- nose ...   (   )
83) *see* WEASEL ----- easel ...   (   )
84) *see* SEA ----- grey-green ...   (   )
85) *see* HEDGEHOG ----- foraging ...   (   )
86) *see* BUTTERFLY ----- garden ...   (   )
87) *see* KETTLE ----- spout ...   (   )
88) *see* TOWEL ----- bathroom ...   (   )

For the next group *be* the first item in each pair

89) *be* PUSHING ----- topple ...   (   )
90) *be* EAGLE ----- could clean eyrie ...   (   )
91) *be* TIPPLING ----- confused ...   (   )
92) *be* TASTE ----- waste ...   (   )
93) *be* BEAR ----- could rob bees' nest ...   (   )
94) *be* TOY ----- sandpit ...   (   )
95) *be* LEOPARD ----- catches gazelle ...   (   )
96) *be* DRIVER ----- could threaten traffic warden ...   (   )

For the next group *see* the first item in each pair

97) *see* TALL ----- see over ...   (   )
98) *see* HANDKERCHIEF ----- square ...   (   )
99) *see* TREE ----- twigs ...   (   )
100) *see* PENCIL ----- thin ...   (   )
101) *see* PONY ----- trotting ...   (   )
102) *see* SMOOTH ----- sheets ...   (   )
103) *see* POLITICIAN ----- worried ...   (   )
104) *see* WHEEL ----- turning ...   (   )

For the next group *say* the first item in each pair

105) *say* SPEECH ----- reach ...   (   )
106) *say* WATER ----- liquid ...   (   )
107) *say* CALM ----- turbulent ...   (   )
108) *say* AIR ----- tight ...   (   )
109) *say* DIRTY ----- clean ...   (   )
110) *say* DRUNKARD ----- could hug lamp-post ...   (   )
111) *say* GROSS ----- negligence ...   (   )
112) *say* SOUGHT ----- taught ...   (   )

For the next group *be* the first item in each pair

113)	*be*	TRAVELLING — — — — arrived . . .	( )
114)	*be*	YELLOW — — — — banana . . .	( )
115)	*be*	CYCLIST — — — — wary . . .	( )
116)	*be*	BEAVER — — — — gnaws tree trunk . . .	( )
117)	*be*	OBLITERATING — — — — gone . . .	( )
118)	*be*	BEREFT — — — — miserable . . .	( )
119)	*be*	RACEHORSE — — — — nervousness . . .	( )
120)	*be*	JELLYFISH — — — — could tickle someone . . .	( )

For the next group *say* the first item in each pair

121)	*say*	ABLE — — — — bodied . . .	( )
122)	*say*	CATCH — — — — hatch . . .	( )
123)	*say*	BROWN — — — — jersey . . .	( )
124)	*say*	HIGH — — — — low . . .	( )
125)	*say*	FREEDOM — — — — of speech . . .	( )
126)	*say*	DRY — — — — wet . . .	( )
127)	*say*	KILO — — — — weight . . .	( )
128)	*say*	REGAL — — — — legal . . .	( )

For the next group *see* the first item in each pair

129)	*see*	BUSH — — — — green . . .	( )
130)	*see*	JACKET — — — — buttons . . .	( )
131)	*see*	PIANIST — — — — concert hall . . .	( )
132)	*see*	SPARROW — — — — nesting . . .	( )
133)	*see*	SKYSCRAPER — — — — tall . . .	( )
134)	*see*	GYMNAST — — — — bending . . .	( )
135)	*see*	FALLING — — — — bruises . . .	( )
136)	*see*	OCTOPUS — — — — tentacles . . .	( )

For the next group *be* the first item in each pair

137)	*be*	END — — — — beginning . . .	( )
138)	*be*	SLICING — — — — small pieces . . .	( )
139)	*be*	DONKEY — — — — carries children . . .	( )
140)	*be*	ATHLETE — — — — determined . . .	( )
141)	*be*	JACKAL — — — — tears carcase . . .	( )
142)	*be*	OX — — — — placidity . . .	( )
143)	*be*	SLAMMING — — — — noise . . .	( )
144)	*be*	CAMEL — — — — arrogant . . .	( )

For the next group *see* the first item in each pair

145)	*see*	BOAT — — — — harbour . . .	( )

146)	see	KANGAROO – – – – – leaps fence . . .	( )
147)	see	BUSINESSMAN – – – – – office . . .	( )
148)	see	HEDGEHOG – – – – – snout . . .	( )
149)	see	CHILDREN – – – – – playing . . .	( )
150)	see	CAR – – – – – steering wheel . . .	( )
151)	see	CLIMB – – – – – stairs . . .	( )
152)	see	BALL – – – – – spherical . . .	( )

For the next group *be* the first item in each pair

153)	be	HAMSTER – – – – – could nibble fingers . . .	( )
154)	be	SWIMMING – – – – – shivering . . .	( )
155)	be	TEACHER – – – – – chastizes pupil . . .	( )
156)	be	FORCED MARCH – – – – – exhausted . . .	( )
157)	be	SEAGULL – – – – – could divebomb people . . .	( )
158)	be	WITCH – – – – – empties cauldron . . .	( )
159)	be	SOPRANO – – – – – meccano . . .	( )
160)	be	TELEPHONIST – – – – – curious . . .	( )
161)	be	LAZY – – – – – failure . . .	( )
162)	be	STRONG – – – – – carry . . .	( )

For the next group *say* the first item in each pair

163)	say	COAL – – – – – fuel . . .	( )
164)	say	LOBSTER – – – – – pot . . .	( )
165)	say	SHARP – – – – – blunt . . .	( )
166)	say	EAST – – – – – direction . . .	( )
167)	say	SHEEP – – – – – timidity . . .	( )
168)	say	FIT – – – – – as a fiddle . . .	( )
169)	say	LONG – – – – – short . . .	( )
170)	say	TRADE – – – – – economics . . .	( )

Please rate how easy you found it, generally, to follow the instructions as regards *see*, *be* and *say*. Circle the appropriate numbers on the scales given below:

	very hard	quite hard	medium	quite easy	very easy
see:	1	2	3	4	5
be:	1	2	3	4	5
say:	1	2	3	4	5

And now, please rate how enjoyable you found these three ways of thinking:

	very unpleasant	quite unpleasant	medium	quite enjoyable	very enjoyable
see:	1	2	3	4	5
be:	1	2	3	4	5
say:	1	2	3	4	5

Scoring the MOTQ

The MOTQ takes 20–30 minutes for most people (students) to complete. It may not be appropriate for much younger, or for less intelligent people.

It is scored as follows: there are 13 structural subscales, where the items are preceded by a representational instruction appropriate to the mode.

Verbal subscales
Phrase completion (thirteen items) Questionnaire item numbers: 1, 5, 7, 40, 52, 73, 77, 108, 111, 121, 125, 164, 168.
Rhyme (six items) 54, 75, 105, 112, 122, 128.
Opposite (eighteen items) 2, 4, 6, 8, 34, 36, 38, 50, 53, 56, 76, 80, 107, 109, 124, 126, 165, 169.
Superordinate (eleven items) 33, 37, 49, 55, 74, 79, 106, 127, 163, 166, 170.

Visual subscales
Environment (ten items) 10, 27, 30, 66, 70, 86, 88, 131, 145, 147.
Attribute (twelve items) 11, 13, 16, 32, 69, 81, 84, 98, 100, 129, 133, 152.
Intransitive action (fourteen items) 9, 12, 15, 26, 29, 65, 67, 72, 85, 101, 104, 132, 134, 149.
Part (ten items) 25, 31, 71, 82, 87, 99, 130, 136, 148, 150.

Enactive subscales
Consequence (nine items) 21, 43, 62, 89, 113, 117, 138, 143, 162.
Affective consequence (ten items) 17, 45, 47, 58, 61, 91, 118, 154, 156, 161.
Affective (fourteen items) 18, 20, 22, 41, 44, 57, 60, 63, 115, 119, 140, 142, 144, 160.
Transitive action (eight items) 48, 64, 95, 116, 139, 141, 155, 158.
Conditional action (eight items) 23, 46, 90, 93, 96, 120, 153, 157.

Cross-modal scale
The cross-modal scale, for use in controlling response bias, uses representational instructions crossed with cognitive structures.
Cross-modal scale (twenty four items) 14, 28, 68, 83; 24, 92, 137, 159; 3, 35, 51, 123; 42, 59, 94, 114; 39, 78, 110, 167; 97, 103, 135, 146.

Ease and *enjoyment* of the three ways of thinking are assessed by the last six questionnaire items.
Buffer items 19, 102, 151.

*

Mode scales
Sum of the means of the relevant subscales times 10. There is one exception to this, which is that we have normally omitted the superordinate subscale from the verbal mode score, as it loads also on the visual factor, see table C.2.

Development of the MOTQ
The version of the MOTQ presented here is the successor to five previous versions. The immediate predecessor involved twenty items on each of fourteen structural subscales. One subscale (instantiations) was eliminated as unreliable, and the others cut down by item analysis to their current lengths. The cross-modal scale was constructed at this stage by using the most reliable of the eliminated items (eight from verbal, eight from visual and eight from enactive subscales), and systematically changing their representational instructions.

The final version of the MOTQ was given to 358 people (181 men and 177 women) to assess internal reliability. Part of this sample (forty-eight people) took the MOTQ again after a seven-week interval to assess test–retest reliabilities. The results are shown in table C.1.

Principal axis factor analysis on the subscale totals for the sample of 358 people (Varimax rotation, using the SPSS package of Nie, Hull, Jenkins, Steinbrenner and Bent, 1975) gave only three factors with eigen values greater than one, which accounted between them for 66.2 per cent of the variance. The rotated factors could be clearly labelled in representational terms (see table C.2). The only major problem arises with the superordinate subscale which loads higher on the visual factor than on the verbal one. This is presumably a reflection of the fact that what superordinate class an object falls into (verbal) is often judged on the basis of what parts and attributes it has (visual). It seems likely that the superordinate subscale assesses something unique to verbalizing, along with something shared with visualizing. The relatively low test–retest reliability (.47) may indicate some drifting between modes over time. The superordinate items use a verbal instruction, and the subscale is treated as a verbal subscale when particular structures are concerned; but it does not contribute to the general verbal mode score.

The factor analysis indicates that while the highest loading subscales on each factor are those appropriate to the relevant mode of representation, other subscales also load significantly, particularly in the case of visual and enactive subscales. A similar relationship emerges in the pattern of intercorrelations

Table C.1 Reliabilities of the Modes of Thought Questionnaire subscales

Scale description	Instruction	N of items	Example item		Cronbach's alpha (N = 358)	Test–retest (7-week interval) N = 48)
opposite	verbal	18	say	WIDE – – – – narrow	.91	.74
phrase completion	verbal	13	say	SCARLET – – – – fever	.76	.80
rhyme	verbal	6	say	REGAL – – – – legal	.82	.69
superordinate	verbal	11	say	ALUMINIUM – – – – metal	.76	.47
environment	visual	10	see	BOAT – – – – harbour	.69	.55
attribute	visual	12	see	HANDKERCHIEF – – – – square	.74	.73
intransitive action	visual	14	see	PENSIONER – – – – strolling	.71	.63
part	visual	10	see	KETTLE – – – – spout	.71	.65
consequence	enactive	9	be	OBLITERATING – – – – gone	.69	.58
affective consequence	enactive	10	be	GREEDY – – – – tummy ache	.65	.65
affective	enactive	14	be	TELEPHONIST – – – – curious	.74	.67
transitive action	enactive	8	be	LEOPARD – – – – catches gazelle	.70	.72
conditional action	enactive	8	be	SECRETARY – – – – could kick boss	.53	.64
cross-modal		24	say / see / be	SHEEP – – – – timidity (affective) / WEASEL – – – – easel (rhyme) / TOY – – – – sandpit (environment)	.78	.73

verbal mode[1] = (opp./18 + phrase/13 + rhy./6) × 10
visual mode = (envir./10 + attrib./12 + intrans./14 + part/10) × 10
enactive mode = (conseq./9 + aff. conseq./10 + affect./14 + trans./8 + condit./8) × 10

					.83	.84
					.88	.69
					.89	.76

1 In calculating mode scores, equal weight is given to the constituent subscales.

between the mode scores, with correlations being reduced, though in the case of the visual–enactive relationship not eliminated, by partialling out the cross-modal scores (see table C.3).

Sex differences on the MOTQ scales, and differences between students 'in different faculties, are shown in tables C.4 and C.5.

Table C.2   Rotated factor matrix of MOTQ subscales (Varimax rotation, N = 358)

Subscale	Factor 1 (Visual)	Factor 2 (Enactive)	Factor 3 (Verbal)
opposite	.175	−.082	.478
phrase completion	.239	.216	.553
rhyme	−.009	.223	.532
superordinate	.518	.232	.269
environment	.761	.267	.229
attribute	.727	.325	.080
intransitive action	.708	.386	.155
part	.725	.296	.228
consequence	.455	.533	.315
affective consequence	.429	.598	.167
affective	.362	.786	.032
transitive action	.334	.683	.166
conditional action	.232	.698	.209
cross-modal	.341	.514	.570

Table C.3   Intercorrelations of MOTQ mode scales (N = 358)

Pearson correlations

	Verbal	Visual	Enactive
Verbal		.35***	.37***
Visual			.70***

Controlling for cross-modal scores

	Verbal	Visual	Enactive
Verbal		.07	.02
Visual			.52***

*** p < .001.

Table C.4   MOTQ subscale and mode scores: means and standard deviations for men and women

subscale	N of items	All (N = 358) mean	SD	Men (N = 181) mean	SD	Women (N = 177) mean	SD	t-tests between sexes
opposite	18	70.2	12.2	69.2	11.8	71.2	12.6	
phrase completion	13	43.1	8.0	42.9	6.8	43.4	9.0	
rhyme	6	12.7	4.8	12.3	4.5	13.0	5.2	
superordinate	11	39.2	6.5	39.3	6.4	39.1	6.5	
environment	10	37.0	5.3	36.5	4.8	37.5	5.8	
attribute	12	43.2	7.0	42.2	6.8	44.3	7.1	women > men**
intransitive act	14	50.0	6.8	49.1	6.5	50.2	7.0	
part	10	35.3	5.8	34.8	5.4	35.7	6.1	
consequence	9	30.0	5.5	30.1	5.1	28.9	5.7	men > women*
affective conseq.	10	31.7	5.9	30.8	5.8	32.6	5.9	women > men**
affective	14	40.3	8.3	40.0	8.3	40.6	8.2	
transitive action	8	23.8	5.5	24.6	5.3	23.1	5.7	men > women**
conditional action	8	17.9	4.9	18.2	4.6	17.7	5.2	
cross-modal	24	61.4	10.6	61.0	9.3	61.9	11.7	

Mode scales

Verbal (R)		93.2	15.5	91.9	13.4	94.7	17.3	
Visual (V)		143.8	18.9	141.6	17.5	146.0	20.1	women > men*
Enactive (E)		145.3	25.6	146.1	24.5	144.5	26.7	
paired t-tests within sexes[1]				E > V*		V > E*		

* $p < .05$; ** $p < .01$; all tests two-tailed.   1 Paired t-tests between modes carried out on standardized scores.

Table C.5   Cognitive biases by faculty

	Total sample	Arts (A)	Commerce (C)	Engineer. (G)	Soc. sci. (S)	t-tests between faculties
Men N =	181	29	27	101	24	
Verbal (R)	91.9	92.6	92.5	90.7	95.2	
Visual (V)	141.6	140.6	136.8	143.0	142.4	
Enactive (E)	146.1	146.9	137.7	148.3	145.0	G > C*
paired t-tests within faculties[1]				E > R**		
Women N =	172	94	13	17	48	
Verbal	94.7	94.2	100.1	99.2	92.6	
Visual	146.0	146.3	133.6	143.8	148.8	A > C*
Enactive	144.5	143.6	134.8	149.7	145.0	
paired t-tests within faculties		V > E**	R > E*			
All N =	353	123	40	118	72	
Verbal	93.2	93.8	95.0	91.5	93.4	
Visual	143.8	145.0	135.8	143.1	146.6	A > C**, S > C*, G > C*
Enactive	145.3	144.3	136.8	148.5	145.0	G > C**
paired t-tests within faculties			R > V**	E > R*		
			R > E*	E > V*		

* $p < .05$; ** $p < .01$; all tests two-tailed.   1 Paired comparisons on standardized scores.

Appendix D
Cognitive correlates of the MOTQ

The tests used in conjunction with the MOTQ were as follows: the Betts Questionnaire upon Mental Imagery (the QMI, in Sheehan's 1967 version); the Gordon Test of Visual Imagery Control (the TVIC, in the modified form given by Richardson, 1969); Pettigrew's (1958) test for category width; Divergent thinking (uses of three objects in 10 minutes and scored for fluency, taken from Hudson, 1966); the Spatial Ability section of the Differential Aptitudes Test (the DAT of Bennett, Seashore and Wesman, 1974; because of time limitations, only the first thirty items were used, with time proportionately decreased); and the General Aptitude Test Battery (the GATB; United States Employment Service, 1970) which contains seven subtests: 1) Clerical speed and accuracy, 2) Computation, 3) Space manipulation, 4) Vocabulary, 5) Tool matching, 6) Arithmetic reasoning, and 7) Form matching. Parts 3 and 7 (Space manipulation and Form matching) both require spatial transformations, part 5 (Tool matching) uses visual stimuli but is a straightforward matching task that does not require spatial transformations.

Participants
It was not possible to give all the above tests to a single group of people, and different subgroups contributed to the total pool of results as follows:
Commerce students (27 men and 13 women): MOTQ with Betts QMI, Gordon's TVIC, Pettigrew's category width and Divergence.
Arts (94 women and 27 men): MOTQ with QMI, TVIC and Pettigrew.
Engineers (101 men and 17 women): MOTQ with QMI and TVIC.

Arts two (105 women and 36 men): MOTQ with the DAT spatial abilities test.
Management trainees (56 men and 17 women): MOTQ with the GATB.

Results

Table D.1 shows the significant results of correlations between the MOTQ scales and other cognitive variables, with the MOTQ cross-modal scores partialled out. Straightforward Pearson correlations showed a similar pattern of results, but at generally lower levels of significance. The main body of the table shows results for the total sample, as preliminary analyses by sex showed that this did little violence to most of the data. However, there *are* sex differences on the spatial-ability tests, and results of these are also shown for men and women separately. Though statistically significant, many of the correlations are low, and make most sense discussed as indicative of general patterns of cognitive activity.

Table D.1 Cognitive correlates of the MOTQ scales (Controlling for cross-modal scores)

		N[1]	Verbal subscales				Visual subscales			
			Opp.	Phrase	Rhyme	Super.	Envir.	Attrib.	Intrans.	Part
Betts[2] visual		223					$-.23^c$	$-.26^c$	$-.25^c$	$-.22^c$
auditory							$-.20^b$	$-.16^b$	$-.19^b$	$-.16^a$
touch						$-.15^a$	$-.17^a$	$-.19^b$	$(-.11)$	$(-.12)$
action							$-.22^c$	$-.24^c$	$-.19^b$	$-.19^b$
taste						$-.19^b$	$(-.13)$	$-.15^a$	$(-.11)$	$(-.13)$
smell										
organic							$(-.12)$	$(-.11)$		
Betts total						$-.15^a$	$-.22^b$	$-.24^c$	$-.18^b$	$-.17^a$
Gordon TVIC		223						$(.13)$	$(.13)$	
Pettigrew		94						$(.19)$	$.20^a$	$(.19)$
Divergence		30							$(.30)$	
GATB clerical		59							$(.23)$	
computation										
vocabulary				$.26^a$					$(.23)$	
tool matching										
arith. reason.										
Spatial flexibility tasks										
GATB space	men	46					$.33^a$			
manipulation	women	13								
	all	59		$(.21)$					$(.23)$	
GATB form	men	46								
matching	women	13								
	all	59								
DAT spatial	men	27				$.39^a$				
abilities	women	90			$.22^a$	$-.26^a$				
	all	117								

Table D.1 Cognitive correlates of the MOTQ scales (Controlling for cross-modal scores) (continued)

		Enactive subscales					Mode scales		
		Conseq.	Aff. con.	Aff.	Trans.	Condit.	Verbal	Visual	Enactive
Betts visual		$-.19^b$	$-.15^a$	$-.22^b$	$.16^a$			$-.30^c$	$-.22^b$
auditory		$-.16^a$		$(-.11)$				$-.21^c$	$(-.12)$
touch			$-.13^a$	$-.14^a$				$-.18^b$	
action			$-.14^a$					$-.26^c$	
taste								$-.15^a$	
smell									
organic								$(-.12)$	
Betts total		$-.14^a$	$-.16^a$	$-.15^a$				$-.25^c$	$-.16^a$
Gordon TVIC								$(.12)$	
Pettigrew					$.23^a$			$.25^a$	
Divergence									
GATB clerical			$(.24)$	$.26^a$					
computation				$(-.23)$					
vocabulary				$(.24)$					
tool matching									
arith. reasoning									

Spatial flexibility
tasks

		Conseq.	Aff. con.	Aff.	Trans.	Condit.	Verbal	Visual	Enactive
GATB space	men					$(.25)$			
manipulation	women			$.53^a$					
	all					$.25^a$			$(.21)$
GATB form	men					$.40^a$			$.29^a$
matching	women								
	all					$.35^b$			$.28^a$
DAT spatial	men				$.43^a$	$(.33)$			$(.35)$
abilities	women								
	all								

[a] $p<.05$; [b] $p<.01$; [c] $p<.001$; ( ) $p<.1$; all tests two-tailed.
1 N of cases is approximate, as some people had missing data on some subscales.
2 Note that lower scores on the Betts indicate higher vividness.

Appendix E
Personality correlates of the MOTQ

The portraits study

This involved 110 people (63 women and 47 men) taking psychology, social work or commerce courses, who completed the MOTQ along with an adjective rating scale. The adjective rating scale consisted of 169 adjectives (including a few phrases) selected from dictionary and thesaurus for potential relevance to the three cognitive styles. (It might have been better to use the Gough Adjective Check List, but we did not have it in our test library at the time when this work seemed urgent.) People were asked to rate themselves on each adjective on a 7-point scale: 1 = this adjective is much less (less often) true of me than of the average person; 7 = this adjective is much more (more often) true of me than of the average person. Reference to 'the average person' (which annoyed some participants) was used in an attempt to circumvent the saints-and-sinners syndrome which leads saints to claim for themselves a greater sinfulness than sinners ever would.

The data were treated correlationally, using both straightforward Pearson correlates and partial correlations controlling for the cross-modal scores. The positive correlates of the cross-modal scale itself are given in table E.1. In presenting the rest of the data (tables 6.1 and 6.2 in the text), two simplifications have been employed: the first is to exclude all the negative correlations; the second is to include only those adjectives which correlated uniquely with a particular scale at a particular correlational level (Pearson or partial). This involved first drawing up lists of correlates for men and women separately (adjectives correlating significantly for the total group were assigned to both sexes); then cancelling out any adjective that appeared for more than one mode scale for that sex at that correlational level; and finally reassembling the unique correlates into the format of table 6.1. A similar procedure was then followed for the subscales, resulting in table 6.2.

The psychometric study

Participants
These were the Arts (N=123), Commerce (N=40), Engineering (N=118), Arts two (N=141), and Management trainee (N=73) groups from appendix D, with each group taking the MOTQ along with a number of other cognitive and personality tests.

Procedure and instruments
In addition to the MOTQ the following tests were used: the Wilson-Patterson Attitude Inventory (the WPAI; Wilson, 1975); Rotter's Internal–External Locus of Control Scale (the IE; Rotter, 1966); the Marlowe-Crowne Social Desirability Scale (Crowne and Marlowe, 1964), all of which were completed by the arts and

Table E.1   Correlates of the MOTQ cross-modal subscale in the portraits study

Men only	Total sample	Women only
	admiring	
	hopeful	
	romantic	
	sociable	
	happy	happy
	compassionate	compassionate
	friendly	friendly
	dutiful	dutiful
	relaxed	relaxed
	open	open
	enthusiastic	enthusiastic
	excited	excited
	sympathetic	sympathetic
	gentle	gentle
	interested	interested
	elated	elated
	feeling of anticipation	feeling of anticipation
	grateful	grateful
	independent	independent
	peaceful	peaceful
unmotivated		understanding

Table E.2 Personality correlates of the MOTQ scales (above, light – Pearson correlates; below, bold – cross-modal scores controlled)   i. Cattell's 16 PF

Factor description (negative pole in parentheses)	Verbal subscales											
	opposite			phrase completion			rhyme			superordinate		
	all	men	women	all	men	women	all	men	women	all	men	women
N¹	73	56	17									
C1 outgoing (reserved)												
C2 high IQ (low IQ)												
C3 emotionally stable (affected by feelings)												
C4 assertive (humble)							-.30[b]		-.69[b] **-.67[b]**			
C5 happy-go-lucky (sober)												-.59[a]
C6 conscientious (expedient)			+.56[a]			+.69[a]		+.31[a]				
C7 venturesome (shy)											+.28[a]	
C8 tenderminded (tough)							+.24[a]	+.34[b]			**+.30[a]**	
C9 suspicious (trusting)												
C10 imaginative (practical)												
C11 shrewd (forthright)				-.26[a]	-.28[a] **-.31[a]**							
C12 apprehensive (self-assured)						+.56[a] **+.61[a]**						
C13 experimenting (conservative)										-.27[a]		
C14 self-sufficient (group dependent)												
C15 controlled (undisciplined self-conflict)												
C16 tense (relaxed)												

Table E.2 Personality correlates of the MOTQ scales (above, light – Pearson correlates; below, bold – cross-modal scores controlled) i. 16 PF (continued)

	Visual subscales											
	environment			attribute			intransitive action			part		
	all	men	women	all	men	women	all	men	women	all	men	women
C1 outgoing												
C2 high IQ												
C3 emotionally stable			$-.62^a$									
C4 assertive												
C5 happy-go-lucky						$-.66^b$					$+.32^a$	
C6 conscientious												
C7 venturesome												
C8 tenderminded		$+.29^a$						$+.28^a$	$-.55^a$			
C9 suspicious												
C10 imaginative												
C11 shrewd												
C12 apprehensive										$-.24^a$	$-.29^a$	
C13 experimenting												
C14 self-sufficient												$+.58^a$
C15 controlled								$+.28^a$				
C16 tense	$-.24^a$	$-.27^a$			$-.29^a$			$-.31^a$		$-.24^a$		

Table E.2 Personality correlates of the MOTQ scales (above, light – Pearson correlates; below, bold – cross-modal scores controlled)   i. 16 PF (continued)

| | Enactive subscales | | | | | | | | | | | | | | |
| | consequence | | | affective consequence | | | affective | | | transitive action | | | conditional action | | |
	all	men	women	all	men	women	all	men	women	all	men	women	all	men	women
C1 outgoing									−.52[a] / **−.57[a]**			−.50[a] / **−.55[a]**			−.62[b] / **−.68[b]**
C2 high IQ													−.29[a]	−.30[a]	
C3 emotionally stable									+.59[a] / **+.55[a]**						
C4 assertive															
C5 happy-go-lucky			−.49[a]					+.31[a]							−.48[a] / **−.60[a]**
C6 conscientious															
C7 venturesome			−.52[a]			−.62[a] / **−.63[a]**			−.78[c] / **−.87[c]**						
C8 tenderminded															
C9 suspicious															
C10 imaginative															
C11 shrewd															
C12 apprehensive															
C13 experimenting															
C14 self-sufficient						**+.72[a]**			**+.55[a]**			**+.59[a]**	−.24[a]	−.33[a]	
C15 controlled			−.55[a]												
C16 tense															

Table E.2 Personality correlates of the MOTQ scales (above, light – Pearson correlates; below, bold – cross-modal scores controlled) i. 16 PF (continued)

	Mode scales											
	cross-modal scale			verbal mode			visual mode			enactive mode		
	all	men	women	all	men	women	all	men	women	all	men	women
C1 outgoing												$-.53^a$ **$-.67^b$**
C2 high IQ												
C3 emotionally stable												
C4 assertive												
C5 happy-go-lucky			-62^b					$+.28^a$				
C6 conscientious						$+.54^a$						
C7 venturesome												$-.62^b$ **$-.72^b$**
C8 tenderminded					$+.34^a$							
C9 suspicious												
C10 imaginative												
C11 shrewd					$-.29^a$ **$-.34^a$**							
C12 apprehensive												
C13 experimenting												
C14 self-sufficient							**$+.26^a$**		$+.63^a$			
C15 controlled												$+.73^b$
C16 tense							$-.26^a$	$-.31^a$				

Table E.2   Personality correlates of the MOTQ scales (above, light – Pearson correlates; below, bold – cross-modal scores controlled)
ii. The Personal Orientation Inventory

| | N | | | Verbal subscales | | | | | | | | | | | |
| | | | | opposite | | | phrase completion | | | rhyme | | | superordinate | | |
	all	men	women	all	men	women	all	men	women	all	men	women	all	men	women
	33	22	11												
Tc Time competence															
I Inner-directed															
SAV Self-actualizing values															
Ex Existentiality															
Fr Feeling reactivity															
S Spontaneity															
Sr High self-regard															
Sa Self-acceptance															
Nc Constructive view of man															
Sy Synergy – – opposites related															+.71[a]
A Accept aggression															
C Capacity for intimate contact															

Table E.2 Personality correlates of the MOTQ scales (above, light – Pearson correlates; below, bold – cross-modal scores controlled)
ii. The Personal Orientation Inventory (continued)

	Visual subscales											
	environment			attribute			intransitive action			part		
	all	men	women	all	men	women	all	men	women	all	men	women
Tc												
I												
SAV												
Ex												
Fr												
S	$-.38^a$											
Sr												
Sa												
Nc							$+.42^a$	$+.54^a$				
Sy	$-.38^a$											
A				$-.39^a$						$-.36^a$		
C				**$-.46^b$**						**$-.42^a$**	**$-.54^a$**	

Table E.2 Personality correlates of the MOTQ scales (above, light – Pearson correlates; below, bold – cross-modal scores controlled)
ii. The Personal Orientation Inventory (continued)

	Enactive subscales														
	consequence			affective consequence			affective			transitive action			conditional action		
	all	men	women	all	men	women	all	men	women	all	men	women	all	men	women
Tc															
I															
SAV															
Ex															
Fr															
S										$-.49^{b}$	$-.48^{a}$				
Sr										**-.40**[a]					
Sa											$-.51^{a}$				
Nc															
Sy															
A															
C					**+.48**[a]										

Table E.2 Personality correlates of the MOTQ scales (above, light – Pearson correlates; below, bold – cross-modal scores controlled)
ii. The Personal Orientation Inventory (continued)

	Mode scales											
	cross-modal			verbal mode			visual mode			enactive mode		
	all	men	women	all	men	women	all	men	women	all	men	women
Tc												
I												
SAV												
Ex												
Fr												
S	−.37[a]											
Sr				+.48[b]	+.48[a]							
Sa												
Nc												
Sy												
A							**−.35[a]**					
C				**+.38[a]**								

Table E.2 Personality correlates of the MOTQ scales (above, light – Pearson correlates; below, bold – cross-modal scores controlled) iii. Other tests

	N			Verbal subscales									superordinate		
				opposite			phrase completion			rhyme					
	all	men	women	all	men	women	all	men	women	all	men	women	all	men	women
WPAI conservatism	123	48	75												
realism													-.21[a]		
militarism-punitiveness						+.23[a] **+.25[a]**									
anti-hedonism													+.18[a]		+.35[b]
ethnocentrism															**+.26[a]**
religion-puritanism												+.25[a]			
IE scale (external)	121	50	71								-.31[a]		-.34[c]	-.34[a]	-.35[b]
CM social desirability	105	44	61										-.25[b]		-.27[a]
EPQ extraversion	250	148	102										+.33[c] **+.21[a]**		+.44[c] **+.27[a]**
neuroticism													**-.13[a]**		**-.22[a]**
psychoticism															
lie										+.14[a]	+.18[a]		+.16[a]		+.23[a]
CK acquiescence	141–	36	105				+.17[a]								

Table E.2 Personality correlates of the MOTQ scales (above, light – Pearson correlates; below, bold – cross-modal scores controlled)   iii. Other tests (continued)

| | Visual subscales | | | | | | | | | | | |
| | environment | | | attribute | | | intransitive action | | | part | | |
	all	men	women	all	men	women	all	men	women	all	men	women
WPAI conservatism												
realism	-.21[a]	-.36[a] / **-.31[a]**								-.23[a]		
militarism-punitiveness												
anti-hedonism	+.17[a]		+.29[a]									+.31[b] / **+.23[a]**
ethnocentrism				-.25[b] / **-.28[b]**	-.34[a] / **-.36[a]**						-.34[a] / **-.36[a]**	
religion-puritanism										-.22[a]		
IE scale (external)	-.22[a]		-.25[a]				**+.29[a]**					
CM social desirability	+.35[c] / **+.25[b]**		+.38[b]	+.22[a]		+.27[a]	+.20[a]		+.29[a]			+.26[a]
EPQ extraversion	**-.20[b]**	**-.22[b]**					**-.13[a]**	**-.19[a]**		-.12[a] / **-.21[c]**	-.17[a] / **-.22[b]**	
neuroticism									-.20[a]			
psychoticism	-.14[a] / **-.19[b]**	-.18[a] / **-.25[b]**					-.16[a] / **-.20[b]**	-.24[b] / **-.28[b]**				
lie	+.25[c] / **+.16[b]**	+.20[a]	+.30[b]	+.14[a]			+.19[b]		+.26[b]			
CK acquiescence												

Table E.2 Personality correlates of the MOTQ scales (above, light – Pearson correlates; below, bold – cross-modal scores controlled)   iii. Other tests (continued)

	Enactive subscales														
	consequence			affective consequence			affective			transitive action			conditional action		
	all	men	women	all	men	women	all	men	women	all	men	women	all	men	women
WPAI conservatism															
realism	-.25[a]	-.35[a]		-.25[b] **-.22[a]**		-.26[a] **-.27[a]**	-.20[a]								
militarism-punitiveness															
anti-hedonism			+.28[a]			+.29[a]									+.24[a]
ethnocentrism															
religion-puritanism										-.24[a]		-.29[a]			
IE scale (external)	-.24[b]		-.25[a]												
CM social desirability		+.27[b]	+.35[b]										+.20[a]		+.26[a]
EPQ extraversion	**-.15[a]**														
neuroticism	-.13[a]														
psychoticism															
lie	+.17[b]	+.18[a]		+.17[b]		+.23[a]	+.13[a]								+.20[a]
CK acquiescence										**-.26[b]**	**-.58[c]**			-.37[a]	

Table E.2 Personality correlates of the MOTQ scales (above, light – Pearson correlates; below, bold – cross-modal scores controlled)   iii. Other tests (continued)

	Mode scales											
	cross-modal			verbal mode			visual mode			enactive mode		
	all	men	women	all	men	women	all	men	women	all	men	women
WPAI conservatism				$[a] @[a]								
realism							-.27[b] **-.21[a]**			-.20[a]		
militarism-punitiveness												
anti-hedonism									+.29[a]			+.29[a]
ethnocentrism							-.20[a] **-.26[b]**	-.39[b] **-.42[b]**				
religion-puritanism												
IE scale (external)	-.24[b]		-.25[a]		-.32[a]							
CM social desirability	+.26[b]		+.37[b]			**+.24[a]**	+.28[b]		+.35[b]	+.21[a]		+.26[a]
EPQ extraversion							-.21[b]	-.23[b]				
neuroticism												
psychoticism							**-.14[a]**	**-.18[a]**				
lie	+.20[b]		+.28[b]	+.13[a]			+.22[c]	+.19[a]	+.26[b]	+.16[a]		+.21[a]
CK acquiescence											**-.37[a]**	

1 Ns approximate, as some people had missing values for some subscales.
$ Correlations with both ease and enjoyment of verbalizing.
@ As above, controlling for cross-modal scores.
a p<.05; b p<.01; c p<.001; all tests two-tailed.

commerce groups; the Eysenck Personality Questionnaire (the EPQ; Eysenck and Eysenck, 1975), completed by arts, commerce and engineering groups; the Personal Orientation Inventory (the POI; Shostrom, 1974), completed by the commerce group; Cattell's 16PF (Form A, Cattell and Eber, 1966), completed by the management trainee group; and the Couch Keniston measure of Acquiescence (Couch and Keniston, 1960), completed by the arts two group.

The data were analysed according to Pearson and partial correlations (controlling for the cross-modal scores) to relate the personality scales to the MOTQ scales. Statistically significant results are shown in table E.2.

Appendix F
Animal favourites

Study on favourite creatures

Participants
First-year arts students, 109 in all, 84 women and 25 men.

Materials and procedure
Twenty four animals' names: donkey, stallion, elephant, fox, stray dog, bulldog, cat, goldfish, sheep, goat, pig, rat, hedgehog, tiger, gorilla, seagull, crow, vulture, snake, lizard, scorpion, crab, fly, spider. These were ordered randomly, four to a page in a booklet handed out during a class period. Instructions on the first page explained that the study was on the relationship between thought and feeling, and involved: 1) rating each of twenty four animals on a 7-point evaluation scale (+3 = feel strongly positive towards; 0 = indifferent, neutral; −3 = feel strongly negative towards); 2) briefly describing their precise attitude or feeling to the animal; 3) giving reasons for this attitude.

The results relating kind of reason to evaluative rating (across animals as 'subjects') are shown in table 7.2. The more specialized details on reasons for feelings about specific animals are shown in table F.1. In these data it is difficult to disentangle *reasons* for evaluations from *rationalizations about* evaluations. In fact what people typically did was less provide reasons than to express their evaluations in more focused ways.

Table F.1 Evaluations: reasons evoked by specific animals

reason[1]	stallion	donkey	stray dog	elephant	seagull	fox	sheep	goldfish	hedgehog	tiger	cat	goat	pig
nice part	8[2]	9	2	6	1	9	6	4	16	7	4	5	1
attrib.	48	7	0	27	19	18	14	37	9	40	14	9	6
action	28	8	0	12	34	9	3	13	15	21	11	1	2
character	43	48	4	32	6	43	28	11	12	21	24	16	9
anything nice	79	64	8	56	55	61	49	61	46	61	39	31	18
nasty attrib.	1	2	0	3	7	2	4	1	3	4	10	5	57
action	2	1	0	2	10	7	1	1	0	2	12	2	5
other	0	0	1	1	2	0	0	0	0	1	1	0	1
anything nasty	4	6	3	6	23	21	16	6	10	17	37	10	64
anything dissonant	2	0	0	24	1	0	2	4	10	3	9	7	4
understandable	3	43	83	12	2	17	14	11	10	6	24	6	7
domestic/useful	8	16	0	11	0	6	20	5	1	0	5	5	17
harmful	4	2	12	1	1	3	0	0	4	26	2	6	0
phobic	0	0	1	0	1	0	0	0	2	1	8	1	0
superordinate	0	1	0	0	18	2	0	4	1	9	1	0	0
mean evaluation	2.15	2.06	1.81	1.35	1.04	1.01	0.96	0.92	0.80	0.54	0.29	-0.20	-0.30

Table F.1   Evaluations: reasons evoked by specific animals (continued)

reason[1]	bulldog	crow	spider	gorilla	crab	lizard	fly	scorpion	vulture	snake	rat	total
nice part	6	0	2	1	0	1	0	0	1	1	0	90
attrib.	8	7	3	8	2	4	1	1	6	12	0	300
action	0	2	24	2	2	1	1	0	4	5	0	198
character	11	3	2	3	3	0	1	0	0	2	0	322
anything nice	21	12	29	22	8	11	4	5	7	20	1	768
nasty attrib.	34	42	9	26	12	33	28	9	9	30	38	369
action	2	13	12	2	12	15	10	7	57	23	16	214
other	2	3	3	4	2	3	5	1	5	2	13	50
anything nasty	59	56	27	33	29	41	40	18	78	53	62	719
anything dissonant	8	12	27	26	11	19	7	7	1	19	14	217
understandable	12	6	3	8	0	0	2	1	1	1	0	272
domestic/useful	2	1	5	0	7	0	1	0	4	1	1	116
harmful	14	1	3	22	54	6	39	62	11	53	54	380
phobic	0	3	32	0	2	13	1	6	1	11	9	92
superordinate	0	29	3	5	4	19	9	8	17	5	2	137
mean evaluation	−0.44	−0.52	−0.61	−0.69	−1.08	−1.31	−1.44	−1.70	−1.75	−1.83	−2.41	

1 Types of reason relating significantly to evaluation only.
2 No. of participants who gave this reason for this animal.

Study on typicality and liking

Participants
First-year arts students, 99 in all, 78 women and 21 men.

Materials and procedure
The same twenty four animals were used. The instructions explained that although many different things were classed by *biologists* as animals, most people felt that some animals were closer to their idea of the Standard Animal, or Animal in General, or Prototype Animal than others. The instructions asked people to: 1) rate each animal for prototypicality on a 7-point scale (from −3 to +3 with 0 as neutral, average or don't know); 2) give reasons for their ratings.

At the end of the booklet the same animals were re-presented in a different random order with a request that they be rated for liking on a 7-point scale (−3 to +3).

Results are given in table 7.2 in the text.

Appendix G
Study on the phenomenology of emotions

One hundred and eleven people took part, 78 women and 33 men. Most were first-year students in their first few weeks of a psychology course, and the remainder were a variety of interested others. The students wrote their descriptions during a class period, though it was stressed that this was not a mandatory activity, and that people should only do it if they wanted to. Results of phenomenological analysis of the descriptions are shown in table G.1, which details the most important constituents for emotional experiences in general (summing over the entire corpus); and for particular types of emotional experience (happiness, anger, etc.). Surprise is counted as an 'emotion' in the table because it is conventionally; shock is not because it is not conventionally, though in many ways it is a stronger candidate.

Table G.1 Constituents of emotional experiences, for the total sample and for particular emotions (figures are percentage of experiences containing particular constituents)

	total sample	subsamples of particular emotions												
		happy	anger	sad	anxiety	confusion	love	depression	lonely	guilt	hurt	fear	disappointment	surprise
N (= 100% for its column)[1]	111	38	37	28	27	21	20	20	15	14	12	12	11	8
Constituents[2] I: Emotions[3]														
happiness, delight, relief	34	—	14	18	59	43	60[4]	25	33	21	17	17	46	0
anger, fury, hatred	33	13	—	29	19	33	25	65	13	50	50	25	36	75
sadness, grief	25	13	22	—	7	19	25	35	40	21	17	0	9	38
anxiety, worry	24	42	14	7	—	43	15	35	20	21	8	17	64	13
confusion, fuddled, bewildered	19	24	19	14	33	—	45	25	40	36	33	8	36	25
love, sexual and other	18	32[5]	14	18	11	43	—	5	20	21	33	0	27	13
depression, futility	18	13	35	25	26	24	5	—	27	29	25	0	9	38
loneliness	14	13	5	21	11	29	15	20	—	0	8	0	0	25
guilt	13	8	19	11	11	24	15	20	0	—	8	25	9	25
hurt, betrayal	11	5	19	7	4	19	20	15	7	7	—	0	27	38
fear (physical threats)	11	5	8	0	7	5	0	0	7	21	0	—	9	13
disappointment	10	13	11	4	26	19	15	5	0	7	25	8	—	13
surprise	7	0	16	11	4	10	5	15	13	14	25	8	9	—

Table G.1 Constituents of emotional experiences, for the total sample and for particular emotions (figures are percentage of experiences containing particular constituents) (continued)

	total sample	happy	anger	sad	anxiety	confusion	love	depression	lonely	guilt	hurt	fear	disappointment	surprise
Constituents II: Other														
environment, place experience occurred	44	37	46	32	56	29	10	50	13	57	25	92	55	38
future, thoughts of what to do next, or what will happen	42	53	35	32	85	50	30	50	53	43	25	67	73	38
body, activation of	35	47	32	18	48	29	35	20	33	36	17	75	18	25
plan, e.g. for future career	30	50	24	7	63	48	30	35	20	29	17	25	46	13
action – in regard to precipitant of emotion	28	34	35	18	26	29	40	35	20	50	17	67	27	38
family member precipitates feeling	26	29	27	46	15	19	40	15	33	29	8	8	27	38
crying	23	16	24	43	19	19	30	35	33	50	17	33	9	25
friend precipitates feeling	22	18	27	21	4	19	25	20	27	29	50	17	9	13
waiting, e.g. for exam results	21	42	11	4	63	24	15	10	7	7	8	8	55	0
realization of meaning delayed	21	16	16	25	19	19	20	25	27	7	25	17	18	25
learning from experience	20	16	24	25	15	14	25	30	7	36	33	25	18	25
death provokes experience	19	8	11	64	4	10	15	20	13	36	0	0	0	25
shock, being 'hit' by news or event	19	8	16	21	7	10	15	25	13	21	67	42	18	38
paralysis of action, rooted to the spot	18	16	14	18	15	14	10	25	7	14	33	50	18	38
bad feelings endure after experience	18	16	24	14	4	14	30	30	27	14	42	8	9	13
'injustice' to self, e.g. being slighted	18	8	35	7	15	24	20	30	7	21	67	17	18	38
wanting to act, to do something	17	24	22	7	7	24	45	15	13	29	17	8	9	13

subsamples of particular emotions

Table G.1 Constituents of emotional experiences, for the total sample and for particular emotions (figures are percentage of experiences containing particular constituents) (continued)

	total sample	happy	anger	sad	anxiety	confusion	love	depression	lonely	guilt	hurt	fear	disappointment	surprise
		subsamples of particular emotions												
frantic behaviour, displacement activities	14	16	27	7	22	14	15	10	13	7	8	17	27	38
social group provokes experience	14	18	8	11	11	19	5	20	40	7	0	17	9	0
sexual partner provokes experience	14	18	11	11	7	29	45	15	13	7	67	0	18	38
response out of proportion (retrospective)	13	11	30	0	11	14	10	5	13	14	8	17	18	13
disbelief, denial, e.g. on news of death	12	8	16	14	4	14	15	15	7	29	33	17	18	50
prayer	12	11	14	25	4	5	5	20	7	14	8	25	9	13
social support	12	16	14	14	7	5	0	25	20	0	25	8	0	25
good feelings endure after experience	12	26	11	4	15	5	25	5	13	7	0	8	9	0
other's injustice to others	11	5	32	11	0	5	5	15	7	14	8	8	0	25
laughing, often hysterical	11	11	11	14	4	5	0	5	13	0	0	17	0	25
external self-awareness	11	16	8	7	15	10	5	15	7	21	0	25	0	13

1 Many descriptions fell under more than one heading. Summing Ns for particular emotions gives 263, whereas there were only 111 descriptions. Thus on average, each description contains references to 2.4 different emotions, and the columns in the table are not fully independent.

2 Inter-rater agreement assessed using Spearman's r_s with categories as subjects = .96. In fact data in table uses only judgments upon which both judges agreed.

3 All the emotional constituents are included (though surprise is rather infrequent). Other constituents are only included in the table if they occur in >10% of the descriptions.

4,5 On how to read this rather complex table: these two cells show that 60% of the 20 descriptions of love contain references also to happiness, whereas 32% of the 38 descriptions of happiness contain references to love, i.e. most loving involves happiness, but there are also many happinesses from other sources.

Notes

Chapter 1 Introduction

1 There are terminological problems here. Bruner actually uses the terms *symbolic, ikonic* and *enactive*. I have preferred *verbal, visual* and *enactive: verbal* and *visual* because they follow conventional practice, and *enactive* because for this there is little convention and it seems the best of a number of alternatives. The only problem with it is that in speech people tend to hear it as *inactive*, which it precisely is not. Horowitz (1978) also uses the term *enactive*, though not perhaps in quite the same way. Alternatives include *histrionic* (Galton, 1907), *motor* (e.g. Colvin, 1909), *kinaesthetic* (Aylwin, 1977, among others), *personal analogy* (Gordon, 1961), *covert role play* (via psychotherapy), and *empathetic* (common parlance).

2 Bower's recent work (1981) on mood and memory is an exception. It tends to assimilate the affective to the cognitive, and is perhaps better viewed as an account of how we represent *descriptions* of cognitive and affective phenomena, than of how we experience those phenomena themselves.

3 Psychologists have sometimes espoused an odd view of what it means to be scientific, assuming that formal experimentation is scientific but observation and description are not. Qualitative work in fact lies at the heart of science, and indeed formal quantitative experimentation can be viewed as a refinement and clarification of it. When quantitative work is inadequately grounded on qualitative work, a number of things happen. It is tacitly assumed that *we already know what there is*, and need only set out to quantify it. It is then necessary to interpret laboriously the

quantitative results in order to construct 'theories' which are little more than the qualitative descriptions ordinary people would have given had we thought to ask, or which would have been obvious had we done the experiment using ourselves as subjects.

This is not an argument against quantitative research, and indeed qualitative and quantitative are not mutually exclusive. Each has its place.

There are a number of good texts on qualitative (or content, or phenomeno-logical) analysis, e.g. van Kaam (1969), Krippendorff (1980), Patton (1980), Bliss, Monk and Ogborn (1983). I suspect that content analysis is, in the end, an art, to be learnt only in practice, and the texts tend to be better on how to apply category systems than on the trickier business of actually generating a category system in the first place. For what they are worth, I have found the following strategies useful in addition to advice available in the texts.

The first is that whatever one wants to get other people to do, it is important to do it oneself beforehand. This provides an epistemological foundation for understanding what other people are writing or saying. It also provides an ethical safeguard, which is important because phenomenological techniques can pene-trate to the core of a person's life in a way in which experimental ones typically cannot. This might not matter very much in looking at why people like animals (chapter 7), but it does matter when people are writing about emotional experiences (chapter 9).

The second is that to generate content categories I have found it useful first to précis the entire corpus of data, using where possible the writers' or speakers' own words; then to cut up this précis with a pair of scissors into the smallest meaningful fragments; and to organize these into groups of items with similar meanings (which will be the 'categories'), by spreading them out over the floor and playing something like conceptual scrabble. At this stage it is important to aim for the greatest number of categories. They can always be collapsed later. This is a time consuming but immensely satisfying process. It provides general categories whose interpretation is given by the elements making up the group. This means that one ends up with categories which have arisen from the data rather than being imposed on it, and which are already 'interpreted' in the words of the people contributing the data. It is of course then necessary to take the category system back to the original data and to refine it as necessary; and then to refine it further by seeing whether a second judge can use it reliably.

Chapter 2   Preliminary sketches of the three modes of thought

1 The notion of case is taken from such languages as Latin, in which words having particular roles in the sentence take particular case endings (nominative, accusative, dative, ablative, etc.). In Latin these cases are a relatively superficial feature of language. Fillmore's case grammar applies at a deeper level, enabling cases to be responsive to meanings.

2 While supporting the dependence of linguistic structures on prior cognitive-semantic ones, Slobin (1982) cautions against taking this dependence too far. He points to the diversity of languages as suggesting that the semantic-to-linguistic mapping is not that simple, and as a reminder that we do need to consider some structural features as specifically linguistic.

3 Strictly, all we can yet say scientifically about some of these techniques is that they may be useful for some people. Some of the work on imagery is higher on clinical enthusiasm than on scientific rectitude.

Chapter 3   Free-associative structures

1 In fact intransitive verbs characterize visual imagery only when people are allowed to use free-flowing speech in their associative response (as in Aylwin, 1981). The restriction to single-word responses leads to verbs of all kinds being confined to enactive imagery.

2 It has been suggested by a number of authors that there may be a limited number of action types (verb families, in Dixon's terms). Murray (1951) specified twelve 'action tendencies', which he saw as being probably adequate for a theory of social action. Most of these are used in Klinger, Barta and Maxeiner's (1981) classification of 'current concerns'. Schank (1975) also proposes eleven primitive actions, which show some overlap with the above.

3 The free-association data, and particularly the division of temporal and spatial labour between visual and enactive representations, suggest that the Hopi world view (Whorf, 1958) may be more appropriate to a study of time than the common-sense English one. The Hopi divided time into two aspects: the Manifested, consisting of everything present and accessible to the senses now, plus whatever had actually happened or been present to the senses in the past (roughly visual); and the Manifesting, which included the future and all thoughts and feelings in the minds (or strictly, hearts) of human and other beings (roughly enactive).

4 This discussion is loosely based on arguments by Diver (1964) on systems of agency in the Latin noun, and by Braine and Hardy (1982) on the development of case grammar in children.

Chapter 4   Day-dreams, fantasies and other idle thoughts

1 I say we advisedly. I was one of my innocent subjects. Hurlburt and Sipprelle (1978) had to discontinue use of a thought sampling technique with a patient subject to anxiety attacks because the method was too effective. The patient also could not tolerate what he found was going on at this normally preconscious level.

2 This iron fist in a humorous glove combination can be a powerful means of social control. Evans-Pritchard (1962) describes how among the Azande, there is a

special language of insult, called *Sanza*, consisting of ambiguous utterances which have innocent appearance but spiteful intent. These things are sometimes easier to see in alien cultures, but most people must recognize the combination.

3 As Frenkel-Brunswik remarked, 'not only the id but also the super-ego may be imbued with unconscious sadistic and primitive tendencies' (1954, p. 265). None of this can be of any reassurance whatsoever to those who unwittingly threaten the conceptual system, as did the Jews and other non-Aryans in Nazi Germany. The only comfort we can hold on to here is that what goes on inside the head need not necessarily go on outside it. There is rather little clear-cut evidence on this issue, and a considerable amount of controversy (see Klinger, 1971), but the balance of the evidence suggests that fantasy aggression can be prevented from leaking out of the head into the real world by the firm application of civilized values; which is often to say, parental disapproval (Lesser, 1957, 1959).

Chapter 5 A cognitive interlude: individual differences in modes of thought

1 In some ways the men in the social-sciences group were somewhat similar to the commerce students with their verbal bias. This is similar to Roe's (1953) findings which indicated a verbal bias in the (male) social scientists of the time, and it may be that men and women go into the social sciences for rather different reasons.

2 Work on sex differences in the lateralization of various psychological functions can be taken to support this idea, as it has been shown that there is stronger right-hemisphere lateralization of spatial abilities for men than women (Hannay, 1976; Hannay & Malone, 1976; Witelson, 1976); and stronger right-hemisphere lateralization of emotional processing for women than for men (Suberi and McKeever, 1977; Davidson, Schwartz, Pugash and Bromfield, 1976).

3 Similar arguments have been made about imagery vividness. Certainly, *general* vividness measures correlate less well with learning or therapeutic improvement than vividness measures of the imagery actually used in the learning or the therapy (see chapter 2, section on: 'Role of vividness').

Chapter 6 Aspects of identity

1 This may be why, as Gilbert Ryle noted, thinking is not itself a school subject. We do not need to be taught thinking itself, though we may indeed need to be taught how to channel our thinking effectively.

2 Dunn, Bliss and Siipola (1958), relating personal values to free associations, found that people with exteroceptive and especially with economic values tended to show contrast (oppositional) responses. This supports the picture of the verbalizer emerging from the MOTQ work.

3 In a rather informal confirmation of the association between the need for

power and the use of criticism, Winter (1973) asked people the following question: if you were allowed to say one thing, to anyone in the world, with absolutely no consequences, what would it be? Those high in the need for power usually wanted to say something extremely rude.

4 Segal and Nathan's findings (1964) support this picture of a humanitarian visualizer: their vivid visualizers characterized themselves as sympathetic, dependable, sociable, efficient, persistent and mannerly.

5 This is important as there were no engineers in the portraits study, and the enactive portrait is therefore not an artefact of the sample used. There were commerce and social-science (psychology and social-work) students. That the verbal and visual portraits (respectively) are simple consequences of the use of these two groups seems unlikely, as analysing the groups separately gives similar patterns of results. The gloominess of the enactive portrait may be because the highly enactive people in the sample are trapped in commerce or social science when something like engineering would have given them more scope and less frustration.

6 Neurolinguistic programming (Bandler and Grinder, 1975; Grinder and Bandler, 1976; Gordon, 1978) also sees different personality types as deriving from different forms of representation; and claims that these forms of representation can be picked up from the language used, as well as from non-verbal cues. The relevant personality types are the ultra-reasonable *computer* (verbal; and a good fit to the current data); the disagreeing *blamer* (visual; and a good fit only to the indignant aspect of the visualizer protrait); and the agreeing *placator* (kinaesthetic; and possibly interpretable as reflecting the low self-esteem aspect of the enactive personality, as it emerges in social relations, but this is generally not a good fit). The parallels here are clearly of interest, though they are not perfect.

Chapter 7 Values in inner speech: preference for categorical clarity

1 Klahr (1969) and Cooper (1973) both found that people make decisions about preferences on the same dimensions they use to make judgments about similarity. In so far as prototypes summarize within-group similarities these findings are along the same lines as the current data.

Zajonc (1968) has shown a 'mere exposure' effect on liking, replicated under various conditions by Brickman, Redfield, Harrison and Crandall (1972); Zajonc, Markus and Wilson (1974). Though this need not be mediated by stimulus recognition (Moreland and Zajonc, 1977; Wilson, 1979), it does indicate that we tend to like what we know. It is interesting therefore to note the relationship between familiarity, evaluation and typicality in the two studies. Familiarity relates to typicality in table 7.2, but not to evaluation in 7.1. That there should be a *general* association between familiarity and typicality is probably inevitable: as Rosch stated, the world exhibits a correlational structure, which is what is abstracted in categories. A category system will always be *with regard to* the experience it organizes.

In general, categories rest on recurring patterns of experience, and in general familiarity will play a part here. In particular cases however, there may be rare entities, such as tigers, which are more prototypical than common ones, such as rats. Furthermore, Tsujimoto (1978) has shown that, provided something is prototypical, people will *assume* it is familiar, even though they have never seen it before.

Zajonc's mere exposure effect may thus be mediated by more complex happenings than mere exposure itself.

2 Berlin, Breedlove and Raven (1966) argue that scientific taxonomies in fact build on folk ones.

3 People differed as to whether they thought real animals should be ferocious and dangerous (as is tiger), or gentle and biddable (as is stray dog), though particular individuals appeared to apply their chosen criterion fairly consistently. Which pole people opt for on the ferocity dimension seems to be a matter of personal preference, but the dimension as a whole appears to be important for most people. This is in loose agreement with the work of Henley (1969) and Caramazza, Hersh and Torgerson (1976), who found ferocity to be an important dimension governing the semantic space occupied by animals.

4 These remarks about non-mammals have to be speculative, as we have no ratings on typicality within subordinate categories. For mammals, however, the argument is sounder.

5 Categorical features are not all that is important in phobias (see e.g.: Rachman, 1968; Wolpe, 1973). Even with small-animal phobias, quality of action may be important regardless of its contribution to atypicality, and some phobias may derive from traumatic events such as being bitten by a dog as a child. Yet other phobias, such as fear of high places or fear of public speaking, do not seem amenable to a taxonomic analysis at all. Within a limited range, however, the hypothesis may have some use.

6 Reptiles and arthropods would see the matter quite differently, I think.

7 There has been much excellent thought recently on the idea that social cognition generally, including stereotyping, is a consequence of normal cognitive processing (e.g.: Nisbett and Ross, 1980; Taylor and Crocker, 1981; L. Z. McArthur, 1982), though little attention has yet been paid to the role of differences. Attention is paid to differences by those who are oppressed by them. Thus feminist literature is a poignant source here. See e.g. Belotti (1975), and Heilbrun (1979).

8 Ickes and Barnes (1978) confirm in the real world that stereotyped males and females don't have very much to say to one another. However, the magic was not evident in the 5-minute encounters they used.

9 No place here for any notion that androgyny may be better than stereotypy, as Bem's work suggests, or even than adequate description requires two dimensions instead of one (see Bem, 1974, 1975; Bem and Lenney, 1976).

10 I cannot leave this section without worrying a little about the effects that stereotypes may have on real behaviour. Locksley, Borgida, Brekke and Hepburn

(1980) present some optimistic evidence suggesting that people only use stereotypes when not enough information is available about particular cases. The possession of concrete evidence is thus crucial. As we usually have less evidence about members of outgroups than we do of our own group, we are more liable to stereotype them than us. This lack of evidence also leads us to make more extreme evaluations of them (Linville, 1982; Linville and Jones, 1980). Even if we depart from the concrete evidence to the smallest extent, to think about it rather than confronting it, attitudes begin to be polarized (Tesser, 1978).

Psychologists are discovering here what artists, mystics and lovers have long known: that abstract knowledge may be a screen in front of reality, and attention to particulars is the only way to avoid being misled by it.

11   This is not quite the same as saying verbalizers prefer the typical. There was no significant correlation with the MOTQ verbal-mode scale, which does not include the superordinate subscale. When this scale is included, the correlation creeps only to the $p < .1$ (two-tailed) level.

Chapter 8   Visualizing, the environment and the sentiments of self

1   In the decade since the original work, the topic has become more complex. Fenigstein, Scheier and Buss (1975) produced a Self-consciousness scale, which measures public and private self-consciousness; and Snyder (1974, 1979) has a Self-monitoring scale. Both these look at aspects of self-awareness as dispositions rather than experiences. There are theoretical divergences as well. Duval and Wicklund use a motivational theory; Carver (1979), and Carver and Scheier (1981) give a cybernetic account; and Hull and Levy (1979) offer an account stressing the processing of information in terms of its self-relevance.

2   This study was actually half of a two-part investigation into liking and interest. In describing what they like, people are tacitly contrasting the two, which amounts to contrasting play with work.

Chapter 9   Emotions and enactive representation

1   Aristotle might have spoken of 'the practical syllogism' here. In the practical syllogism the major premiss is a judgment of value (car crashes are bad for people) or an imperative (car crashes ought to be avoided). The minor premiss would be something like this is a potential car crash situation; and the conclusion resulting from the combination of the two is not a statement but an action – the person brakes and avoids the car crash. This is Aristotle's solution to the fact that we are rational animals, in which the rational and the animal have somehow to interact and promote each other's welfare.

2   Whether objective physiological measures would show any isomorphism to these statements is unclear. In general, verbal reports of autonomic symptoms show rather poor relations with objective measures (Shields and Stern, 1979).

3 Laughter and crying are both primarily facial expressions. It is worth commenting that there were no other facial expressions mentioned with any frequency in the data. The importance of this negative finding is that some theorists (e.g.: Tomkins, 1962; Izard, 1971, 1977) have claimed that emotion primarily is an awareness of our facial expression. The data offer no support for this. Indeed only two people in the entire sample (of 111) referred to facial expressions at all (apart from in laughing and crying).

4 Nigro and Neisser (1983) report some relevant data from their work on memory. Memories which are recalled from a perspective of externalized self-awareness tend to be more emotional than those recalled from an experiencer perspective. However, people only report feelings from the experiencer perspective, not from an externalized one.

5 Bower (1981) explains mood-dependent memory in terms of the mood being a node in a network, to which memories are attached. This may be the only way in which artificial intelligence (and models based on it) can currently cope with moods, but it does not seem to accord very well with their human phenomenology. Moods just are not the same sort of thing as the memories to which, in Bower's model, they are extrinsically attached.

Chapter 10   Mind and time

1 I do not think this is a necessary criticism of all possible (including future) information processing models. It is a defect that has arisen from what is really a metaphysical error, not from the essential nature of computers.

2 A possible bonus of an intentional account of memory would be a link to the phenomena described in a number of meditative traditions, which claim that all there is is the present.

3 There may be an important exception to the one-way movement of thought and the irrecoverable nature of mental events. This involves images of the environment. If we have an image of the location which serves as the background of an object, then it seems possible, through that locative image, to return over and over again to the object. This may be one aspect of the mnemonic power of such images. It is probably better, however, not to rely on internal representations, but to use external ones. Notes in a notebook are not worn away by being looked at over and over again, and objects in the real world can code for memories in a very powerful way. Romanyshyn (1982) describes a book in his study as being the memory of the dead friend who gave it to him. It is an account that has a profound appeal.

4 These anatomical differences between the coding of where and the coding of what may underlie some of the odd features of the coding of environments. Their mnemonic power has already been referred to. Another unique feature is that environments may essentially be grounds: that is, they exist only relative to a figure. Attention to the environment leads to part of it becoming an articulate figure, the

rest remaining unarticulated ground. Polanyi (1958) points out that we can never attend to the ground *as such*, for attention always converts it to a figure.

5 I was once piloting an STM study with one of our postgraduate students. I was to read out a string of digits at approximately one per half-second, and he was supposed to reply at the same rate, with no break after the end of presentation. He managed the rate all right, but there was always a pause before he started his recall. When asked what he was doing in the interval he said that he was turning the string of digits into 'an icon'. This appears to have been his way of saying that he was recoding them into this atemporal form.

6 None of this is to deny that mental representations may have spatial extension. Visual images do have some extension, and in spatial-flexibility tasks people do mentally manipulate objects in space. But this space is not a distinct mental space, ontologically distinguished from the real one; it is the same as that of the real world. When I day-dream about a city I used to live in, the images of its places are overlaid on the real world which is in front of my eyes. Our idea of mental space probably arises from as simple a fact as that we have eyelids. Mental space is what is inside them when they are closed, and real space is what is outside them. In fact, shutting our eyes may shut out the apprehension of particular spaces, but it does not shut out the spatiality itself. It does not shut out, in Kant's terms, space as the form of perception, which is held in common by our real and imaginary worlds.

Chapter 11   The psychology of science

1 Kelly (1955) and Lévi-Strauss (1968), dealing respectively with individual and societal meanings, both put forward theories with a major emphasis on opposed-category pairs. In Kelly's Personal Construct Theory these are expanded to dimensions; in the work of Lévi-Strauss and other structuralists, opposed categories often find a mediator in some third category which has magical or sacred status.

2 Physicists have recently been concerned with the existence of the parts of these subatomic particles: quarks. Foucault (1972) uses the phrase 'the archaeology of knowledge' to refer to the fact that all knowledge is structured in this relative way, never being based on absolutes.

3 Some nuclear physicists claim that atomic structure has now passed beyond the point at which visual metaphors are useful. For example, is light a shower of pebbles, or waves in a bath-tub? Visual imagination can only cope with these two separately, and not with the conception provided by quantum mechanics, which allows light, in mathematical symbolism, to be both.

4 The story goes deeper than this, since there is a change of identity also at the level of subatomic particles (from proton plus electron to neutron plus neutrino). This change in turn is assumed to rest on the shuffling of quarks into new combinations, the identity of these quarks, however, being preserved.

5 It perhaps needs to be said that the value placed on conflict and change by the scientific ethos does not always extend to individual scientists. Merton (1969, 1973), Mitroff (1974), and Mahoney (1976), have all stressed the divergence between the objectivity of 'science' and the lack of objectivity of many scientists. Polanyi (1958) would go further and say that this is a *necessary* lack of objectivity.

References

Allport, G. W. (1955) Becoming. Basic Considerations for a Psychology of Personality, New Haven and London, Yale University Press.

Alpert, R. and Haber, R. N. (1960) 'Anxiety in academic achievement situations', Journal of Abnormal and Social Psychology, 61, 207–15.

Anderson, J. R. (1978) 'Arguments concerning representations for mental imagery', Psychological Review, 85, 249–77.

Anderson, J. R. (1983) 'A spreading activation theory of memory', Journal of Verbal Learning and Verbal Behavior, 22, 261–95.

Anderson, R. C. and McGaw, B. (1973) 'On the representation of meanings of general terms', Journal of Experimental Psychology, 101, 301–6.

Anderson, R. C. and Pichert, J. W. (1978) 'Recall of previously unrecallable information following a shift in perspective', Journal of Verbal Learning and Verbal Behavior, 17, 1–12.

Anderson, R. C., Pichert, J. W., Goetz, E. T., Schallert, D. L., Stevens, K. V. and Trollip, S. R. (1976) 'Instantiation of general terms', Journal of Verbal Learning and Verbal Behavior, 15, 667–79.

Angell, J. R. (1910) 'Methods for the determination of mental imagery', Psychological Monographs, 13, 61–107.

Apter, M. J. (1982) The Experience of Motivation. The Theory of Psychological Reversals, London, Academic Press.

Arieti, S. (1970) 'Cognition and feeling', in Arnold, M. B. (ed.) Feelings and Emotions, New York, Academic Press, pp. 135–43.

Aristotle (1976) The Ethics of Aristotle. The Nicomachean Ethics, trans. J. A. K. Thompson, revised by H. Tredinnick, Harmondsworth, Penguin.

Arnold, M. B. (1960) Emotion and Personality. vol. I: Psychological Aspects, New York, Columbia University Press.

Asch, S. E. (1958) 'The metaphor: A psychological inquiry', in Tagiuri, R. and Petrullo, L.

(eds) *Person Perception and Interpersonal Behavior*, Stanford, Stanford University Press, pp. 86–94.

Ashton, R., McFarland, K., Walsh, F. and White, K. (1978) 'Imagery ability and the identification of hands: A chronometric analysis', *Acta Psychologica*, 42, 253–62.

Ashton, R. and White, K. D. (1980) 'Sex differences in imagery vividness: An artefact of the test', *British Journal of Psychology*, 71, 35–38.

Atwood, G. (1971) 'An experimental study of visual imagination and memory', *Cognitive Psychology*, 2, 290–9.

Averill, J. R. (1974) 'An analysis of psychophysiological symbolism and its influence on theories of emotion', *Journal for the Theory of Social Behavior*, 4, 147–90.

Averill, J. R. (1980) 'A constructivist view of emotion', in Plutchik, R. and Kellerman, H. (eds) *Emotion: Theory, Research and Experience. vol. I: Theories of Emotion*, New York, Academic Press, pp. 305–39.

Aylwin, S. (1977) 'The structure of visual and kinaesthetic imagery: A free association study', *British Journal of Psychology*, 68, 353–60.

Aylwin, S. (1981) 'Types of relationship instantiated in verbal, visual and enactive imagery', *Journal of Mental Imagery*, 5 (1), 67–84.

Baker, S. (1984) 'Human hibernation', *Omni*, 6, 68–74.

Bandler, R. and Grinder, J. (1975) *The Structure of Magic I. A Book about Language and Therapy*, Palo Alto, Science and Behavior Books.

Bandura, A. (1977) 'Self-efficacy: Toward a unifying theory of behavioral change', *Psychological Review*, 84, 191–215.

Bandura, A. (1980) 'Gauging the relationship between self-efficacy judgments and action', *Cognitive Therapy and Research*, 4, 263–8.

Barthes, R. (1972) *Mythologies*, trans. A. Lavers, London, Jonathan Cape (1st publ. 1957).

Bartlett, F. C. (1921) 'The functions of images', *British Journal of Psychology*, 11, 320–37.

Beck, A. T. (1963) 'Thinking and depression. I. Idiosyncratic content and cognitive distortions', *Archives of General Psychiatry*, 9, 36–45.

Beck, A. T., Rush, A. J., Shaw, B. F. and Emery, G. (1979) *Cognitive Therapy of Depression*, Chichester, Wiley.

Belotti, E. G. (1975) *Little Girls. Social Conditioning and its Effects on the Stereotyped Role of Women during Infancy*, London, Writers and Readers Publishing Cooperative (1st publ. 1973).

Bem, S. (1974) 'The measurement of psychological androgyny', *Journal of Consulting and Clinical Psychology*, 42, 155–62.

Bem, S. L. (1975) 'Sex role adaptability: One consequence of psychological androgyny', *Journal of Personality and Social Psychology*, 31, 634–43.

Bem, S. L. and Lenney, E. (1976) 'Sex typing and the avoidance of cross-sex behavior', *Journal of Personality and Social Psychology*, 33, 48–54.

Bennett, G. K., Seashore, H. G. and Wesman, A. G. (1974) *Manual for the Differential Aptitude Tests: Forms S and T* (5th edn), New York, The Psychological Corporation.

Berger, G. H. and Gaunitz, S. C. B. (1977) 'Self-rated imagery and vividness of task pictures in relation to visual memory', *British Journal of Psychology*, 68, 283–8.

Berger, P. L. and Luckman, T. (1966) *The Social Construction of Reality*, New York, Doubleday.

Berlin, B., Breedlove, D. E. and Raven, P. H. (1966) 'Folk taxonomies and biological classification', *Science*, 154, 273–5.

Bersted, C. T. (1983) 'Memory scanning of described images and undescribed images: Hemispheric differences', *Memory and Cognition*, 11, 129–36.

Betts, G. (1909) *The Distribution and Functions of Mental Imagery*, New York, Teachers College, Columbia University.

Bever, T. G. (1970) 'The cognitive basis for linguistic structures', in Hayes, J. R. (ed) *Cognition and the Development of Language*, New York, Wiley, pp. 279–362.

Bion, W. R. (1962) 'A theory of thinking', International Journal of Psychoanalysis, 43, 306–10.

Bliss, J., Monk, M. and Ogborn, J. (1983) Qualitative Data Analysis for Educational Research, London, Croom Helm.

Borgida, E., Locksley, A. and Brekke, N. (1981) 'Social stereotypes and social judgment', in Cantor, N. and Kihlstrom, J. F. (eds) Personality, Cognition, and Social Interaction, Hillsdale, NJ: Erlbaum, pp. 153–69.

Borkovec, T. D. (1976) 'Physiological and cognitive processes in the regulation of anxiety', in Schwartz, G. E. and Shapiro, D. (eds) Consciousness and Self-regulation. Advances in Research. vol. I, New York, Plenum, pp. 261–312.

Bower, G. H. (1972) 'Mental imagery and associative learning', in Gregg, L. W. (ed.) Cognition in Learning and Memory, New York, Wiley, pp. 51–88.

Bower, G. H. (1978) 'Experiments on story comprehension and recall', Discourse Processes, 1, 211–32.

Bower, G. H. (1981) 'Mood and memory', American Psychologist, 36, 129–48.

Braine, M. D. S. and Hardy, J. A. (1982) 'On what case categories there are, why they are, and how they develop: An amalgam of a priori considerations, speculation, and evidence from children', in Wanner, E. and Gleitman, L. R. (eds) Language Acquisition: The State of the Art, Cambridge, Cambridge University Press, pp. 219–39.

Braine, M. D. S. and Wells, R. S. (1978) 'Case-like categories in children: The Actor and some related categories', Cognitive Psychology, 10, 100–22.

Brenner, M. (ed.) (1980) The Structure of Action, Oxford, Blackwell.

Brickman, P., Redfield, J., Harrison, A. A. and Crandall, R. (1972) 'Drive and predisposition as factors in the attitudinal effects of mere exposure', Journal of Experimental Social Psychology, 8, 31–44.

Brooks, L. (1968) 'Spatial and verbal components of the act of recall', Canadian Journal of Psychology, 22, 349–68.

Broverman, I. K., Broverman, D. M., Clarkson, F. E., Rosencrantz, P. S. and Vogel, S. R. (1970) 'Sex-role stereotypes and clinical judgments of mental health', Journal of Consulting and Clinical Psychology, 34, 1–7.

Bruner, J. S. (1966) 'On cognitive growth', in Bruner, J. S., Olver, R. R., Greenfield, P. M., et al. Studies in Cognitive Growth, New York, Wiley, pp. 1–29.

Bruner, J. S. (1975) 'The ontogenesis of speech acts', Journal of Child Language, 2, 1–19.

Bruner, J. S. (1981) 'The organization of action and the nature of adult–infant transaction', in d'Ydewalle, G. and Lens, W. (eds) Cognition in Human Motivation and Learning, Louvain, Leuven University Press, pp. 1–13.

Bruner, J. S. and Postman, L. (1949) 'On the perception of incongruity: A paradigm', Journal of Personality, 18, 206–23.

Bucci, W. (1982) 'The vocalization of painful affect', Journal of Communication Disorders, 15, 415–40.

Bull, N. (1951) 'The attitude theory of emotion', Nervous and Mental Disease Monographs, 81.

Buytendijk, F. J. J. (1950) 'The phenomenological approach to the problem of feelings and emotions', in Reymert, M. L. (ed.) Feelings and Emotions. The Mooseheart Symposium, New York, Hafner, pp. 127–41.

Calvano, M. A. (1974) 'Predicting the use of imagery as a mediation strategy', Audiovisual Communication Review, 22, 269–77.

Camp, B. W. (1977) 'Verbal mediation in young aggressive boys', Journal of Abnormal Psychology, 86, 145–53.

Cannon, W. B. (1929) Bodily Changes in Pain, Hunger, Fear and Rage; an Account of Researches into the Function of Emotional Excitement (2nd edn), New York, Appleton-Century-Crofts.

Cantor, N. and Mischel, W. (1977) 'Traits as prototypes: Effects on recognition memory', Journal of Personality and Social Psychology, 35, 38–48.

Cantor, N. and Mischel, W. (1979) 'Prototypes in person perception', *Advances in Experimental Social Psychology*, 12, 3–52.

Caramazza, A., Hersh, H. and Torgerson, W. S. (1976) 'Subjective structures and operations in semantic memory', *Journal of Verbal Learning and Verbal Behavior*, 15, 103–17.

Cartwright, R. D. and Munroe, L. J. (1968) 'Relation of dreaming and REM sleep: The effects of REM deprivation under two conditions', *Journal of Personality and Social Psychology*, 10, 69–74.

Carver, C. S. (1979) 'A cybernetic model of self-attention processes', *Journal of Personality and Social Psychology*, 37, 1251–81.

Carver, C. S., Blaney, P. H. and Scheier, M. F. (1979) 'Focus of attention, chronic expectancy, and responses to a feared stimulus', *Journal of Personality and Social Psychology*, 37, 1186–95.

Carver, C. S. and Scheier, M. F. (1981) *Attention and Self-Regulation: A Control-Theory Approach to Human Behavior*, New York and Heidelberg, Springer Verlag.

Cattell, R. B. and Eber, H. W. (1966) *The Sixteen Personality Factor Questionnaire*, Champaign, Ill., Institute for Personality and Ability Testing.

Cautela, J. R. (1970) 'Covert reinforcement', *Behavior Therapy*, 1, 33–50.

Cautela, J. R. and Kastenbaum, R. (1967) 'A reinforcement survey schedule for use in therapy, training, and research', *Psychological Reports*, 20, 1115–30.

Cautela, J. R. and Wisocki, P. (1971) 'Covert sensitization for the treatment of sexual deviations', *The Psychological Record*, 21, 37–48.

Cawelti, J. G. (1976) *Adventure, Mystery, and Romance: Formula Stories as Art and Popular Culture*, Chicago, Chicago University Press.

Chafe, W. L. (1970) *Meaning and the Structure of Language*, Chicago, Chicago University Press.

Chance, M. A. (1980) 'An ethological assessment of emotion', in Plutchik, R. and Kellerman, H. (eds) *Emotion: Theory, Research, and Experience. vol. I. Theories of Emotion*, New York, Academic Press, pp. 81–111.

Chomsky, N. (1959) 'Review of B. F. Skinner's *Verbal Behavior*', *Language*, 35, 26–58.

Claparède, E. (1928) 'Feelings and emotions', in Reymert, M. L. (ed.) *Feelings and Emotions. The Wittenberg Symposium*. Worcester, Mass.: Clark University Press, pp. 124–39.

Colvin, S. S. (1909) 'Methods of determining ideational types', *Psychological Bulletin*, 6, 223–37.

Cooley, C. H. (1902) *Human Nature and the Social Order*, New York, Charles Scribners Sons.

Cooper, L. A. and Shepard, R. N. (1973) 'Chronometric studies of the rotation of mental images', in Chase, W. G. (ed.) *Visual Information Processing*, New York, Academic Press, pp. 75–176.

Cooper, L. G. (1973) 'A multivariate investigation of preferences', *Multivariate Behavior Research*, 8, 253–72.

Couch, A. and Keniston, K. (1960) 'Yeasayers and naysayers: Agreeing response set as a personality variable', *Journal of Abnormal and Social Psychology*, 60, 151–74.

Craik, F. I. M. and Lockhart, R. S. (1972) 'Levels of processing: A framework for memory research', *Journal of Verbal Learning and Verbal Behavior*, 11, 671–84.

Cramer, P. (1968) *Word Association*, New York, Academic Press.

Cranach, M. von, Kalbermatten, U., Indermühle, K. and Gugler, B. (1982) *Goal-Directed Action*, trans. M. Turton, New York, Academic Press.

Crowne, D. P. and Marlowe, D. (1964) *The Approval Motive: Studies in Evaluative Dependence*, New York, Wiley.

Csikszentmihalyi, M. (1975) *Beyond Boredom and Anxiety. The Experience of Play in Work and Games*, San Francisco, Jossey-Bass.

Dahl, H. (1979) 'The appetite hypothesis of emotions: A new psychoanalytic model of motivation', in Izard, C. E. (ed.) *Emotions in Personality and Psychopathology*, New York, Plenum Press, pp. 201–25.

Danaher, B. G. and Thoresen, C. E. (1972) 'Imagery assessment by self-report and behavioral measures', *Behavior Research and Therapy*, 10, 131–8.

Danehy, E. Z. (1980) 'Centering movement and the visualization of transformational imagery', in Shorr, J. E. Sobel, G. E., Robin, P. and Connella, J. A. (eds) *Imagery: Its Many Dimensions and Applications*, New York, Plenum, pp. 243–50.

Darwin, C. (1872) *The Expression of the Emotions in Man and Animals*, London, John Murray.

Davidson, R. J., Schwartz, G. E., Pugash, E. and Bromfield, E. (1976) 'Sex differences in patterns of EEG asymmetry', *Biological Psychology*, 4, 119–38.

Davitz, J. R. (1969) *The Language of Emotion*, New York, Academic Press.

Davitz, J. R. (1970) A dictionary and grammar of emotion', in Arnold M. B., (ed.) *Feelings and Emotions*, New York, Academic Press, pp. 251–8.

de Charms, R. (1968) *Personal Causation: The Internal Affective Determinants of Behaviour*, New York, Academic Press.

de Rivera, J. (1977) *A Structural Theory of the Emotions*, New York, International Universities Press.

De Soto, C., London, M. and Handel, S. (1965) 'Social reasoning and spatial paralogic', *Journal of Personality and Social Psychology*, 2, 513–21.

Deese, J. (1965) *The Structure of Associations in Language and Thought*, Baltimore, John Hopkins Press.

Deese, J. (1973) 'Cognitive structure and affect in language', in Pliner, P., Krames, L. and Alloway T., (eds) *Communication and Affect: Language and Thought*, New York, Academic Press, pp. 9–20.

Dembo, T. (1976) 'The dynamics of anger', in de Rivera, J. (ed.) *Field Theory as Human–Science*, New York, Gardner Press, pp. 324–422.

Dendinger, R. A. (1980) 'Imagination and movement therapy', in Shorr, J. E., Sobel, G. E., Robin, P., and Conella, J. A. (eds) *Imagery: Its Many Dimensions and Applications*, New York, Plenum, pp. 237–41.

Diehl, C. F. and England, N. C. (1958) 'Mental imagery', *Journal of Speech and Hearing Research*, 1, 268–74.

Diener, E. (1977) 'Deindividuation: Causes and consequences', *Social Behavior and Personality*, 5, 143–55.

Diener, E. (1979) 'Deindividuation, self-awareness, and disinhibition', *Journal of Personality and Social Psychology*, 37, 1160–71.

Diener, E., Lusk R., DeFour, D, and Flax, R. (1980) 'Deindividuation: Effects of group size, density, number of observers, and group member similarity on self-consciousness and disinhibited behavior', *Journal of Personality and Social Psychology*, 39, 449–59.

Dilling, C. A. and Rabin, A. I. (1967) 'Temporal experience in depressive states and schizophrenia', *Journal of Consulting Psychology*, 31, 604–8.

Diver, W. (1964) 'The system of agency in the Latin noun', *Word*, 20, 178–96.

DiVesta, F. J., Ingersoll, G. and Sunshine, P. A. (1971) 'Factor analysis of imagery tests', *Journal of Verbal Learning and Verbal Behavior*, 10, 471–9.

Dixon, R. (1971) 'A method of semantic description', in Steinberg, D. and Jakobovits, L. A. (eds) *Semantics. An Interdisciplinary Reader in Philosophy, Linguistics and Psychology*, Cambridge, Cambridge University Press, pp. 436–71.

Doise, W. (1978) *Groups and Individuals: Explanations in Social Psychology*, trans. D. Graham, Cambridge, Cambridge University Press (1st publ. 1976).

Dollard, J., Doob, L. W., Sears, R. R., Miller, N. E. and Mowrer, O. H. (1939) *Frustration and Aggression*, New Haven, Yale University Press.

Dosamantes-Alperson, E. (1980) 'Contacting bodily-felt experiencing in psychotherapy', in Shorr, J. E., Sobel, G. E., Robin, P. and Connella, J. A. (eds) *Imagery: Its Many Dimensions and Applications*, New York, Plenum, pp. 223–36.

Duffy, E. (1962) *Activation and Behaviour*, New York, Wiley.

Dunn, S., Bliss, J. and Siipola, E. (1958) 'Effects of impulsivity, introversion, and individual values upon association under free conditions', *Journal of Personality*, 26, 61–76.

Duval, S. and Wicklund, R. (1972) *A Theory of Objective Self-Awareness*, New York, Academic Press.

Dyckman, J. M. and Cowan, P. A. (1978) 'Imaging vividness and the outcome of in vivo and imagined scene desensitization', *Journal of Consulting and Clinical Psychology*, 46, 1155–6.

Easterbrook, J. A. (1959) 'The effect of emotion on cue utilization and the organization of behavior', *Psychological Review*, 66, 183–201.

Eibl-Eibesfeldt, I. (1971) *Love and Hate. On the Natural History of Basic Behaviour Patterns*, trans. G. Strachan, London, Methuen (1st publ. 1970).

Eibl-Eibesfeldt, I. (1980) 'Strategies of social interaction', in Plutchik, R. and Kellerman H., (eds), *Emotion: Theory, Research, and Experience. vol. I: Theories of Emotion*, New York, Academic Press, pp. 57–80.

Einstein, A. (1954) 'Letter to Jacques Hadamard', reprinted in Ghiselin, B. (ed.) *The Creative Process. A Symposium.* Berkeley and Los Angeles: University of California Press.

Ekman, P. (ed.) (1982) *Emotion in the Human Face* (2nd edn), Cambridge, Cambridge University Press.

Ekman, P. and Friesen, W. V. (1971) 'Constants across culture in the face and emotion', *Journal of Personality and Social Psychology*, 17, 124–9.

Eliade, M. (1976) *Myths, Rites, Symbols: A Mircea Eliade Reader. vol. I*, ed. Beane, W. C. and Doty, W. G., New York, Harper Colophon.

Elkind, D., Koegler, R. R. and Go, E. (1964) 'Studies in perceptual development: II. Part–whole perception,' *Child Development*, 35, 81–90.

Ellenberger, H. F. (1958) 'A clinical introduction to psychiatric phenomenology and existential analysis', in May, R., Angel, E., and Ellenberger, H. F. (eds) *Existence. A New Dimension in Psychiatry and Psychology*, New York, Basic Books, pp. 92–123.

Emmons, M. (1980) 'The inner source and meditative therapy', in Shorr, J. E., Sobel, G. E., Robin, P. and Connella, J. A. (eds) *Imagery: Its Many Dimensions and Applications*, New York, Plenum Press, pp. 321–42.

Epstein, S. (1972) 'The nature of anxiety with emphasis upon its relationship to expectancy', in Spielberger, C. D. (ed.) *Anxiety: Current Trends in Theory and Research. vol. 2*, New York, Academic Press, pp. 291–331.

Ernest, C. H. (1977) 'Imagery ability and cognition: A critical review', *Journal of Mental Imagery*, 1(2), 181–216.

Ernest, C. H. and Paivio, A. (1971) 'Imagery and sex differences in incidental recall', *British Journal and Psychology*, 62, 67–72.

Euse, F. J. and Haney, J. N. (1975) 'Clarity, controllability, and emotional intensity of image: Correlations with introversion, neuroticism, and subjective anxiety', *Perceptual and Motor Skills*, 40, 443–7.

Evans-Pritchard, E. (1962) 'Sanza: A characteristic feature of Zande language and thought', reprinted in his *Essays in Social Anthropology*, London, Faber & Faber (1st publ. 1956).

Eysenck, H. J. and Eysenck, S. B. G. (1975) *Manual of the Eysenck Personality Questionnaire*, Sevenoaks, Kent, Hodder & Stoughton Educational.

Fell, J. P. (1977) 'The phenomenological approach to emotion', in Candland, D. K. and others (eds), *Emotion*, Monterey, Calif., Brooks Cole, pp. 253–85.

Fenigstein, A., Scheier, M. F. and Buss, A. H. (1975) 'Public and private self-consciousness: Assessment and theory', *Journal of Consulting and Clinical Psychology*, 43, 522–7.

Festinger, L. (1957) *A Theory of Cognitive Dissonance*, Stanford, Calif., Stanford University Press.

Fillmore, C. J. (1968) 'The case for case', in Bach, E. and Harms, R. (eds) *Universals in Linguistic Theory*, New York, Holt, Rinehart & Winston, pp. 1–88.

Fillmore, C. J. (1971) 'Types of lexical information', in Steinberg, D. and Jakobovits, L. A. (eds) *Semantics. An Interdisciplinary Reader in Philosophy, Linguistics and Psychology*, Cambridge, Cambridge University Press, pp. 370–92.

Folkman, S., Schaefer, C. and Lazarus, R. S. (1979) 'Cognitive processes as mediators of stress and coping', in Hamilton, V. and Warburton, D. M. (eds) *Human Stress and Cognition. An Information Processing Approach*, Chichester, Wiley, pp. 265–98.

Forisha, B. D. (1975) 'Mental imagery verbal processes: A developmental study', *Developmental Psychology*, 11, 259–67.

Forisha, B. D. (1978) 'Mental imagery and creativity: Review and speculations', *Journal of Mental Imagery*, 2, 209–38.

Foucault, M. (1972) *The Archaeology of Knowledge*, trans. A. M. Sheridan Smith, London, Tavistock (1st publ. 1969).

Foulkes, D. (1978) *A Grammar of Dreams*, Hassocks, Sussex, Harvester Press.

Frazer, J. G. (1922) *The Golden Bough. A Study in Magic and Religion* (abridged edn), London, Macmillan.

Frenkel-Brunswik, E. (1948) 'A study of prejudice in children', *Human Relations*, 1, 295–306.

Frenkel-Brunswik, E. (1949) 'Intolerance of ambiguity as an emotional and perceptual personality variable', *Journal of Personality*, 18, 108–43.

Frenkel-Brunswik, E. (1954) 'Further explorations by a contributor to "The Authoritarian Personality"', in Christie, R. and Jahoda, M. (eds) *Studies in the Scope and Method of The Authoritarian Personality*, New York, Free Press, pp. 226–75.

Freud, S. (1900) *The Interpretation of Dreams*, New York, Wiley, 1961.

Freud, S. (1908a) 'The relation of the poet to daydreaming' in *Collected Papers. vol. IV*, trans. J. Riviere, London, Hogarth Press, 1949, pp. 173–83.

Freud, S. (1908b) 'Hysterical fantasies and their relation to bisexuality', in *Collected Papers. vol. II*, trans. J. Riviere, London, Hogarth Press, 1957, pp. 51–8.

Freud, S. (1911) 'Formulations regarding the two principles in mental functioning', in *Collected Papers. vol. IV*, trans. J. Riviere, London, Hogarth Press, 1949, pp. 13–21.

Freud, S. (1915) 'Instincts and their vicissitudes', *Standard Edition of the Complete Psychological Works of Sigmund Freud. vol. 14*, trans. J. Strachey and others, London, Hogarth Press, 1957, pp. 109–40.

Freud, S. (1923) 'The ego and the id', *Standard Edition of the Complete Psychological Works of Sigmund Freud. vol. 19*, trans. J. Strachey, London, Hogarth Press, 1961, pp. 12–66.

Freud, S. (1931) 'Libidinal types', in *Collected Papers. vol. V*, ed. J. Strachey, London, Hogarth Press, 1957, pp. 247–51.

Frijda, N. H. (1970) 'Emotion and recognition of emotion', in Arnold, M. B., (ed.) *Feelings and Emotions*, New York, Academic Press, pp. 241–50.

Gale. A., Morris, P. E., Lucas, B. and Richardson, A. (1972) 'Types of imagery and imagery types: An EEG study', *British Journal of Psychology*, 63, 523–31.

Galton, F. (1880) 'Statistics of mental imagery', *Mind*, 19, 301–18.

Galton, F. (1907) *Inquiries into Human Faculty and Its Development* (2nd edn), London, J. M. Dent.

Gardner, R. W. (1969) 'Organismic equilibration and the energy–structure duality in psychoanalytic theory: An attempt at theoretical refinement', *Journal of the American Psychoanalytic Association*, 17, 3–40.

Gardner, R. W., Holzman, P. S., Klein, G. S., Linton, H. B. and Spence, D. P. (1959) 'Cognitive control. A study of individual differences in cognitive behaviour', *Psychological Issues*, 1 (4), Monog. No. 4.

Garfinkel, H. (1955–6) 'Conditions of successful degradation ceremonies', *American Journal of Sociology*, 61, 420–4.

Geer, J. (1965) 'The development of a scale to measure fear', *Behavior Research and Therapy*, 3, 45–53.

Gellhorn, E. (1964) 'Motion and emotion: The role of proprioception in the physiology and pathology of emotions', *Psychological Review*, 71, 457–72.

Gellhorn, E. (1968) 'Attempts at a synthesis: Contribution to a theory of emotion', in Gellhorn, E. (ed.) *Biological Foundations of Emotion*, Glenview, Ill. Scott, Foresman, pp. 144–53.

Gendlin, E. T. (1980) 'Imagery is more powerful with focusing: Theory and practice', in Shorr, J. E., Sobel, G. E., Robin, P. and Connella, J. A. (eds) *Imagery: Its Many Dimensions and Applications*, New York, Plenum Press, pp. 65–73.

Gerard, R. W. (1954) 'The biological basis of imagination', in Ghiselin, B. (ed.) *The Creative Process. A Symposium*, Berkeley and Los Angeles, University of California Press, pp. 236–59.

Giambra, L. M. (1980) 'A factor analysis of the items of the imaginal processes inventory', *Journal of Clinical Psychology*, 36, 383–409.

Gibson, J. J. (1977) 'The theory of affordances', in Shaw, R. and Bransford, J. (eds) *Perceiving, Acting and Knowing. Toward an Ecological Psychology*, Hillsdale, NJ, Erlbaum, pp. 67–82.

Gleitman, L. R. and Wanner, E. (1982) 'Language acquisition: The state of the state of the art', in Wanner, E. and Gleitman L. R. (eds) *Language Acquisition: The State of the Art*, Cambridge, Cambridge University Press, pp. 3–48.

Glucksberg, S. (1984), 'Commentary: The functional equivalence of common and multiple codes', *Journal of Verbal Learning and Verbal Behavior*, 23, 100–4.

Goffman, E. (1955) 'On face work', *Psychiatry*, 18, 213–31.

Goffman, E. (1956) 'Embarrassment and social organization', *American Journal of Sociology*, 62, 264–71.

Gordon, D. (1978) *Therapeutic Metaphors. Helping Others through the Looking Glass*, Cupertino, Calif., META Publications.

Gordon, R. (1949) 'An investigation into some of the factors that favour the formation of stereotyped imagery', *British Journal of Psychology*, 39, 156–67.

Gordon, W. J. J. (1961) *Synectics. The Development of Creative Capacity*, New York, Harper & Row.

Gorman, B. S. and Wessman, A. E. (1977) 'Images, values, and concepts of time in psychological research', in Gorman, B. S. and Wessman, A. E. (eds) *The Personal Experience of Time*, New York, Plenum, pp. 217–63.

Gralton, M. A., Hayes, Y. A. and Richardson, J. T. E. (1979) 'Introversion–extraversion and mental imagery', *Journal of Mental Imagery*, 3, 1–10.

Griffitts, C. H. (1925) *Fundamentals of Vocational Guidance*, New York, Macmillan.

Griffitts, C. H. (1927) 'Individual differences in imagery', *Psychological Monographs*, 37 (3).

Grinder, J. and Bandler, R. (1976) *The Structure of Magic II*, Palo Alto, Science and Behavior Books.

Gross, E. and Stone, S. P. (1964) 'Embarrassment and the analysis of role requirements', *American Journal of Sociology*, 70, 1–15.

Grossberg, J. M. and Wilson, H. K. (1968) 'Physiological changes accompanying the visualization of fearful and neutral situations', *Journal of Personality and Social Psychology*, 10, 124–33.

Gumenik, W. E. (1979) 'The advantage of specific terms over general terms as cues for sentence recall: Instantiation or retrieval?', *Memory and Cognition*, 7, 240–4.

Hannay, H. J. (1976) 'Real or imagined incomplete lateralization of function in females?', *Perception and Psychophysics*, 19, 349–52.

Hannay, H. J. and Malone, D. R. (1976) 'Visual field effects and short-term memory for verbal material', *Neuropsychologia*, 14, 203–9.

Harrington, D. M. (1980) 'Creativity, analogical thinking, and muscular metaphors', *Journal of Mental Imagery*, 4 (2), 13–23.

Hayakawa, S. I. (1965) *Language in Thought and Action* (2nd edn), London, Allen & Unwin.

Hebb, D. O. (1949) *The Organization of Behavior: A Neuropsychological Study*, New York, Wiley.

Heidegger, M. (1967) *Being and Time*, trans. J. Macquarrie and E. Robinson, Oxford, Blackwell.

Heider, F. (1958) *The Psychology of Interpersonal Relations*, New York, Wiley.

Heilbrun, C. G. (1979) *Reinventing Womanhood*, New York, Norton.

Henley, N. M. (1969) 'A psychological study of the semantics of animal terms', *Journal of Verbal Learning and Verbal Behavior*, 8, 176–84.

Hesiod (1876) 'The Theogony of Hesiod', in *The Works of Hesiod, Callimachus, and Theognis*, trans. J. Banks, London, George Bell & Sons.

Higgins, E. T. and Rholes, W. S. (1976) 'Impression formation and role fulfillment: A "holistic reference" approach', *Journal of Experimental Social Psychology*, 12, 422–35.

Hillman, J. (1970), 'C. G. Jung's contributions to "Feelings and Emotions": Synopsis and implications', in Arnold, M. B. (ed.) *Feelings and Emotions*, New York, Academic Press, pp. 125–34.

Hiscock, M. and Cohen, D. B. (1973) 'Visual imagery and dream recall', *Journal of Research in Personality*, 7, 179–88.

Hollandsworth, J. R., Glazeski, R. C., Kirkland, K., Jones, G. E. and van Norman, L. R. (1979) 'An analysis of the nature and effects of test anxiety: Cognitive, behavioral, and physiological components', *Cognitive Therapy and Research*, 3, 165–80.

Hollon, S. D. and Kendall, P. C. (1980) 'Cognitive self-statements in depression: Development of an automatic thoughts questionnaire', *Cognitive Therapy and Research*, 4, 383–95.

Horowitz, M. J. (1978) *Image Formation and Cognition* (2nd edn), New York, Appleton-Century-Crofts.

Hubel, D. H. and Wiesel, T. N. (1979) 'Brain mechanisms of vision', in *The Brain* (Reprints from *Scientific American*, September 1979), San Francisco, Freeman, pp. 84–96.

Huckabee, M. W. (1974) 'Introversion–extraversion and imagery', *Psychological Reports*, 34, 453–4.

Hudson, L. (1966) *Contrary Imaginations. A Psychological Study of the English Schoolboy*, London, Methuen.

Hudson, L. (1968) *Frames of Mind. Ability Perception and Self-Perception in the Arts and Sciences*, London, Methuen.

Hull, J. G. and Levy, A. S. (1979) 'The organizational functions of the self: An alternative to the Duval and Wicklund model of self-awareness', *Journal of Personality and Social Psychology*, 37, 756–68.

Hurlburt, R. T. and Sipprelle, C. N. (1978) 'Random sampling of cognitions in alleviating anxiety attacks', *Cognitive Therapy and Research*, 2, 165–70.

Ickes, W. and Barnes, R. D. (1978) 'Boys and girls together – and alienated: On enacting stereotyped sex roles in mixed-sex dyads', *Journal of Personality and Social Psychology*, 36, 669–83.

Isakower, O. (1939) 'On the exceptional position of the auditory sphere', *International Journal of Psychoanalysis*, 20, 340–8.

Israeli, N. (1935) 'Distress in the outlook of Lancashire and Scottish unemployed', *Journal of Applied Psychology*, 19, 67–9.

Izard, C. E. (1971) *The Face of Emotion*, New York, Appleton-Century-Crofts.

Izard, C. E. (1977) *Human Emotions*, New York, Plenum Press.

Jacobson, E. (1938) *Progressive Relaxation* (2nd edn), Chicago, Chicago University Press,

Jacobson, E. (1970) *Modern Treatment of Tense Patients*, New York, Charles C. Thomas.

Jaffe, D. T. and Bresler, D. E. (1980) 'Guided imagery: Healing through the mind's eye', in Shorr, J. E., Sobel, G. E., Robin, P. and Connella, J. A. (eds) *Imagery: Its Many Dimensions and Applications*, New York, Plenum Press, pp. 253–66.

James, W. (1892) *Psychology. Briefer Course*, London, Macmillan.

James, W. (1902) *The Varieties of Religious Experience*, London, Longmans, Green.

Janis, I. L. (1958) *Psychological Stress*, New York, Wiley.

Janis, I. L. and Mann, L. (1977) *Decision Making*, New York, Free Press.

Johnson, R. D. and Downing, L. L. (1979) 'Deindividuation and valence of cues: Effects on prosocial and antisocial behavior', *Journal of Personality and Social Psychology*, 37, 1532–8.

Jones, H. E. (1935) 'The galvanic skin reflex as related to emotional expression', *American Journal of Psychology*, 47, 241–51.

Jones, H. E. (1950) 'The study of patterns of emotional expression', in Reymert, M. L. (ed.) *Feelings and Emotions. The Mooseheart Symposium*, New York, McGraw Hill, pp. 161–6.

Jones, J. G. (1965) 'Motor learning without demonstration of physical practice, under two conditions of mental practice', *Research Quarterly*, 36, 270–6.

Jung, C. G. (1918) *Studies in Word Association*, trans. M. D. Eder, New York, Russell & Russell.

Kant, I. (1968) *Critique of Pure Reason* (2nd edn), trans. N. Kemp Smith, London, Macmillan (1st publ. 1781).

Kanzer, M. (1958) 'Image formation during free association', *Psychoanalytic Quarterly*, 27, 465–84.

Kelley, H. H. and Stahelski, A. J. (1970) 'The social interaction basis of cooperators' and competitors' beliefs about others', *Journal of Personality and Social Psychology*, 16, 66–91.

Kelly, G. A. (1955) *The Psychology of Personal Constructs* (2 vols), New York, Norton.

Kelly, G. A. (1958) 'Man's construction of his alternatives', in Lindzey, G. (ed.) *Assessment of Human Motives*, New York, Rinehart & Co., pp. 33–64.

Kieras, D. (1978) 'Beyond pictures and words: Alternative information-processing models for imagery effects in verbal memory', *Psychological Bulletin*, 85, 532–54.

Kintsch, W. (1972) 'Notes on the structure of semantic memory', in Tulving, E. and Donaldson, W. (eds) *Organization of Memory*, New York, Academic Press, pp. 249–308.

Kipnis, D. and Vanderveer, R. (1971) 'Ingratiation and the use of power', *Journal of Personality and Social Psychology*, 17, 280–6.

Kirk, G. S. and Raven, J. E. (1966) *The Presocratic Philosophers. A Critical History with a Selection of Texts*, Cambridge, Cambridge University Press.

Klahr, D. (1969) 'Decision making in a complex environment: The use of similarity judgments to predict preferences', *Management Science*, 15, 595–618.

Klein, G. S. (1958) 'Cognitive control and motivation', in Lindzey, G. (ed.) *Assessment of Human Motives*, New York, Rinehart & Co., pp. 87–118.

Klein, G. S. (1967) 'Peremptory ideation: Structure and force in motivated ideas', *Psychological Issues*, 5 (2–3), 80–128.

Klinger, E. (1971) *Structure and Functions of Fantasy*, New York, Wiley.

Klinger, E., Barta, S. G. and Maxeiner, M. E. (1981) 'Current concerns: Assessing therapeutically relevant motivation', in Kendall, P. C. and Hollon, S. D. (eds) *Assessment Strategies for Cognitive-Behavioral Interventions*, New York, Academic Press, pp. 161–96.

Korzybski, A. (1933) *Science and Sanity: An Introduction to Non-Aristotelian Systems and General Semantics*, Lancaster, Pa., Science Press Printing Co.

Kosslyn, S. M. (1973) 'Scanning visual images: Some structural implications', *Perception and Psychophysics*, 14, 90–4.

Kosslyn, S. M. (1978) 'Imagery and internal representation', in Rosch, E. and Lloyd, B. B. (eds) *Cognition and Categorization*, Hillsdale, NJ, Erlbaum, pp. 217–57.

Kosslyn, S. M., Pinker, S., Smith, G. E. and Schwartz, S. P. (1979) 'On the demystification of mental imagery', *The Behavioural and Brain Sciences*, 2, 535–81.

Kosslyn, S. M. and Pomerantz, J. R. (1977) 'Imagery, propositions, and the form of internal representations', *Cognitive Psychology*, 9, 52–76.

Krippendorff, K. (1980) *Content Analysis. An Introduction to Its Methodology*, Beverly Hills, Sage.

Kuhn, T. (1970) *The Structure of Scientific Revolutions* (2nd edn), Chicago, Chicago University Press.

Lacan, J. (1977) 'The mirror stage as formative of the functions of the I', in *Écrits. A Selection*, trans. A. Sheridan, London, Tavistock (1st publ. 1949).

Laing, R. D. (1959) *The Divided Self*, London, Tavistock.

Laird, J. D. (1974) 'Self-attribution of emotion: The effects of expressive behavior on the quality of emotional experience', *Journal of Personality and Social Psychology*, 29, 475–86.

Lakoff, G. (1971) 'On generative semantics', in Steinberg, D. and Jakobovits, L. (eds), *Semantics*, Cambridge, Cambridge University Press, pp. 232–96.

Lakoff, G. and Johnson, M. (1980) *Metaphors We Live by*, Chicago and London, Chicago University Press.

Landau, R. J. (1980) 'The role of semantic schemata in phobic word interpretation', *Cognitive Therapy and Research*, 4, 427–34.

Lang, P. J. (1968) 'Fear reduction and fear behaviour: Problems in treating a construct', in Schlien, J. M. (ed.) *Research in Psychotherapy*. vol. 3, Washington, DC, APA, pp. 90–102.

Lang, P. J. (1979a) 'A bio-informational theory of emotional imagery', *Psychophysiology*, 16, 495–512.

Lang, P. J. (1979b) 'Language, image, and emotion', in Pliner, P., Blankstein, K. R. and Spigel, I. M. (eds), *Perception of Emotion in Self and Others* (*Advances in the Study of Communication and Affect, vol. 5*), New York, Plenum Press, pp. 107–17.

Lang, P. J., Melamed, B. G. and Hart, J. (1970) 'A psychophysiological analysis of fear modification using an automated desensitization procedure', *Journal of Abnormal Psychology*, 76, 220–34.

Langer, E. J. (1978) 'Rethinking the role of thought in social interaction', in Harvey, J. H., Ickes, W. J. and Kidd, R. F. (eds) *New Directions in Attribution Research*, vol. 2, Hillsdale, NJ, Erlbaum, pp. 35–58.

Lanzetta, J. T., Cartwright-Smith, J. and Kleck, R. E. (1976) 'Effects of nonverbal dissimulation on emotional experience and autonomic arousal', *Journal of Personality and Social Psychology*, 33, 354–70.

Lanzetta, J. T. and Kleck, R. E. (1970) 'Encoding and decoding of nonverbal affect in humans', *Journal of Personality and Social Psychology*, 16, 12–19.

Lao Tzu (1963) *Tao Te Ching*, trans. D. C. Lau, Harmondsworth, Penguin.

Laski, M. (1961) *Ecstasy: A Study of Some Secular and Religious Experiences*, London, Cresset Press.

Lazarus, R. S. (1981) 'A cognitivist's reply to Zajonc on emotion and cognition', *American Psychologist*, 36, 222–3.

Lazarus, R. S. (1982) 'Thoughts on the relations between emotion and cognition', *American Psychologist*, 37, 1019–24.

Lazarus, R. S. and Averill, J. R. (1972) 'Emotion and cognition: With special reference to anxiety', in Spielberger, C. D. (ed.) *Anxiety. Current Trends in Theory and Research*. vol. 2, New York, Academic Press, pp. 243–83.

Lazarus, R. S., Kanner, A. D. and Folkman, S. (1980) 'Emotions: A cognitive-phenomenological analysis', in Plutchik, R. and Kellerman, H. (eds) *Emotion: Theory, Research, and Experience*. vol. I: *Theories of Emotion*, New York, Academic Press, pp. 189–217.

Leach, C. (1979) *Introduction to Statistics. A Nonparametric Approach for the Social Sciences*, Chichester, Wiley.

Leach, E. (1964) 'Anthropological aspects of language: Animal categories and verbal abuse', in Lenneberg, E. H. (ed.) *New Directions in the Study of Language*, Cambridge, Mass., MIT Press, pp. 23–63.

Leach, E. (1969) *Genesis as Myth and Other Essays*, London, Cape.

Ledwidge, B. (1978) 'Cognitive behavior modification: A step in the wrong direction?', *Psychological Bulletin*, 85, 353–75.

Lee, T. R. (1981) 'Space cognition and schema theory'. (Paper presented at BPS Annual Conference, Guildford.)

Leeper, R. W. (1948) 'A motivational theory of emotion to replace "emotion as disorganized response" ', *Psychological Review*, 55, 5–21.

Leeper, R. W. (1970) 'The motivational and perceptual properties of emotions as indicating their fundamental character and role', in Arnold, M. B. (ed.) *Feelings and Emotions*, New York, Academic Press, pp. 151–68.

Lefebvre, H. (1971) *Everyday Life in the Modern World*, trans. S. Rabinovitch, London. Allen Lane The Penguin Press (1st publ. 1968).

Leibovitz, M. P., London, P., Cooper, L. M. and Hart, J. T. (1972) 'Dominance in mental imagery', *Educational and Psychological Measurement*, 32, 679–703.

Lesser, G. S. (1957) 'The relationship between overt and fantasy aggression as a function of maternal response to aggression', *Journal of Abnormal and Social Psychology*, 55, 218–21.

Lesser, G. S. (1959) 'Population differences in construct validity', *Journal of Consulting Psychology*, 23, 60–5.

Lettvin, J. Y., Maturana, H. R., McCulloch, W. S. and Pitts, W. H. (1959) 'What the frog's eye tells the frog's brain', *Proceedings of the IRE*, 47, 1940–51.

Leuner, H. (1977) 'Guided affective imagery: An account of its development', *Journal of Mental Imagery*, 1, 73–92.

Leuner, H. (1978) 'Basic principles and therapeutic efficacy of guided affective imagery (GAI)', in Singer, J. L. and Pope, K. S. (eds) *The Power of Human Imagination. New Methods in Psychotherapy*, New York, Plenum Press, pp. 125–66.

Leventhal, H. (1980) 'Toward a comprehensive theory of emotion', *Advances in Experimental Social Psychology*, 13, 139–207.

Lévi-Strauss, C. (1968) *Structural Anthropology*, trans. C. Jacobson and B. Grundfest Schoepf, London, Allen Lane The Penguin Press.

Lévy-Bruhl, L. (1965) *The 'Soul' of the Primitive*, trans. L. A. Clare, London, George Allen & Unwin (1st publ. 1928).

Lewis, H. B. (1979) 'Shame in depression and hysteria', in Izard, C. E. (ed.) *Emotions in Personality and Psychopathology*, New York, Plenum Press, pp. 371–96.

Liem, G. R. (1975) 'Performance and satisfaction as affected by personal control over salient decisions', *Journal of Personality and Social Psychology*, 31, 232–40.

Linville, P. W. (1982) 'The complexity extremity effect and age-based stereotyping', *Journal of Personality and Social Psychology*, 42, 193–211.

Linville, P. W. and Jones, E. E. (1980) 'Polarized appraisals of outgroup members', *Journal of Personality and Social Psychology*, 38, 689–703.

Locksley, A., Borgida, E., Brekke, N. and Hepburn, C. (1980) 'Sex stereotypes and social judgment', *Journal of Personality and Social Psychology* 39, 821–31.

Loftus, G. R. (1972) 'Eye fixations and recognition memory for pictures', *Cognitive Psychology*, 3, 525–51.

Luria, A. R. (1961) *The Role of Speech in the Regulation of Normal and Abnormal Behavior*, New York, Liveright.

Lyons, J. (1968) *Introduction to Theoretical Linguistics*, Cambridge, Cambridge University Press.

McArthur, D. J. (1982) 'Computer vision and perceptual psychology', *Psychological Bulletin*, 92, 283–309.

McArthur, L. Z. (1982) 'Judging a book by its cover: A cognitive analysis of the relationship between physical appearance and stereotyping', in Hastorf, A. H. and Isen, A. M. (eds), *Cognitive Social Psychology*, New York, Elsevier/North Holland, pp. 149–211.

McClelland, D. C. (1955) 'Notes for a revised theory of motivation', in McClelland, D. C. (ed.) *Studies in Motivation*, New York, Appleton-Century-Crofts, pp. 226–34. (Reprinted from McClelland, D. C. (1951) *Personality*, New York, Sloane, pp. 466–75.)

McClelland, D. C. and Winter, D. (1971) *Motivating Economic Achievement*, New York, Free Press.

Maccoby, E. E. and Jacklin, C. N. (1974) *The Psychology of Sex Differences*, Stanford, Calif., Stanford University Press.

McDougall, W. (1928) 'Emotion and feeling distinguished', in Reymert, M. L. (ed.) *Feelings and Emotions. The Wittenberg Symposium*, Worcester, Mass., Clark University Press, pp. 200–5.

McGee, M. G. (1979) 'Human spatial cognition: Psychometric studies and environmental, genetic, hormonal and neurological influences', *Psychological Bulletin*, 86, 889–918.

McKellar, P. (1957) *Imagination and Thinking: A Psychological Analysis*, London, Cohen & West.

MacLean, P. D. (1958) 'Contrasting functions of the limbic and neocortical systems of the brain and their relevance to psychophysiological aspects of medicine', *American Journal of Medicine*, 25, 611–26.

McLemore, C. W. (1972) 'Imagery in desensitization', *Behavior Research and Therapy*, 10, 51–7.

McTaggart, J. M. E. (1927) *The Nature of Existence*. vol. 2, Cambridge, Cambridge University Press.

Mahoney, M. J. (1974) *Cognition and Behavior Modification*, Cambridge, Mass., Ballinger.

Mahoney, M. J. (1976) *Scientist as Subject*, Cambridge, Mass., Ballinger.

Mahoney, M. J. (1979) 'Cognitive skills and athletic performance', in Kendall, P. C. and Hollon, S. D. (eds), *Cognitive-Behavioral Interventions. Theory, Research, and Procedures*, New York, Academic Press, pp. 423–43.

Maier, S. F. and Seligman, M. E. P. (1976) 'Learned helplessness: Theory and evidence', *Journal of Experimental Psychology: General*, 105, 3–46.

Mandler, G. (1975) *Mind and Emotion*, New York, Wiley.

Mandler, G. (1979) 'Thought processes, consciousness, and stress', in Hamilton, V. and Warburton, D. M. (eds), *Human Stress and Cognition. An Information Processing Approach*, Chichester, Wiley, pp. 179–201.

Mandler, G. (1982) 'The structure of value: Accounting for taste', in Clark, M. S. and Fiske, S. T. (eds), *Affect and Cognition*, Hillsdale, NJ, Erlbaum, pp. 3–36.

Mandler, J. M., Seegmiller, D. and Day, J. (1977) 'On the coding of spatial information', *Memory and Cognition*, 5, 10–16.

Marks, D. F. (1973a) 'Visual imagery differences in the recall of pictures', *British Journal of Psychology*, 64, 17–24.

Marks, D. F. (1973b) 'Visual imagery differences and eye movements in the recall of pictures', *Perception and Psychophysics*, 14, 407–12.

Markus, H. (1977) 'Self-schemata and processing information about the self', *Journal of Personality and Social Psychology*, 35, 63–78.

Markus, H. and Sentis, K. (1982) 'The self in social information processing', in Suls, J. (ed.) *Psychological Perspectives on the Self*. vol. 1, Hillsdale, NJ, Erlbaum, pp. 41–70.

Marschark, M. and Paivio, A. (1977) 'Integrative processing of concrete and abstract sentences', *Journal of Verbal Learning and Verbal Behavior*, 16, 217–31.

Marshall, G. D. and Zimbardo, P. G. (1979) 'Affective consequences of inadequately explained physiological arousal', *Journal of Personality and Social Psychology*, 37, 970–88.

Maslach, C. (1979a) 'Negative emotional biasing and unexplained arousal', *Journal of Personality and Social Psychology*, 37, 953–69.

Maslach, C. (1979b) 'The emotional consequences of arousal without reason', in Izard, C. E. (ed.) *Emotions in Personality and Psychopathology*, New York, Plenum Press, pp. 565–90.

Maslow, A. H. (1968) *Toward a Psychology of Being* (2nd edn), New York, Van Nostrand.

Mead, G. H. (1934) *Mind, Self and Society*, Chicago, Chicago University Press.

Meichenbaum, D. (1976) 'Toward a cognitive theory of self-control', in Schwartz, G. and

Shapiro, D. (eds), *Consciousness and Self-Regulation: Advances in Research*. vol. 1, New York, Plenum Press, pp. 223–60.

Meichenbaum, D. and Cameron, R. (1974) 'The clinical potential of modifying what clients say to themselves', in Mahoney, M. J. and Thoreson, C. E. (eds) *Self Control: Power to the Person*, Monterey, Calif., Brooks Cole, pp. 263–90.

Merton, R. K. (1969) 'Behavior patterns of scientists', *American Scientist*, 57, 1–23.

Merton, R. K. (1973) *The Sociology of Science. Theoretical and Empirical Investigations*, Chicago, Chicago University Press.

Miller, G. A. (1979) 'Images and models, similes and metaphors', in Ortony, A. (ed.) *Metaphor and Thought*, Cambridge, Cambridge University Press, pp. 202–50.

Miller, G. A. and Johnson-Laird, P. N. (1976) *Language and Perception*, Cambridge, Cambridge University Press.

Minkowski, E. (1958) 'Findings in a case of schizophrenic depression', in May, R., Angel, E. and Ellenberger, H. F. (eds) *Existence: A New Dimension in Psychiatry and Psychology*, New York, Basic Books, pp. 127–38 (1st publ. 1923).

Mischel, W. (1968) *Personality and Assessment*, New York, Wiley.

Mischel, W. (1979) 'On the interface of cognition and personality', *American Psychologist*, 34, 740–54.

Mitroff, I. I. (1974) *The Subjective Side of Science*, New York, Elsevier.

Modigliani, A. (1968) 'Embarrassment and embarrassibility', *Sociometry*, 31, 313–26.

Modigliani, A. (1971) 'Embarrassment, facework and eye-contact. Testing a theory of embarrassment', *Journal of Personality and Social Psychology*, 17, 15–24.

Moltmann, J. (1972) *Theology of Play*, trans R. Ulrich, New York, Harper & Row.

Moody, R. A. (1976) *Life after Life*, New York, Bantam.

Moreland, R. L. and Zajonc, R. B. (1977) 'Is stimulus recognition a necessary condition for the occurrence of exposure effects?', *Journal of Personality and Social Psychology*, 35, 191–9.

Morelli, G. and Lang, D. (1971) 'Rated imagery and pictures in paired-associate learning', *Perceptual and Motor Skills*, 33, 1247–50.

Morris, P. E. and Gale, A. (1974) 'A correlational study of variables related to imagery', *Perceptual and Motor Skills*, 38, 659–65.

Murray, H. A. (1951) 'Toward a classification of interaction', in Parsons, T. and Shils, E. A. (eds) *Toward a General Theory of Action*, Cambridge, Mass., Harvard University Press, pp. 434–64.

Musante, G. J. and Anker, J. M. (1974) 'Cognitive, physiological, and motor effects of systematic desensitization on complex stimulus generalization', *Behavior Therapy*, 5, 365–80.

Neisser, U. (1967) 'Cognitive psychology', New York, Appleton-Century-Crofts.

Neisser, U. (1970) 'Visual imagery as process and as experience', in Antrobus, J. (ed.) *Cognition and Affect*, Boston, Brown, Little & Co., pp. 159–78.

Neisser, U. (1976) *Cognition and Reality: Principles and Implications of Cognitive Psychology*, San Francisco, Freeman.

Neisser, U. (1978) 'Anticipations, images, and introspection', *Cognition*, 6, 169–74.

Nie, N. H., Hull, C. H., Jenkins, J. G., Steinbrenner, K. and Bent, D. H. (1975) *Statistical Package for the Social Sciences* (2nd edn), New York, McGraw Hill.

Nigro, G. and Neisser, U. (1983) 'Point of view in personal memories', *Cognitive Psychology*, 15, 467–82.

Nisbett, R. E. and Ross, L. D. (1980) *Human Inference*, Englewood Cliffs, NJ, Prentice Hall.

Nisbett, R. E. and Wilson, T. D. (1977) 'Telling more than we can know: Verbal reports on mental processes', *Psychological Review*, 84, 231–59.

Norman, D. A. (1973) 'Memory, knowledge, and the answering of questions', in Solso, R. L.

(ed.) *Contemporary Issues in Cognitive Psychology: The Loyola Symposium*, Washington, DC, V. H. Winston, p. 135–65.

Notarius, C. I. and Levenson, R. W. (1979) 'Expressive tendencies and physiological response to stress', *Journal of Personality and Social Psychology*, 37, 1204–10.

Novaco, R. W. (1979) 'The cognitive regulation of anger and stress', in Kendall, P. C. and Hollon, S. D. (eds) *Cognitive-Behavioral Interventions; Theory, Research and Practice*, New York, Academic Press, pp. 241–85.

Odom, J. V., Nelson, R. O. and Wein, K. S. (1978) 'The differential effectiveness of five treatment procedures on three response systems in a snake phobia analog study', *Behavior Therapy*, 9, 936–42.

Oeltgen, P. R., Walsh, J. W., Hamann, S. R., Randall, D. C., Spurrier, W. A. and Myers, R. D. (1982) 'Hibernation trigger: opioid-like inhibitory action on brain function of the monkey *Macaca mulatta*', *Pharmacology, Biochemistry and Behaviour*, 17, 1271–4.

Ortony, A. (ed.) (1979) *Metaphor and Thought*, Cambridge, Cambridge University Press.

Osgood, C. E. (1971) 'Where do sentences come from?', in Steinberg, D. D. and Jakobovits, L. A. (eds) *Semantics. An Interdisciplinary Reader in Philosophy, Linguistics and Psychology*, Cambridge, Cambridge University Press, pp. 497–529.

Padgett, V. R. and Wolosin, R. J. (1980) 'Cognitive similarity in dyadic communication', *Journal of Personality and Social Psychology*, 39, 654–9.

Paivio, A. (1971) *Imagery and Verbal Processes*, New York, Holt, Rinehart & Winston.

Paivio, A. (1976) 'Images, propositions, and knowledge', in Nicholas, J. M. (ed.) *Images, Perception and Knowledge*, Dordrecht, Reidel, pp. 47–71.

Paivio, A. (1979) 'Psychological processes in the comprehension of metaphor', in Ortony, A. (ed.) *Metaphor and Thought*, Cambridge, Cambridge University Press, pp. 150–71.

Paivio, A. and Csapo, K. (1969) 'Concrete-image and verbal memory codes', *Journal of Experimental Psychology*, 80, 279–85.

Paivio, A. and Foth, D. (1970) 'Imaginal and verbal mediators and noun concreteness in paired-associate learning: The elusive interaction', *Journal of Verbal Learning and Verbal Behavior*, 9, 384–90.

Palmer, S. E. (1977) 'Hierarchical structure in perceptual representation', *Cognitive Psychology*, 9, 441–74.

Palmer, S. E. (1978) 'Fundamental aspects of cognitive representation', in Rosch, E. and Lloyd, B. B. (eds), *Cognition and Categorization*, Hillsdale, NJ, Erlbaum, pp. 259–303.

Parkes, C. M. (1972) *Bereavement; Studies of Grief in Adult Life*, London, Tavistock.

Parsons, T., Shils, E. A. and others. (1951) *Toward a General Theory of Action*, Cambridge, Mass., Harvard University Press.

Patton, M. Q. (1980) *Qualitative Evaluation Methods*, Beverly Hills, Sage.

Pavlov, I. P. (1927) *Conditioned Reflexes. An Investigation of the Physiological Activity of the Cerebral Cortex*, trans. G. V. Anrep, Oxford, Oxford University Press (reprinted by Dover (New York), 1960).

Perky, C. (1910) 'An experimental study of imagination', *American Journal of Psychology*, 21, 422–52.

Persson, L.-O. and Sjöberg, L. (1978) 'The influence of emotions on information processing', *Göteborg Psychological Reports*, 8, (7).

Pettigrew, T. F. (1958) 'The measurement and correlates of category width as a cognitive variable', *Journal of Personality*, 26, 532–44.

Phares, E. J. (1965) 'Internal–external control as a determinant of amount of social influence exerted', *Journal of Personality and Social Psychology*, 2, 642–7.

Phillips, L. W. (1971) 'Training of sensory and imaginal responses in behavior therapy', in

Rubin, R. D., Fensterheim, H., Lazarus, A. A. and Franks, C. M. (eds) *Advances in Behavior Therapy*, New York, Academic Press, pp. 111–22.

Piaget, J. (1954) *The Construction of Reality in the Child*, trans. M. Cook, New York, Basic Books.

Piaget, J. (1959) *The Language and Thought of the Child* (3rd edn), trans. M. Gabain, London, Routledge & Kegan Paul.

Piaget, J. and Inhelder, B. (1971) *Mental Imagery in the Child*, London, Routledge & Kegan Paul.

Pichert, J. W. and Anderson, R. C. (1977) 'Taking different perspectives on a story', *Journal of Educational Psychology*, 69, 309–15.

Pilkonis, P. A. and Zimbardo, P. G. (1979) 'The personal and social dynamics of shyness', in Izard, C. E. (ed.) *Emotions in Personality and Psychopathology*, New York, Plenum Press, pp. 133–60.

Plessner, H. (1970) *Laughing and Crying. A Study of the Limits of Human Behavior*, trans. J. Churchill and M. Grene, Evanston, Northwestern University Press (from the 3rd German edn, 1961).

Plutchik, R. (1954) 'The role of muscular tension in maladjustment', *Journal of General Psychology*, 50, 45–62.

Plutchik, R. (1970) 'Emotions, evolution, and adaptive processes', in Arnold, M. B. (ed.) *Feelings and Emotions*, New York, Academic Press, pp. 3–24.

Plutchik, R. (1980) *Emotion: A Psychoevolutionary Synthesis*, New York, Harper & Row.

Polanyi, M. (1958) *Personal Knowledge*, London, Routledge & Kegan Paul.

Popper, K. (1945) *The Open Society and Its Enemies* (2 vols), London, Routledge & Kegan Paul.

Proust, M. (1936) *Within a Budding Grove*, Part 2, trans. C. K. Scott Moncrieff, London, Chatto & Windus.

Pylyshyn, Z. W. (1973) 'What the mind's eye tells the mind's brain. A critique of mental imagery', *Psychological Bulletin*, 80, 1–24.

Pylyshyn, Z. W. (1979) 'The rate of "mental rotation" of images: A test of a holistic analogue hypothesis', *Memory and Cognition*, 7, 19–28.

Rachman, S. (1968) *Phobias: Their Nature and Control*, Springfield, Ill., Thomas.

Rapaport, D. (1953) 'On the psycho-analytic theory of affects', *International Journal of Psychoanalysis*, 34, 177–98.

Rapaport, D. (1959) 'The structure of psychoanalytic theory: A systematizing attempt', in Koch, S. (ed.) *Psychology: A Study of a Science. vol. 3: Formulations of the Person and the Social Context*, New York, McGraw Hill, pp. 55–183.

Rapaport, D., Gill, M. M. and Schafer, R. (1968) *Diagnostic Psychological Testing* (ed. R. R. Holt), New York, International Universities Press.

Reed, A. W. (1946) *Myths and Legends of Maoriland*, Wellington, A. H. & A. W. Reed.

Rehm, L. P. (1973) 'Relationships among measures of visual imagery', *Behavior Research and Therapy*, 11, 265–70.

Reich, W. (1968) *The Function of the Orgasm*, trans. T. P. Wolfe, London, Panther (1st publ. 1942).

Reing, A. B. (1978) 'Imaginal behavioral analysis: A multisensory imagery scale for evaluating a specific teacher competency', *Journal of Special Education*, 12, 153–70.

Reyher, J. (1963) 'Free imagery: An uncovering procedure', *Journal of Clinical Psychology*, 19, 454–9.

Reyher, J. and Smeltzer, W. (1968) 'Uncovering properties of visual imagery and verbal association', *Journal of Abnormal Psychology*, 73, 218–22.

Richardson, A. (1967a) 'Mental practice: A review and discussion. Part I', *Research Quarterly*, 38, 95–107.

Richardson, A. (1967b) 'Mental practice: A review and discussion. Part II', *Research Quarterly*, 38, 263–73.

Richardson, A. (1969) *Mental Imagery*, London, Routledge & Kegan Paul.

Richardson, A. (1977a) 'Verbalizer–visualizer: A cognitive style dimension', Journal of Mental Imagery, 1, 109–26.

Richardson, A. (1977b) 'The meaning and measurement of memory imagery', British Journal of Psychology, 68, 29–43.

Richardson, J. T. E. (1978) 'Mental imagery and memory: Coding ability or coding preference?', Journal of Mental Imagery, 2, 101–16.

Riding, R. J. and Calvey, I. (1981) 'The assessment of verbal-imagery learning styles and their effect on the recall of concrete and abstract prose passages by 11-year-old children', British Journal of Psychology, 72, 59–64.

Riding, R. J. and Dyer, V. A. (1980) 'The relationship between extraversion and verbal-imagery learning style in 12-year-old children', Personality and Individual Differences, 1, 273–9.

Riesman, D. (1950) The Lonely Crowd: A Study of the Changing American Character, New Haven, Yale University Press.

Robbins, D., Barresi, J., Compton, P., Furst, A., Russo, M. and Smith, M. A. (1978) 'The genesis and use of exemplar vs. prototype knowledge in abstract category learning', Memory and Cognition, 6, 473–80.

Roe, A. (1953) 'A psychological study of eminent psychologists and anthropologists and a comparison with biological and physical scientists', Psychological Monographs, 67 (2).

Rolf, I. P. (1977) Rolfing: The Integration of Human Structures, Santa Monica, Dennis Landman.

Romanyshyn, R. D. (1982) Psychological Life: From Science to Metaphor, Milton Keynes, The Open University Press.

Rosch, E. (1975a) 'Cognitive reference points', Cognitive Psychology, 7, 532–47.

Rosch, E. (1975b) 'Cognitive representations of semantic categories', Journal of Experimental Psychology: General, 104, 192–233.

Rosch, E. (1978) 'Principles of categorization', in Rosch, E. and Lloyd, B. B. (eds), Cognition and Categorization, Hillsdale, NJ, Erlbaum, pp. 27–48.

Rosch, E. and Mervis, C. B. (1975) 'Family resemblances: Studies in the internal structure of categories', Cognitive Psychology, 7, 573–605.

Rosch, E., Mervis, C. B., Gray, W. D., Johnson, D. M. and Boyes-Braem, P. (1976) 'Basic objects in natural categories', Cognitive Psychology, 8, 382–439.

Rosch, E., Simpson, C. and Miller, R. S. (1976) 'Structural bases of typicality effects', Journal of Experimental Psychology: Human Perception and Performance, 2, 491–502.

Rosenberg, S. and Simon, H. A. (1977) 'Modeling semantic memory: Effects of presenting semantic information in different modalities', Cognitive Psychology, 9, 293–325.

Rotter, J. B. (1966) 'Generalized expectancies for internal versus external control of reinforcement', Psychological Monographs, 80, 1–28.

Rubinstein, B. B. (1967) 'Explanation and mere description: A metascientific examination of certain aspects of the psychoanalytic theory of motivation', Psychological Issues, 5 (2–3), 18–77.

Rumelhart, D. E., Lindsay, P. H. and Norman, D. A. (1972) 'A process model for long-term memory', in Tulving, E. and Donaldson, W. (eds) Organization of Memory, New York, Academic Press, pp. 198–246.

Russell, J. A. (1978) 'Evidence of convergent validity on the dimensions of affect', Journal of Personality and Social Psychology, 36, 1152–68.

Russell, J. A. (1979) 'Affective space is bipolar', Journal of Personality and Social Psychology, 37, 345–56.

Ryle, G. (1949) The Concept of Mind, London, Hutchinson.

Sarason, I. G. (1972) 'Experimental approaches to test anxiety: Attention and the uses of information', in Spielberger, C. D. (ed.) Anxiety: Current Trends in Theory and Research. vol. 2, New York, Academic Press, pp. 381–403.

Sarbin, T. R. (1972) 'Imagining as muted role-taking: A historical-linguistic analysis', in Sheehan, P. W. (ed.) *The Function and Nature of Imagery*, New York, Academic Press, pp. 333–54.

Sartre, J.-P. (1957) *Being and Nothingness*, trans. H. E. Barnes, London, Methuen (1st publ. 1943).

Sartre, J.-P. (1962) *Sketch for a Theory of the Emotions*, London, Methuen.

Sattler, J. M. (1965) 'A theoretical, developmental and clinical investigation of embarrassment', *Genetic Psychology Monographs*, 71, 19–59.

Schachter, S. and Singer, J. E. (1962) 'Cognitive, social and physiological determinants of emotional state', *Psychological Review*, 69, 379–99.

Schafer, R. (1975) 'Psychoanalysis without psycho-dynamics', *International Journal of Psychoanalysis*, 56, 41–55.

Schank, R. C. (1975) 'The structure of episodes in memory', in Bobrow, D. G. and Collins, A. (eds) *Representation and Understanding: Studies in Cognitive Science*, New York, Academic Press, pp. 237–72.

Schank, R. C. and Abelson, R. P. (1977) *Scripts, Plans, Goals and Understanding. An Inquiry into Human Knowledge Structures*, Hillsdale, NJ, Erlbaum.

Scheier, M. F. and Carver, C. S. (1977) 'Self-focused attention and the experience of emotion: Attraction, repulsion, elation, and depression', *Journal of Personality and Social Psychology*, 35, 625–36.

Scheier, M. F., Carver, C. S. and Gibbons, F. X. (1981) 'Self-focused attention and reactions to fear', *Journal of Research in Personality*, 15, 1–15.

Scherer, K. R. (1979) 'Voice and speech correlates of perceived social influence in simulated juries', in Giles, H. and St Clair, R. N. (eds) *Language and Social Psychology*, Oxford, Blackwell, pp. 88–120.

Schlosberg, H. (1954) 'The three dimensions of emotion', *Psychological Review*, 61, 81–8.

Schneider, G. E. (1969) 'Two visual systems', *Science*, 163, 895–902.

Schulz, R. (1976) 'Some life and death consequences of perceived control', in Carroll, J. S. and Payne, J. W. (eds) *Cognition and Social Behavior*, Hillsdale, NJ, Erlbaum, pp. 135–53.

Schwartz, G. E. and Weinberger, D. A. (1980) 'Patterns of emotional responses to affective situations: Relations among happiness, sadness, anger, fear, depression, and anxiety', *Motivation and Emotion*, 4, 175–91.

Scott, J. P. (1980) 'The function of emotions in behavioral systems: A systems theory analysis', in Plutchik, R. and Kellerman, H. (eds) *Emotion: Theory, Research, and Experience. vol. I: Theories of Emotion*, New York, Academic Press, pp. 35–56.

Segal, S. (1971) 'Processing of the stimulus in imagery and perception', in Segal, S. (ed.), *Imagery, Current Cognitive Approaches*, New York, Academic Press, pp. 69–100.

Segal, S. J. and Nathan, S. (1964) 'The Perky effect: Incorporation of an external stimulus into an imagery experience under placebo and control conditions', *Perceptual and Motor Skills*, 18, 385–95.

Seligman, M. (1971) 'Phobias and preparedness', *Behavior Therapy*, 2, 307–20.

Seligman, M. E. P. (1975) *Helplessness. On Depression, Development, and Death*, San Francisco, Freeman.

Senden, M. von (1960) *Space and Sight*, trans. P. Heath, London, Methuen (1st publ. 1932).

Sheehan, P. W. (1967) 'A shortened form of Betts' questionnaire upon mental imagery', *Journal of Clinical Psychology*, 23, 386–9.

Sheehan, P. W. and Neisser, U. (1969) 'Some variables affecting the vividness of imagery in recall', *British Journal of Psychology*, 60, 71–80.

Shepard, R. N. (1978) 'Externalization of mental images and the act of creation', in Randhawa, B. S. and Coffman, W. E. (eds) *Visual Learning, Thinking, and Communication*, New York, Academic Press, pp. 133–89.

Shepard, R. N. and Metzler, J. (1971) 'Mental rotation of three-dimensional objects', *Science*, 171, 701–3.

Shields, S. and Stern, R. M. (1979) 'Emotion: The perception of bodily changes', in Pliner, P., Blankstein, K. R. and Spigel, I. M. (eds) *Advances in the Study of Communication and Affect*. vol. 5: *Perception of Emotion in Self and Others*, New York, Plenum Press, pp. 85–106.

Shostrom, E. L. (1974) *Manual for the Personal Orientation Inventory*, San Diego, Calif., Educational and Industrial Testing Service.

Siegman, A. W. (1961) 'The relationship between future time perspective, time estimation, and impulse control in a group of young offenders and in a control group', *Journal of Consulting Psychology*, 25, 470–5.

Sifneos, P. E. (1975) 'The prevalence of "alexithymic" characteristics in psychosomatic patients', *Psychotherapy and Psychosomatics*, 26, 65–70.

Siipola, E., Walker, W. N. and Kolb, D. (1955) 'Task attitudes in word association, projective and nonprojective', *Journal of Personality*, 23, 441–59.

Simon, H. A. (1967) 'Motivational and emotional controls of cognition', *Psychological Review*, 74, 29–39.

Singer, J. L. (1966) *Daydreaming. An Introduction to the Experimental Study of Inner Experience*, New York, Random House.

Singer, J. L. (1974) *Imagery and Daydream Methods in Psychotherapy and Behavior Modification*, New York, Academic Press.

Singer, J. L. (1976) *Daydreaming and Fantasy*, London, George Allen & Unwin (1st publ. 1975).

Singer, J. L. and Antrobus, J. S. (1963) 'A factor-analytic study of daydreaming and conceptually related cognitive and personality variables', *Perceptual and Motor Skills*, 17, 187–209 (Monogr. Suppl. 3-V17).

Singer, J. L. and Antrobus, J. S. (1967) 'Signal performance by subjects differing in predisposition to daydreaming', *Journal of Consulting Psychology*, 31, 487–91.

Singer, J. L. and Antrobus, J. S. (1972) 'Daydreaming, imaginal processes, and personality: A normative study', in Sheehan, P. W. (ed.) *The Function and Nature of Imagery*, New York, Academic Press, pp. 175–202.

Singer, J. L. and McCraven, V. G. (1961) 'Some characteristics of adult daydreaming', *Journal of Psychology*, 51, 151–64.

Skinner, B. F. (1957) *Verbal Behavior*, New York, Appleton-Century-Crofts.

Slee, J. A. (1980) 'Individual differences in visual imagery ability and the retrieval of visual appearances', *Journal of Mental Imagery*, 4, 93–113.

Slobin, D. I. (1982) 'Universal and particular in the acquisition of language', in Wanner, E. and Gleitman, L. R. (eds) *Language Acquisition. The State of the Art*, Cambridge, Cambridge University Press, pp. 128–70.

Snodgrass, J. G. (1984) 'Concepts and their surface representations', *Journal of Verbal Learning and Verbal Behavior*, 23, 3–22.

Snyder, M. (1974) 'The self-monitoring of expressive behavior', *Journal of Personality and Social Psychology*, 30, 526–37.

Snyder, M. (1979) 'Cognitive, behavioral, and interpersonal consequences of self monitoring', in Pliner, P., Blankstein, K. R. and Spigel, I. M. (eds) *Advances in the Study of Communication and Affect*. vol. 5: *Perception of Emotion in Self and Others*, New York, Plenum Press, pp. 181–201.

Sokolov, A. N. (1972) *Inner Speech and Thought*, trans. G. T. Onischenko, New York, Plenum Press (1st publ. 1968).

Solomon, R. L. and Corbit, J. D. (1974) 'An opponent-process theory of motivation: I. Temporal dynamics of affect', *Psychological Review*, 81, 119–45.

Spindler, F. N. (1907) 'Memory types in spelling', *Education*, 28, 175–81.

Starker, S. (1974) 'Daydreaming styles and nocturnal dreaming', *Journal of Abnormal Psychology*, 83, 52–5.

Start, K. B. (1960) 'Relationship between intelligence and the effect of mental practice on the performance of a motor skill', *Research Quarterly*, 31, 644–9.

Start, K. B. and Richardson, A. (1964) 'Imagery and mental practice', *British Journal of Educational Psychology*, 34, 280–4.

Steiner, R. (1979) *Occult Science. An Outline*, trans. G. and M. Adams, London, Pharos, Rudolf Steiner Press (1st publ. 1909).

Storms, M. D. (1979) 'Sexual orientation and self-perception', in Pliner, P., Blankstein, K. R. and Spigel, I. M. (eds) *Advances in the Study of Communication and Affect. vol. 5: Perception of Emotion in Self and Others*, New York, Plenum Press, pp. 165–80.

Strauss, E. W. (1947) 'Disorders of personal time in depressive states', *Southern Medical Journal*, 40, 254–8.

Stricklin, A. B. and Penk, M. L. (1980) 'Vividness and control of imagery in personality types', *Journal of Mental Imagery*, 4, 111–14.

Strosahl, K. D. and Ascough, J. C. (1981) 'Clinical uses of mental imagery: Experimental foundations, theoretical misconceptions, and research issues', *Psychological Bulletin*, 89, 422–38.

Suberi, M. and McKeever, W. F. (1977) 'Differential right hemispheric storage of emotional and non-emotional faces', *Neuropsychologia*, 15, 757–68.

Suomi, S. J. and Harlow, H. F. (1976) 'The facts and functions of fear', in Zuckerman, M. and Spielberger, C. D. (eds), *Emotions and Anxiety: New Concepts, Methods and Applications*, Hillsdale, NJ, Erlbaum, pp. 3–34.

Swann, W. B. and Miller, L. C. (1982) 'Why never forgetting a face matters: Visual imagery and social memory', *Journal of Personality and Social Psychology*, 43, 475–80.

Tajfel, H. and Billig, M. (1974) 'Familiarity and categorization in intergroup behavior', *Journal of Experimental Social Psychology*, 10, 159–70.

Tajfel, H. and Wilkes, A. L. (1963) 'Classification and quantitative judgement', *British Journal of Psychology*, 54, 101–14.

Tauber, E. S. and Green, M. R. (1959) *Prelogical Experience: An Inquiry into Dreams and Other Creative Processes*, New York, Basic Books.

Taylor, S. E. and Crocker, J. (1981) 'Schematic bases of social information processing', in Higgins, E. T., Herman, C. P. and Zanna, M. P. (eds), *Social Cognition. The Ontario Symposium. vol. I*, Hillsdale, NJ, Erlbaum, pp. 89–134.

Teahan, J. E. (1958) 'Future time perspective, optimism, and academic achievement', *Journal of Abnormal and Social Psychology*, 57, 379–80.

Tendler, A. D. (1945) 'Significant features of disturbance in free association', *Journal of Psychology*, 20, 65–89.

Tesser, A. (1978) 'Self-generated attitude change', *Advances in Experimental Social Psychology*, 11, New York, Academic Press.

Thorndike, E. and Lorge, I. (1944) *The Teacher's Word Book of 30,000 Words*, New York, Teachers College Press.

Titchener, E. (1909) *Lectures on the Experimental Psychology of the Thought Processes*, New York, Macmillan.

Tolstoy, L. (1904) *War and Peace*, trans. C. Garnett, London, Heineman (repr. in association with Pan, 1972).

Tomkins, S. S. (1962) *Affect, Imagery, Consciousness. vol. I: The Positive Affects*, New York, Springer.

Tomkins, S. S. (1963) *Affect, Imagery, Consciousness. vol. II: The Negative Affects*, New York, Springer.

Tomkins, S. S. (1979) 'Script theory: Differential magnification of affects', in Howe, H. E. and Dienstbier, R. A. (eds) *Nebraska Symposium on Motivation. vol. 26*, Lincoln, Nebraska University Press.

Tomkins, S. S. (1980) 'Affect as amplification: Some modifications in theory', in Plutchik, R. and Kellerman, H. (eds) *Emotion: Theory, Research, and Experience. vol. I: Theories of Emotion*, New York, Academic Press, pp. 141–64.

Tower, R. B. and Singer, J. L. (1981) 'The measurement of imagery: How can it be clinically useful?', in Kendall, P. C. and Hollon, S. D. (eds) *Assessment Strategies for Cognitive-Behavioral Interventions*, New York, Academic Press, pp. 119–59.

Tsujimoto, R. N. (1978) 'Memory bias toward normative and novel trait prototypes', *Journal of Personality and Social Psychology*, 36, 1391–401.

Turner, R. C., Brown, R. J. and Tajfel, H. (1979) 'Social comparison and group interest in ingroup favouritism', *European Journal of Social Psychology*, 9, 187–204.

United States Employment Service (1970) *Manual for the General Aptitude Test Battery*, Washington, US Department of Labor and Manpower Administration.

Upanishads, The (1965) trans. J. Mascaro, Harmondsworth, Penguin.

van Kaam, A. (1969) *Existential Foundations of Psychology*, New York, Image (1st publ. 1966).

Vandell, R. A., Davis, R. A. and Clugston, N. A. (1943) 'Function of mental practice in the acquisition of motor skills', *Journal of General Psychology*, 29, 243–50.

Varendonck, J. (1921) *The Psychology of Daydreams*, London, George Allen & Unwin.

Vygotsky, L. S. (1962) *Thought and Language*, trans. E. Hanfman and G. Vakar, Cambridge, Mass., MIT Press.

Walkup, L. (1965) 'Creativity in science though visualization', *Perceptual and Motor Skills*, 21, 35–41.

Wallace, M. and Rabin, A. I. (1960) 'Temporal experience', *Psychological Bulletin*, 57, 213–36.

Washburn, M. F. (1916) *Movement and Mental Imagery. Outlines of a Motor Theory of the Complexer Mental Processes*, Boston, Houghton Mifflin.

Weerts, T. C. and Lang, P. J. (1978) 'The psychophysiology of fear imagery: Differences between focal phobia and social performance anxiety', *Journal of Consulting and Clinical Psychology*, 46, 1157–9.

Wegner, D. M. and Giuliano, T. (1980) 'Arousal-induced attention to the self', *Journal of Personality and Social Psychology*, 38, 719–26.

Weimer, W. B. (1974) 'Overview of a cognitive conspiracy: Reflections on the volume', in Weimer, W. B. and Palermo, D. S. (eds) *Cognition and the Symbolic Processes*, Hillsdale, NJ, Erlbaum, pp. 415–42.

Weimer, W. B. (1977) 'A conceptual framework for cognitive psychology: Motor theories of the mind', in Shaw, R. and Bransford, J. (eds) *Perceiving, Acting, and Knowing*, Hillsdale, NJ, Erlbaum, pp. 267–311.

Weinberg, M. S. (1968) 'Embarrassment: Its variable and invariable aspects', *Social Forces*, 46, 382–8.

Weiner, B., Russell, D. and Lerman, D. (1978) 'Affective consequences of causal ascriptions', in Harvey, J. H., Ickes, W. and Kidd, R. F. (eds) *New Directions in Attribution Research. vol. 2*, Hillsdale, NJ, Erlbaum, pp. 59–90.

Weiner, B., Russell, D. and Lerman, D. (1979) 'The cognition-emotion process in achievement-related contexts', *Journal of Personality and Social Psychology*, 37, 1211–20.

Werner, H. and Kaplan, B. (1963) *Symbol Formation. An Organismic-Developmental Approach to Language and the Expression of Thought*, New York, Wiley.

Wessman, A. E. and Ricks, J. H. (1966) *Mood and Personality*, New York, Holt, Rinehart & Winston.

White, K. D., Ashton, R. and Brown, R. M. D. (1977) 'The measurement of imagery vividness: Normative data and their relationship to sex, age, and modality differences', *British Journal of Psychology*, 68, 203–11.

White, K., Sheehan, P. W. and Ashton, R. (1977) 'Imagery assessment: A survey of self-report measures', *Journal of Mental Imagery*, 1, 145–70.

White, R. W. (1959) 'Motivation reconsidered: The concept of competence', *Psychological Review*, 66, 297–333.

Whorf, B. L. (1958) *Language, Thought and Reality* (ed. J. Carroll), Cambridge, Mass., MIT Press.

Wicklund, R. A. (1975) 'Objective self-awareness', *Advances in Experimental Social Psychology*, 8, 233–75.

Wicklund, R. A. (1978) 'Three years later (comments on Wicklund 1975)', in Berkowitz, L. (ed.) *Cognitive Theories in Social Psychology*, New York, Academic Press, pp. 509–21.

Wicklund, R. A. (1979) 'The influence of self-awareness on human behavior', *American Scientist*, 67, 187–93.

Wicklund, R. A. (1982) 'How society uses self-awareness', in Suls, J. (ed.) *Psychological Perspectives on the Self*. vol. I, Hillsdale, NJ, Erlbaum, pp. 209–30.

Wiggins, D. (1967) *Identity and Spatio-Temporal Continuity*, Oxford, Blackwell.

Wilson, G. D.. (1975) *Manual for the Wilson-Patterson Attitude Inventory*, Windsor, NFER.

Wilson, W. R. (1979) 'Feeling more than we can know: Exposure effects without learning', *Journal of Personality and Social Psychology*, 37, 811–21.

Winograd, T. (1972) *Understanding Natural Language*, New York, Academic Press.

Winograd, T. (1975) 'Frame representations and the declarative/procedural controversy', in Bobrow, D. G. and Collins, A. (eds) *Representation and Understanding: Studies in Cognitive Science*, New York, Academic Press, pp. 185–210.

Winter, D. G. (1973) *The Power Motive*, New York, Free Press.

Wisocki, P. (1973) 'A covert reinforcement program for the treatment of test anxiety: Brief report', *Behavior Therapy*, 4, 264–6.

Witelson, S. F. (1976) 'Sex and the single hemisphere: Specialization of the right hemisphere for spatial processing', *Science*, 193, 425–7.

Witkin, H. A. (1976) 'Cognitive styles in academic performance and in teacher–student relations', in Messick, S. (ed.) *Individuality in Learning*, San Francisco, Jossey-Bass, pp. 38–72.

Witkin, H. A., Dyk, R. B., Faterson, H. F., Goodenough, D. R. and Karp, S. A. (1962) *Psychological Differentiation: Studies of Development*, New York, Wiley.

Witkin, H. A., Lewis, H. B., Hertzman, M., Machover, K., Meissner, P. B. and Wapner, S. (1954) *Personality through Perception*, New York, Harper.

Wolpe, J. (1958) *Psychotherapy by Reciprocal Inhibition*, Palo Alto, Calif., Stanford University Press.

Wolpe, J. (1973) *The Practice of Behavior Therapy* (2nd edn), New York, Pergamon.

Wolpe, J. (1978a) 'Cognition and causation in human behavior and its therapy', *American Psychologist*, 33, 437–46.

Wolpe, J. (1978b) 'Self-efficacy and psychotherapeutic change: A square peg for a round hole', *Advances in Behavior Research and Therapy*, 1, 231–6.

Wolpe, J. and Lang, P. J. (1964) 'A fear survey schedule for use in behavior therapy', *Behavior Research and Therapy*, 2, 27–30.

Wolpin, M. and Kirsch, I. (1974) 'Visual imagery, various muscle states and desensitization procedures', *Perceptual and Motor Skills*, 39, 1143–9.

Wundt, W. (1907) *Outlines of Psychology*, trans. C. H. Judd, Leipzig, Wilhelm Engelman.

Yates, F. A. (1966) *The Art of Memory*, London, Routledge & Kegan Paul.

Young, P. T. (1961) *Motivation and Emotion. A Survey of the Determinants of Human and Animal Activity*, New York, Wiley.

Yuille, J. C. and Catchpole, M. J. (1977) 'The role of imagery in models of cognition', *Journal of Mental Imagery*, 1, 171–80.

Zaehner, R. C. (1957) *Mysticism Sacred and Profane. An Inquiry into Some Varieties of Praeternatural Experience*, Oxford, Clarendon Press.

Zajonc, R. B. (1968) 'Attitudinal effects of mere exposure', *Journal of Personality and Social Psychology Monographs*, 9 (2, Part 2, 1–27).

Zajonc, R. B. (1980) 'Feeling and thinking: Preferences need no inferences', *American Psychologist*, 35, 151–75.

Zajonc, R. B., Markus, H. and Wilson, W. R. (1974) 'Exposure effects and associative learning', *Journal of Experimental Social Psychology*, 10, 248–63.

Zajonc, R. B., Pietromonaco, P. and Bargh, J. (1982) 'Independence and interaction of affect and cognition', in Clark, M. S. and Fiske, S. T. (eds) *Affect and Cognition*, Hillsdale, NJ, Erlbaum, pp. 211–27.

Index of names

Index of subjects

abstract information, 9, 22, 26–7, 185
abuse, 11, 52–3, 149
access, 13, 15, 18, 41–3, 120, 160
acoustic properties, 22, 26
acquiescence, 88–9, 91, 216–20
action, 16–20, 22, 32–9, 60, 98, 123–5, 163–6, 168, 180, 186 (*see also* intransitive action, transitive action); and instrumental parts, 31, 38–9, 177; as epistemological foundation, 8, 16–17, 152; blocked/inhibited, 18, 34–6, 58, 84–7, 131, 142, 154, 167, 169 (*see also* paralysis of action); conditional/potential, 25, 35–7, 166 (*see also* MOTQ conditional action); general theory of, 16; imagined/internalized, 5, 20, 38, 58, 70; in emotion, 130–3, 135, 140–8, 151–4, 227, 235; involuntary v willed, 142; primitives, 231; social action, 16, 120–1, 231
adjective rating scale, 75, 206–7
affect, 4, 8, 22, 25, 34–5, 166 (*see also* emotion, evaluation, feeling, MOTQ affective, preferences, sentiments); in day-dreams, 47–50, 63–4; primacy of, 4, 132–3, 144–5
affective consequence, 25, 166, 186 (*see also* MOTQ affective consequence)
affiliation, 82–4, 88, 90–2, 121, 167–8
agency, 10, 17–18, 20, 32–4, 38; agentive case, 10, 32, 130, 151, 160, 231; and emotions, 129, 151–2; self as agent, 84–5, 130, 151–2, 166, 169, 177
aggression, 63, 77, 85–7, 130, 141, 150, 232

alexithymia, 63
alienation, 49, 51, 54, 190
ambiguous stimuli (*see* misfits)
ambition, 77–9, 169
analysis in science, 174–6
anger, 9, 59, 131–4, 136, 139–42, 147, 149–50, 153–4, 225–8
animals, 132, 150; in free association studies, 22–46, 185–6; preferences for, 96–110, 164–5, 221–4, 234
anxiety, 14, 53, 115, 125, 130, 134, 136–7, 139–41, 145–8, 153–4, 167, 169, 226–8, 231
apathy/emptiness, 77, 81, 83, 111, 118, 167
appearance, 55–8, 64, 83, 111–15, 119, 127–8, 150, 166, 168–9 (*see also* persona)
appraisal, 61, 131, 143–5
arousal, 130–3, 137, 145–8, 180 (*see also* bodily activation)
articulation, 8, 46, 172–81, 236–7
artificial intelligence, 16–18, 158–60, 236 (*see also* information processing)
arts students, 69–70
association, 14, 21–45, 191, 231 (*see also* free association); as transition, 32, 44–6
atomism in science, 173
attention, 18, 88, 122–3, 125, 128, 161, 168, 173, 178; and cognitive structures, 44–6, 74–5, 162–4, 168; and personality, 74–5, 88, 91, 168; in emotion, 125, 131, 139, 148, 150–4; in

and spatial representations, 25, 32, 34–5, 70–1, 205
transparency of social behaviour, 119–21, 126, 169
triptych, 38–40, 63, 67, 88, 171
type-token relationship, 44–5, 173
typical instances, 23–6, 51, 96, 173–4 (*see also* norm, prototype); preference for, 99–106, 109–10, 153, 164, 167, 169, 224, 233

uncertainty, 137–40
unconscious, 13, 143, 152
unity with nature, 121–8, 152–3, 165, 167, 169
utility (as value), 97, 222–3

value (*see* evaluation)
value conflict in category systems, 108–9
value judgment, 61, 64, 129–30, 152–4, 235 (*see also* appraisal, evaluation, preferences)
verb families, 32, 231
verbal fluency, 68, 71, 169
verbal reports, 41–2; analysis of, 229–30
verbal representation, 4–6, 8–11, 20–7, 166–70, 185–6; and abstract/conceptual information, 5, 9, 20, 22, 26, 39; and dereferentialized language, 23–4, 26–7, 80, 166–8, 174; and emotion, 148–9; and idle thoughts, 49–54, 59, 61, 64, 80, 187–90; and liking for power, 78–82, 88–9, 91–2, 166; and order, 51–4, 64, 78–80, 88, 95, 99, 106, 152–3, 164–6, 169–70, 174; and preferences, 95–110, 129, 152–4; and stereotyping, 106–8; and tradition-directedness, 88–9, 91, 166, 168; as cognitive style, 5–6, 68–9, 76–82, 88–9, 166–70; cognitive correlates, 68–9, 71, 203–5; distinguished from language, 11; personality correlates, 76–82, 89, 208, 211–12, 215–16, 219; structures in, 9–11, 21–7, 38–40, 46, 163, 166–8 (*see also* MOTQ verbal); words in, 26–7, 38, 166, 173–4 (*see also* naming)
verbal stratum in science, 172–4

verbalizers, 6, 78–82, 89 (*see also* verbal representation as cognitive style)
verbal-visual idle thoughts, 49, 61–2, 188–90
violence, 34, 63, 146, 148 (*see also* aggression)
visual imagery, 4–6, 8, 11–16, 21–2, 24–5, 27–33, 42, 44–6, 166–70, 185–6; and belonging, 115, 121, 126, 128, 152–3, 164–6, 169–70; and emotion, 148–51; and idle thoughts, 49, 54–8, 61, 64, 82–3, 187–90; and metaphor, 24, 27, 31–2, 45, 122–3, 174–6, 237; and need for affiliation, 82–4, 88, 90–2, 167–8; and objective self-awareness, 57, 82–3, 111–21, 167–9; and other-directedness, 88–91, 166; and sentiments, 111–29, 152–4; and spatial representations, 12, 19–20, 24, 27–30, 175–6, 231, 237; and unity with nature, 121–6; as cognitive style, 5–6, 69–70, 82–4, 88–90, 166–70; as mnemonic, 12, 15, 20, 151, 236; cognitive correlates, 69–71, 203–5; in psychotherapy, 12–13, 125, 231; ontological depth, 30–1 (*see also* levels of discourse); personality correlates, 81–4, 89–90, 209, 211, 213, 215, 217, 219; structures in, 14–16, 21–2, 24–5, 27–33, 38–9, 46, 125–6, 163, 166–8 (*see also* MOTQ visual); vividness, 13–14, 18–20, 24, 66, 69–71, 90, 203–5, 232–3
visual stratum in science, 174–6
visual-enactive idle thoughts, 49, 50, 62, 188–90
visualizers, 6, 82–4, 89–90 (*see also* visual imagery as cognitive style)
vividness, 13–14, 18–20, 24, 66, 69–71, 90, 203–5, 232–3; as an attribute, 69
Vividness of Visual Imagery Questionnaire, 66–7
vocabulary, 68, 71

whole-part structure, 30–1, 38–9, 44, 125–6 (*see also* part, MOTQ part)
will, 142–3
Wilson-Patterson Attitude Inventory, 88–91, 207, 216–19
wish fulfilment, 47
wonder, sense of, 77, 81–2, 111–12, 126